ROBBER'S CAVE
Truths, Legends, Recollections

ROBBER'S CAVE
Truths, Legends, Recollections

Joel Green

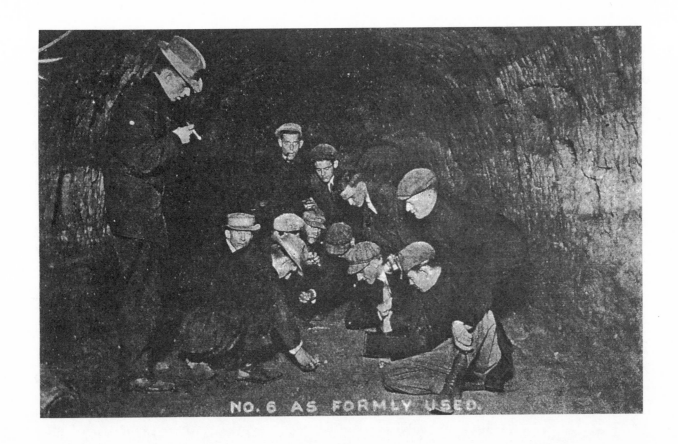

NO. 6 AS FORMLY USED.

(printed book) 978-0-9998297-0-7

First Printed Edition - April 2018
Cover Design by Pixel Bakery, Lincoln, Nebraska

Lincoln, Nebraska

Foreword

It was a dark and stormy night when I first met Joel Green . . . well, okay, it was a cool Saturday morning at The Mill, a local coffee shop, over glasses of White Heat. As Joel introduced himself and began relating parts of his own history and the writing of this book, it quickly became apparent that I was in the presence of an extraordinary young man.

As he continued, I found myself quickly enthused, excited, and drawn into his writing adventure. It dawned on me as the morning progressed that Joel is as much a treasure as Robber's Cave. I was astonished to see the range of knowledge, insight, research, time, effort, and obvious love he has brought to this project.

This portrait of Robber's Cave is anchored with meticulous research and enthusiasm. As you read this marvelous gift to the legacy of Lincoln, you might recognize a few names. I believe you will be drawn into the adventure, the legends, the history, the famous, and the infamous.

No one knows Robber's Cave better than Joel Green. His beautifully presented story will make a place in the heart of every Lincolnite, spelunker, Nebraskan, historian, or anyone who loves a story well told!

~ Frosty Chapman

Writer and early-1950s explorer of Robber's Cave (with his fellow Cub Scouts)

Contents

For my daughter, Brooklyn, a fellow writer,
Husker fan, cave tour guide, and all-around lover
of life. You inspire me, keep me young, and bring
joy into my life in so many ways.

"Even the faintest ink is better than the best memory."

–Chinese Proverb

"Our memories of a place, no matter how fond we were of it, are little more than a confusion of lights on a ground of darkness."

–Edwin Muir

Preface

A cave in Lincoln, Nebraska, seems a bit out of place considering the relatively flat terrain the city is laid out upon, but there is a cave that dates back further than the city itself. Surprisingly though, many Nebraskans today, including current residents of Lincoln, still do not realize the cave exists and have never entered into its network of tunnels.

However, the cave will no longer linger in obscurity, because all the secrets and folklore surrounding it are documented together for the first time in the publication of this compelling book—*ROBBER'S CAVE: Truths, Legends, Recollections*—by Joel Green.

The sesquicentennial year of 2017 for the State of Nebraska and its capital city of Lincoln provided all the inspiration necessary for Joel to compile facts and write a comprehensive history of Lincoln's original "underground attraction"—Robber's Cave.

No one has been more passionate than Joel in pursuing the history of Lincoln's intriguing and visually interesting cave through the years, stretching from its earliest oral and recorded history right up to the present time. His years of effort for this history project have now culminated with the publication of this book.

Joel's personal investment of research time in separating truths from legends regarding the cave; documenting detailed facts about the cave; conducting multiple personal interviews with people who had first-hand knowledge of Robber's Cave, such as former longtime owner of the cave Edwin Scarborough Jr.; and documenting as many personal stories as possible from people who visited the cave over the years—are all a tribute to Joel's heartfelt interest in the cave's history, personified by the fact he has enjoyed serving as a cave tour guide since the cave's reopening to the public. Joel's dedication to Robber's Cave has resulted in the first book focused exclusively on the history of Lincoln, Nebraska's, very own legendary sandstone cave.

The first personal exposure many of us locals had to Robber's Cave through the years came in connection with group field trips to the cave as young school children. Those trips produced a lifetime of memories for most of us about our cave experience. My first visits to the cave were in the late 1950s. I returned to the cave for a tour decades later on October 9, 2016, after Blue Blood Brewery reopened the cave to the public. On March 1, 2017, the actual sesquicentennial birthday for both the city of Lincoln and the state of Nebraska, Joel gave my wife and me a private tour of the cave. I told Joel later that there was no place else I would have preferred to be that day than in a part of Lincoln that was already here before Lincoln became Lincoln on March 1, 1867.

I truly believe people of all ages will find stories to enjoy from this book about Robber's Cave, packed full with fascinating and very rare photographs.

~ Dale V. Nobbman
Historian and Author

*Dale Nobbman is an author and historian from Emerald, Nebraska, and his information about the cave provided an excellent historical overview.

Introduction—An Unforeseen Journey to Robber's Cave

The shell of a graffiti-covered structure crumbling in the middle of Lincoln's Wilderness Park. The remains of collapsing kilns hiding behind overgrown weeds at Yankee Hill's Brick Yard. A former men's reformatory, although abandoned and vandalized, standing with an eerie beauty in summer moonlight.

Whenever I'd encounter such places, I'd think to myself: I wonder what's happened here over the years? If only the walls could talk. Anything abandoned, dilapidated, or left behind by time has always seemed to intrigue me simply because these forgotten places can serve as windows into another time. The world goes on regardless, but as author Kieron Connolly once explained, "While each generation remakes the world to suit current tastes [abandoned places] provide a glimpse into a past where humanity stood still and only nature marched on."

Where and when I developed my interest for local history I cannot say for sure. The curiosity could have taken root while growing up on West R Street near Capitol Beach Lake where as a youngster I often joined friends in a wooded area near West S Street to play on the remnants of the once-popular Capitol Beach amusement park. Gone were the roller coaster, Ferris wheel, skating rink, and fun house, but a few abandoned structures and paint-chipped rides remained and still spun with a push or pull. Unlike many guests, I did not grow up playing in Robber's Cave as it had closed by the time I moved on to Park Middle School from Lakeview Elementary. Although, I imagine it would have been a blast.

Once while pondering future occupations at a younger age, I remember wondering if *timeologists* existed—people whose actual job was to study time, memory, and change. It seemed like a commendable career. Memory is another other subject I've always found thought-provoking, and I enjoy discussing the topic with young and old alike. I find it entertaining to converse about memories with my daughter as well as my middle school students. So it should come as no surprise that along with my interest in time, memory, and change (and *Goonies*-like passageways), I have had for years an uncommon interest in a certain legendary, local location. Simply put, one place where time and memory seem to slow, or even stand still, is Robber's Cave.

Like many with an interest in history, I've always loved movies. Certain films, like music, have the ability to instantly transport me to my youth, especially when I hear parts of the score or soundtrack. I clearly remember several wood-paneled storage drawers filled with my family's collection of VHS tapes. The movies sat high on my family's faux-wood entertainment center—just out of my eight-year-old reach. I distinctly recall sitting at my mom's feet listening attentively while she read through the titles: *Indiana Jones, Star Wars, Back to the Future* . . . Some of my favorites were *The Goonies, Stand by Me,* and *Legend.* The obvious thread that connects these films is adventure, but all my favorites also contained an aspect of time and memory that has always intrigued me and still does to this day.

Growing up a devoted NBA basketball fan, I worked all through college with one goal in mind: to land a job with an NBA team. I feel very fortunate to have fulfilled that childhood dream at such a young age as I moved to Philadelphia, Pennsylvania, to work for NBA Hall-of-Famer Harvey Pollack and the Philadelphia 76ers. Sylvester Stallone's character Rocky Balboa served as a boyhood hero to me and "The Round Mound of Rebound" Charles Barkley topped my favorite NBA player list until his retirement. So of all the cities I could have worked, landing in the "City of Brotherly Love," home to Rocky Balboa and (at one time) Sir Charles, seemed quite the coincidence.

My time with the 76ers led me to Cleveland, Ohio, to work in the Cleveland Cavaliers' Public Relations Department during the 2003–04 season. At that time, an incredibly talented phenom named LeBron James had just won the NBA's Rookie-of-the-Year Award and had begun what many knew would become an historic NBA career. Maybe one day I'll write another book about my weekly encounters with professional athletes as some might find a few of my brief brushes with extravagance quite comical. For example, I once received an invite to go bowling with a few of the Cavalier Girls after work on a random weekday (of course I accepted), and we were actually chauffeured from the arena to the bowling alley in a Hummer limousine. I've stored quite a few NBA anecdotes in my memory that might someday find their way to the page.

One final coincidence, I later learned that just down the street from where I lived sat the famed home in Cleveland's Tremont neighborhood where Bob Clark directed the holiday classic *A Christmas Story* in 1983, which just so happened to be one of my favorite films. The renowned leg lamp still glows in the front window as the home opened as a museum in 2006. Happenstances such as these could simply be mere serendipity, but it's more meaningful, and fun, if they can serve to reinforce the comforting idea that I'm exactly where I'm supposed to be in my life.

I'm often asked why I no longer work with the NBA, and the answer is simple: I had a desire to start a family, and arriving at the arena at 8 A.M. to prepare for games and not leaving the arena until 1 A.M. some nights can wear on a person. It can be done, but a lot is missed as time flies, especially when having as many good times as we did. At times, we might have been having a little too much fun.

I decided to explore ways I could directly have a palpable impact on lives. I felt I could always return to professional basketball later in life if I really wanted to. My youthful dream had been accomplished, and I didn't want to be just another suit. I had once learned from a rabbi that "few people can truly excel at occupations about which they entertain moral reservations." So I followed that internal voice of noble authority and returned to Lincoln, Nebraska, with the intent to replenish my funds and begin my next ambition: helping people with developmental disabilities and mentoring highly gifted students (which I continue to do to this day). While doing so, I found an unexpected and newfound interest for my hometown.

Although Lincoln had grown and changed significantly from when I had last lived there, I enjoyed talking with Lincolnites who were quick to share a nostalgic tale. It has never been difficult for me to find people who enjoy reminiscing about a bygone era. As a self-proclaimed history nerd, I once cruised around my childhood neighborhood, Capitol Beach, with two of my dad's friends, Jim Kyles and Jack Merril, and listened as the two talked nonstop about what used to be where and who owned what.

I've always found it gratifying to listen to those older and wiser than me—it's endearing, and I learn a lot. Considering how much I enjoy conversing with people and listening to their stories, it should come as no surprise to me that in addition to being a middle school writing mentor, I've also begun guiding guests through Robber's Cave. Yet I still have a hard time believing that everything has come together as well as it has.

My wife doesn't quite share an interest for history as much as I do, but because she is such a special spouse, she accompanied me to Nebraska historian Jim McKee's classes: "The History of Lincoln" and "The History of Lincoln's Suburbs," offered through Southeast Community College's Continuing Education program. I highly recommend them, as Mr. McKee is an absolute treasure to the city of Lincoln and the State of Nebraska. I had also attended several informative presentations given by Lincoln's Historic Preservation Planner Ed Zimmer, who is another walking, talking encyclopedia. As I absorbed all of this fascinating knowledge about Lincoln, there still remained much I wanted to know regarding Robber's Cave, which at the time of these classes remained sealed and closed to the public.

Years ago during the fall, my Aunt Peggy would take me for a cruise in her sleek, black Lincoln Town Car to visit a few of the locations described in Alan Boye's book *A Guide to the Ghosts of Lincoln*. At the time, to a youngster like me, this seemed as if my aunt chauffeured me along on a personalized ghost hunt. After she showed me a few locations near Antelope Park, Lake Street Lake, and Washington Street, we headed to Robber's Cave. The element of the unknown drew me in, as it has for countless others over the years. I shared the same sentiments as Dick Cavett: for one reason or another, we both were really bothered that nothing had been done with the cave. *What a waste*, I thought.

While my wife attended the University of Nebraska—Lincoln, she needed to write a paper about Robber's Cave for a place conscious writing class. I jumped at the chance to help her with the research. In the Jane Pope Geske Heritage Room of Nebraska Authors at the Bennett Martin Library and at the Nebraska State Historical Society, I spent hours looking over articles, booklets, and photos. I even purchased an old photograph of the Palladian Literary Society in the cave back in 1912 from Mr. Scott Wendt at Bluestem Books in Lincoln, Nebraska. Needless to say, I had a great deal of interest in the cave for years and I'd always become a bit frustrated when someone referred to the cave as nothing more than "an old hole in the ground."

Recently my wife came across an old email I had sent to Margaret Reist at the *Lincoln Journal Star* dated October 24, 2005. I can still sense my eagerness even when I read the message years later:

My name is Joel Green and I am hoping you can answer a few questions for me regarding Robber's Cave [. . .] I have been helping my girlfriend research the cave for a paper . . . then an idea came to me. Why not write a book about Robber's Cave that separates the facts and the folklore? I graduated from Buena Vista University with degrees in English and

Spanish and have been working in Philadelphia and Cleveland for the past few years, but I have returned to my hometown rejuvenated and ready to write my first book. The article you wrote in July of 2000 was excellent! I saved it because the cave has always intrigued me and I hope that one day it will reopen [. . .] Simply put, I think the cave was and is tremendously underappreciated, and I find it hard to believe that no one has published a book about it.

I went on to ask Ms. Reist what she thought of my book idea, but I never received a response. Ten years later, luck struck in 2015 when Sam Manzitto (Robbers Cave LLC) purchased the cave from developer Tom White. The two wanted to reopen the cave and build a restaurant, brewery, and tap room above it. Not surprisingly, I was ecstatic upon hearing the news! My daughter and I would frequently drive by on Sundays to see the progressing construction. As an added bonus, Blue Blood hired my lovely little sister, Jamie Schack, as the events and training coordinator. I quickly offered to meet with Blue Blood's marketing coordinator at the time, Jullia Grossman, and we compared our cave research. Grossman showed me the ropes, and after I learned about Blue Blood's brewery and beer, I began giving tours in September of 2016.

From the large holiday parties and company gatherings, to the smaller private tours and family outings, I have immensely enjoyed leading guests through Robber's Cave. I especially appreciate the visitors who came to the cave long ago and have returned years later for another peek. They usually mention how the cool, damp smell hasn't changed, and how the tunnels seem larger due to the improved lighting. Always entertaining are the wide variety of admittances by guests who become caught in the moment. Stories ranging from first dates, kisses, and marriage proposals to tales of the risqué variety of which include a bit too much information—I have chosen to exclude these in good taste. Nonetheless, when guests learn that I had begun to write a book about Robber's Cave years ago, I have since received overwhelming encouragement to finish it. So here we are just in time for Nebraska's sesquicentennial—the state's 150th anniversary.

Although Robber's Cave may not boast the historical or geological significance of Carlsbad Caverns in New Mexico or Mammoth Cave in Kentucky, it is unique enough to Nebraska and contains within it stories that should be shared and enjoyed. Not to mention, I've met many guests who were born and raised in Lincoln that have never visited, nor had any idea that a cave exists beneath the city and just south of downtown. What's more are the comments after tours such as, "Lincoln needed something like this!" and "We just moved here and this is by far the coolest thing we've done!" In 1924 the cave was named "one of Lincoln's most notorious and interesting institutions." In short, a book about Robber's Cave has been well overdue.

Joel Green
Author

A Story That Deserves to Be Told

To those who view Robber's Cave as nothing more than an old hole in the ground, I've included plenty of anecdotes from guests who would say otherwise. Countless locals have eagerly shared their cave tales with me, and for that, I'm very thankful. Since Robbers Cave LLC purchased the cave, built a brewpub atop it, rejuvenated the property, and opened in 2016, nearly 60,000 guests have toured the tunnels in about three years. As a guide who is used to giving 45-minute tours, enjoy my "extended tour" of Lincoln, Nebraska's, legendary underground attraction. I believe the story of Robber's Cave, considering the facts along with the folklore, is truly a story that deserves to be told.

The Comeback Cave

From its unique physical origins and folklore, to its return in popularity as a local attraction—not to mention its colorful owners—I've always been fascinated by Robber's Cave. I began writing this book years ago, but I placed the project aside as the city of Lincoln bulldozed the entrance to seal the cave (mostly) from the public. With Nebraska's 150th anniversary in full swing, 2017 seemed to be the perfect time to finish what I had started. When I first read about a brewery purchasing the property with plans to reopen the cave, you can imagine my excitement. I am so thankful to the members of Robbers Cave LLC. for not only reopening, cleaning, and lighting the cave, but for giving me an opportunity to share my interest for the cave with thousands of guests through public and private tours.

Robber's Cave tours have far exceeded the expectations of many, but their success comes as no surprise to me. I pursued becoming a guide with full confidence that I could provide guests with informative, entertaining, and for some, nostalgic experiences. I was certain that guests from all generations would tour the cave—not just those who visited many years ago, but younger generations that never had a chance to legally experience the mysterious piece of Lincoln's lore. As with many of life's scenarios, luck can play a major role. When my younger sister, Jamie, accepted a position at the new brewery atop Robber's Cave, I knew something special was in the works.

In order to explain why I remained hopeful that someone one day would do something with Robber's Cave, consider the cranky opinion of this local in 1946. While researching the cave, I came across an amusing article in the "Minerva's Mail" section from a March 1946 issue of *The Lincoln Star.* In this article, a Lincolnite named Lolita complains how entertaining activities have gone downhill in Lincoln and that there is little fun to be had anymore. For instance, she mentions how nice Lincoln was back in the 1905 to 1914 period, but now—this was in 1946, mind you—so many of the landmarks are gone. Here is a portion of her complaint:

> Then Robbers Cave—a very popular place—scarcely heard of now. To one who has lived here in those days it is truly a ghost town now with nothing to take their places. [. . .] Capitol Beach was really a lovely place, with the big double-deck boat that took trips around the lake with refreshments, and band music, dancing, etc. on board. Then there were the row boats for hire and the free shows, vaudeville and the diving horses, a man shot from a cannon, and other attractions. It was a lovely place at Electric Park also, and not to forget the Epworth

encampments at beautiful Epworth Park. Why did all these things go to smash the way they did? There isn't a thing worth going to anymore that interests young or old.

This goes to show that some things never change. Robber's Cave was open to the public from 1906 to 1973, again from 1986 to 1989, and yet again in 2016. Places and amusements will always become old and outdated. What's incredible is that sometimes they can make a comeback.

Allure of the Underground

Consider what draws people underground. What is so interesting about the subterranean? Gary Soule, one of America's preeminent show cave historians, discovered caving as a teen and has had a lifetime of discovery and adventure exploring Wisconsin's underground treasures. He helped preserve the Dorchester Cave in downtown Sturgeon Bay, Wisconsin, after it was discovered by accident beneath a nursing home! I agree with Soule's explanation regarding the allure of caves. "Caves are truly the last frontier. Any one of us could discover a hidden underground world right beneath our very feet. And that's that lure of the unknown that makes it so exciting." Much like Robber's Cave has been reopened, Soule is considering the possibility of reopening Horseshoe Bay Cave near Murphy County Park to the public for tours. "More people have been on the moon than have been in certain sections of that cave" (Waldinger). Also like Robber's Cave, much of Horseshoe Bay Cave has been vandalized, but it has actually begun to repair itself.

For me, while attending Lincoln High School, my ears would perk up anytime I'd hear someone mention the school's tunnels that extended beneath the school (and farther if there is truth to the rumors). During one particular tornado warning my sophomore year, I remember having to descend with my class into to LHS's basement where a few students and I noticed that chicken wire impeded entry to a certain passageway. I didn't know it at the time, but I later learned that the tunnel crosses beneath Capitol Parkway from Lincoln High to the maintenance building to the east. Some might be surprised how popular urban spelunking has become with thrill seekers traversing old tuberculosis tunnels, steam tunnels, and sewage drains and then reporting their findings via blogs.

Caves being natural subterranean destinations have served as a source of safety for humans for ages, not just for people, but also for snakes, bats, and even prehistoric cave bears. Caves have always played a major role in mythology and ritual. From the dragon's den in fairytales to the home of Tom Sawyer's dark and dangerous enemy, Injun Joe, in American literature, caves have demanded a sense of respect as they have always represented shadow and risk. For *Star Wars* fans, how about when Luke Skywalker meets Darth Vader after entering the cave while training as a Jedi? As mythographer and author Joseph Campbell explains, part of the hero's journey is to descend into the underworld. As an English teacher, I think of Odysseus visiting Hades in Homer's *Odyssey* or Virgil guiding Dante's descent in *The Inferno*. This *katabasis*, as it's known, is clearly evident in film as well, everything from *Dumbo* and *Pinocchio* to *Citizen Kane* and *The Shining*. Walter Wright Arthen accurately describes how people are drawn to caves in his essay "The Magic of Caves":

To enter [a cave] is to meet the Jungian shadow side: our fears, the parts of ourselves we refuse to recognize in the light, the dark places of the soul. This perception of the cave as danger persists in our thought of caves today [. . .] Like water, we flow into low spaces and fill them. Like water, we are drawn gravitationally toward centers. [. . .] The cave is a kind of magnet.

Taking into account that Robber's Cave has existed in its current physical form for nearly 150 years, one can only imagine all that has occurred within its tunnels. Plenty of good-spirited fun I'm sure, but knowing the duality of imperfect beings, there have been plenty of sordid situations too. So why have so many people been drawn to caves for so long if they're often frightening or perilous? What do people gain by venturing into darkness and danger? After considering ancient and modern uses of caves, I've learned that many people believe caves contain a sacred or spiritual power; they represent death and rebirth, and they serve as a place between worlds. It is for these reasons Robber's Cave has been used by groups for countless initiation ceremonies through the years (more on that later).

Several years ago, I purchased a rare photograph of the UNL Palladian party (a literary society) taken in tunnel two of Robber's Cave circa 1910. I bought it from Mr. Wendt, the owner of Bluestem Books in Lincoln, and the black-and-white photo depicts individuals holding candles as they pose body to body facing west. Many guests are struck with a sense of awe when they see this photo during tours because it provides a look back in time—they can see what their exact location looked like over 100 years ago. One local historian thought Willa Cather was among the group. (I later learned from a Cather Scholar at the University who closely analyzed the photo that it most likely was not her).

The Palladian Party photo reminds me of the 1989 film *The Dead Poets Society* directed by Peter Weir. This film is particularly poignant in showing how caves can be a special place, especially for youth who are caught in the complicated process of shaping their lives. "They assemble in a candlelit circle to release the inhibitions of their regimented prep school existence." I'm sure many of the youth who visited Robber's Cave over the years could relate as they seized the day. Initially, to the unknowing, a cave is dark and mysterious—a place where daring kids sneak to in the middle of the night to break the rules and express their adolescent courage—but that's not the only reason. Visitors young and old have returned in droves to recapture a bit of their past or to discover what has been sealed from the public for many years. People have come to the cave from not only all over the United States, but from Australia, Brazil, Belgium, England, Germany, and Mexico. I have sincerely enjoyed giving tours to the thousands that have returned for a cave visit, as well as to those seeing it for the first time.

I don't claim to be an expert geologist or spelunker, and I didn't grow up wanting to study or spend countless hours underground. I simply became intrigued by Robber's Cave at a young age and continued to learn more and more about it from various sources over the years. Whether it is a primal experience or a connection to cave-dwelling ancestors, descending into darkness affects people in many ways. This effect becomes evident even today while holding open the cave entrance door to obtain my head count. Depending on the makeup of the tour group, the cave's atmosphere can evoke several emotions. *Fear*: "Has anyone died down here? Are there bats? Is it haunted?" All common questions I'll get from wide-eyed youth immediately upon entering the first tunnel. *Humor*: "I remember having a helluva good time down here. Those stairs were terrible to carry kegs down. Don't ask me the details, but we had a bathtub in here once!" a guest with a hefty laugh recalled.

Surprise: "I've lived in Lincoln my entire life and had no idea . . ." *Excitement*: "This is incredible! Who would've thought, in Lincoln, Nebraska? Can it be rented for dinners? Private parties?" No matter the crowd, a certain thrill is conveyed by almost everyone when initially entering Robber's Cave.

The Cave's Origin—A General Background

Robber's Cave, located on what is now 1.5 acres of land in the northeast quarter of Section 2–9–6 in Yankee Hill Precinct of Lancaster County, Nebraska, has been known, not only as Robber's Cave, but also Lincoln Cave, Penitentiary Cave, Notorious Old Cave, Pawnee Council Cave, or Original Council Cave Tunnel. On December 16, 1864 (one source states December 18), President Abraham Lincoln granted a military warrant of ownership (Warrant #92803) to Harriet Green, the widow of Roswell Huntington, a War of 1812 veteran who died in 1827. At that time, it was common for the government to grant bounty land as a reward for military service. The first series of warrants resulted from acts passed in 1811 and 1812, in which Congress provided that noncommissioned officers and soldiers serving for five years (unless discharged sooner) or their heirs would be entitled to 160 acres of land from the public domain in partial compensation for military service. A total of six million acres were to be surveyed and reserved for this purpose:

> Families usually sold their warrants for cash to third parties who then presented them to the General Land Office as payments for parcels of public land . . . For the most part the veterans sold their rights to warrant brokers who flourished on the purchase and sale of them. They were quoted daily in the New York papers, and large numbers were acquired by speculators for entering public land at prices as low as 50 cents an acre, although more commonly the warrants sold for 70 cents to $1.10 (Oberly).

The warrant of ownership for the cave property actually reads *"In testimony whereof, I, Abraham Lincoln, PRESIDENT OF THE UNITED STATES OF AMERICA, have caused these Letters to be made Patent, and the SEAL OF THE GENERAL LAND OFFICE to be hereunto affixed . . ."* After looking into the signature, I found that Congress passed a law in March 1833 authorizing the president to appoint a special secretary to sign patents in order to alleviate the chief from the time-consuming task of having to sign thousands of land grants. I know a few employees, including me, were excited to see Abe Lincoln's name at the bottom. I had to serve as somewhat of a killjoy when I found that Andrew Jackson was actually the last president to *personally* sign these types of land grants. However, the document remains a nice piece of cave history, and I have Emerald Historian Dale Nobbman to thank for it.

The widow Harriet Green immediately assigned the rights of her land to Daniel Low, Andrew Cochran, and W. W. Chipman, just six months before her death in May 1865. Low, Cochran, and Chipman ruined the natural entrance while operating a stone quarry business above the cave from 1865 to 1867. I found it intriguing that the 1938 *NSM* article states, "Stone quarried from beneath the top of the ground over the cave was used in constructing the foundation to the first building that was erected at Lincoln." The natural entrance and stone quarry are also mentioned in the Federal Writers Project in 1939, but there is a discrepancy in the 1865 date. Soule explains, "In 1863, when a stone quarry was started by three men who had acquired the title to the land from the Government, the removal of the cap rock destroyed the original entrance to the cave." Folklorist Louise Pound added in her 1949 *Nebraska History* that "very little quarrying was done. If anything, it opened up the cave for discovery."

Initially, what I'll refer to as the natural entrance was actually more of a pock or fissure in the side of the sandstone bluff. Being an estuary deposit, running water from creeks or rivers formed the original tunnel's opening over time. According to former Robber's Cave owner Ed Scarborough Jr., Jacob Andra would have barely been able to stand up in the first tunnel, which is why he lowered the floor. The ceiling's vaulted, pointed, or teardrop-shape is the natural water-formed shape. The other tunnels, however, were enlarged by Andra from the ceiling down, as evidenced by the pickaxe markings. He seemingly enlarged the areas where water had already begun to create depressions or cavities. Before overflow dams were built, Salt Creek would flood the area and water would erode the soft Dakota Sandstone. At certain times, the water level would reach the bottom of the bluff. Receding floodwaters also left small ponds and pools near the cave referenced later as "Old Lady Scarborough's lily ponds off of the west side of the house."

While Low and Chipman, both New Yorkers, were related through marriage, Cochran was a single man from Philadelphia. On July 25, 1867, the three men, along with Low's and Chipman's wives, sold the cave to the city of Lincoln for $760.00. The warranty deed for land ownership change was filed with the Lancaster Country clerk on October 15, 1867. (Nobbman also notes that at this same time William T. Donovan platted Section 2 of Yankee Hill Precinct to become a part of Lincoln, the new capital city.) The land and cave would soon be purchased by two brewers from Wisconsin and Minnesota, and from that point, the cave would no longer be a small, singular tunnel in the sandstone bluff.

A Record of the Property's Ownership

Roswell Huntington (1795–1827)
Harriet (Green) Huntington (1800–1865)

Daniel Low (1792–1876)
Evelina (Tilden) Low (1829–1886)

William Wirt Chipman (1834–1924)
Ellen Maria (Redfield) Chipman (1833–1910)

Andrew Cochran

Michael Ulmer

Andrew Lindner

Note: In 1877 The Lincoln Brewery property south of town (Pioneer Brewery) was in court for foreclosure on a mortgage. (2/11/37)

John Lutz

Frank Beeser

Chris Rocke (1850–1930)
Amanda (Stockfeld) Rocke (1853–1949)

John Wesley Scarborough (1852–1922)
Mary Susannah (Wilmeth) Scarborough (1857–1931)

Fred Carl Scarborough (1877–1949)
Esther Belle (Stevens) Scarborough (1890–1965)

Edwin Lee (Newnom) Scarborough Sr.
(1909–1983) Agnes Elizabeth (Carter)
Scarborough (1909–)

Note: The Yeany family managed the cave while renting the property from the Scarboroughs in the 1960s.

Edwin Lee Scarborough Jr. (1931–)
Viola E. Maybin (1934–1992)

John C. Brager (Ridge Development Company)

Tom White (ZSA Realty Group)

Sam Manzitto Sr. and the members of Robbers Cave LLC

The Brewers
Come to Lincoln

In April 1869, two brewers arrived scouting a location to build the first brewery in Lincoln, Nebraska, the Pioneer Brewery. Ulmer and Lindner were no strangers to caves and breweries. Thanks to two brewery cave specialists and authors from Minnesota and Wisconsin, Tim Wolter and Doug Hoverson, I learned that Michael Ulmer had previously operated a brewery in Pepin, Wisconsin, on the Mississippi River just southwest of Eau Claire, Wisconsin. Hoverson provides what little info exists about Ulmer in his encyclopedic book *Land of Amber Waters, The History of Brewing in Minnesota*:

> Charles Saile started the Pepin Brewery sometime before 1860 . . . Saile and his partner, Michael Ulmer, built a new brewery in 1862 . . . and sold between fifteen and twenty barrels of lager each month. In fall 1866, Saile sold his brewery to Gottlieb Walty and moved to Hastings (275).

After following Saile to Hastings, Minnesota, Ulmer ran a second brewery with Michael Schaller. The Schaller/Ulmer Brewery operated from 1856–1867 until disaster struck. In March 1867, Ulmer and his employees jumped from a second-floor window after a fire gutted the brewery. Hoverson lists Ulmer's uninsured loss at approximately $7,000.00 (229-30).

Andrew Lindner is said to be from Waukesha, Wisconsin, but I later learned of an Andrew Lindner who was a twentieth century proprietor of the Cassville Brewery (also in Wisconsin). Whether this was Lindner's son or a man staying in the brewing business for an unusually long time is unclear. "They were familiar with the brewing business as Aulmer [*sic*] had run a brewery and he had had caves connected with the plant." Since the two brewers were familiar with using caves for storing beer, they understood that the constant 55-degree temperature (the natural temperature in Robber's Cave) would be perfect for lagering caverns.

Until January of 2018, it was thought that Michael Ulmer was Michael *Aulmer* and that he was from Red Wing, Minnesota, (25 miles southeast of Hastings), but with Wolter and Hoverson's help, we were able to rectify the common German misspelling with the use of a log book of Minnesota Brewers.

Minnesota has hundreds of natural and man-made sandstone caves. In fact, approximately 150 miles of storm sewers and utility tunnels beneath the Minneapolis–St. Paul area were enlarged from these caves. Nancy Wagner wrote a feature for USA Today's "Travel Tips" section specifically on Minnesota's sandstone caves in which she describes the caves' formation in that particular area:

> Many sandstone caves were formed from the erosion of a sandstone bed. The sandstone was washed away by groundwater that created pipe-shaped cavities in the sandstone. Over the years, more groundwater helped shape the cavities, filling many of them with stream sediments. Most of these caves formed in the walls of the valleys along deep rivers, including the Mississippi.

Several of the caves beneath Minnesota's Twin Cities are still used for storage of temperature-sensitive foods and beverages to this day. Red Wing is a city most known for its quality stoneware, pottery, and boots; however, it also has breweries and caves. Hoverson, who also happens to be the associate editor of *American Breweriana Journal*, describes Red Wing's popular brewing history:

> The state of Minnesota is situated in what has long been known as America's Grain Belt, and the City of Red Wing located on the Mississippi River has historically been one of the thriving ports used to ship grain to other markets. One of the historical markers in Red Wing's Bay Point Park states, "Fertile fields within and beyond Red Wing yielded abundant harvests, supplying grain for grist and four mills and later for the malting companies and breweries." It was natural, then, that brewing would evolve as one of the earliest industries of Red Wing. In fact, by 1867, the city once boasted a total of five breweries.

If one were to travel to the Redwing, Minnesota, area today, they could visit Sorin's Bluff, a former limestone mine also known as Memorial Park developed in the 1920s. The most popular cave in that area is Overlook Cave or Cool Cave, but on the opposite side of the bluff is Horseshoe Cave. While I looked into Red Wing's brewery and cave history, I noticed that the archway into Horseshoe Cave in Redwing is strikingly similar to the archway at Robber's Cave. The archway entrance into Robber's Cave was built after J. W. Scarborough purchased the cave in 1908. That specific archway entrance is absent in F. M. Downs's photo of tunnel number one from 1908. The entrance at Horseshoe Cave in Redwing has a gigantic tree growing around it, but it is still passable if one is willing to crawl. I find it interesting that Ulmer decided to leave Hastings and the Red Wing area with its limestone bluffs and caves to come to Lincoln and build a brewery atop a sandstone bluff and have tunnels dug for storage.

The Pioneer Brewing Company and Jacob Andra

The Pioneer Brewery took advantage of a pre-existing cave. According to Wolter, the basic types of brewery caves are simple vaulted cellars (usually built where there is no decent rock structure), industrial level excavations (usually a bit later), and natural caves expanded (vent holes were an issue with these).

Ulmer and Lindner recognized the potential of the sandstone bluff and small tunnel and decided to purchase the four acres. "When his eyes viewed the sandstone hills out near the state penitentiary he decided that he [Ulmer] had struck the right place and his partner agreed with him." Since there was no railroad that led to Lincoln at the time, teams hauled lumber and other material from Nebraska City. A month later on May 20, 1869, Jacob Andra, who had quite the reputation as a digger, began the momentous task of enlarging the cave and digging a well.

To give an idea as to what kind of reputation Andra had at the time, consider the fact that he was a featured character played by someone in a local pageant on Nebraska Field in 1915. (Before Memorial Stadium, the Nebraska football team played at Nebraska Field from 1909 to 1922 located at practically the same site.) The August 1917 *Lincoln Star* article describes Bob Harley, a major in the cadet regiment, taking "the part of that early German brewer of Lincoln, who dug the so-called Robber's Cave south of town." Andra being a featured character in a pageant, along with his impressive tombstone, reiterates that he must have had quite the reputation! Not only was Andra a renowned digger, he served with H. P. Lau as an officer of the Harmonic Musical Society founded in 1875 (Parminter). H. P. Lau emigrated to Nebraska from Fleusburg, Germany, in 1870 and founded the H. P. Lau Company and operated a wholesale grocery on North 8th Street in Lincoln, Nebraska.

At the time *The Daily News* interviewed Mr. Andra in January of 1914, he was considered one of the oldest citizens of Lincoln. Born in Germany, he immigrated to America with his parents in 1852 and married Magdalena Whittman in 1874. Their four children were Herman, Anna, Carl, and Emma. Before moving to Lincoln, Nebraska, Andra lived in Lima, Ohio. "He came in 1868 when a husky youth of only nineteen years. He worked for thirty years for one of the pioneer harness firms of the city." At the time of his interview, Andra had been a stock keeper for Harpham Brothers for six years (Harpham Brothers established in 1884 made fine leather gun belts, holsters, and horse collars in Lincoln). He was also an employee of The Pioneer Brewery, and when he wasn't helping brew, he labored on the beer cellars. Andra also had experience digging wells. He began May 20, 1869, and it would be three years before the caves were ready for storing malt and beer! (The foundations of the brewery, however, were laid in 1870.)

Air shafts were needed to keep the tunnels' temperature constant. Fermenting beer gives off heat that needs to be vented. As for Robber's Cave's airshafts, it is likely that they were created using a drill. Tim Wolter explains in a January 2018 email:

> If you take a good look at them [the airshafts], you might find evidence that they were in effect drilled from down below. I have seen instances where a hole was started then abandoned, leaving some circular cuts. I figure they used something like an ice auger with additional sections that could be bolted on—necessary when some of these air shafts were 30 to 50 feet. I have also seen remains of insets at the top of them, a sort of metal cap in one instance, and actual ceramic pipe in another.

Scarborough Jr. maintains that in the case of the first tunnel, Andra expanded what nature had already begun (which would explain the random layout of the cave) and he added more tunnels for the brewery to use as lagering caverns. The sand was hauled out to an incline by wheelbarrow, and it has been reported that some of the sand was used in the construction of Lincoln's second state capitol building and original state penitentiary. The 1914 Andra interview also states:

> Before the brewery building was erected a small cellar about thirty feet square had been dug and the three caves radiated from it. [. . .] A well was dug to furnish water for the brewery.

It was about sixty feet deep. When the bottom was reached, petrified pecans and other nuts were found.

After Andra extended the cave for the brewery, it would be years before he'd return. When he did return, he was entertained by the rumors that the tunnels had produced. "I have been much amused over the romantic stories that have been circulated concerning the caves. [. . .] I think these stories are mere fancy the products of fertile imaginations." Andra doesn't specify which stories he believes were thought up, but I believe he is referring to the more outlandish tales of the Pawnee Indians, Jesse James, and the Underground Railroad. However, such a prediction doesn't mean the cave didn't see its fair share of interesting and mysterious happenings.

After one particular cave tour, a man gave me a copy of a 1908 Robber's Cave flyer, and in it Andra remarks, "The Cave is a very interesting place and was undoubtedly a mysterious Robbers' Cave long after I worked there over forty years ago. I will assure anyone that he will not regret a visit to The Cave." At one time, Andra and his wife lived not far from the cave at 920 Rose St. Although Lena died in 1914, he remained in Lincoln until his death in 1935 and is buried, as is Magdalena, in Lincoln's Wyuka Cemetery.

Later into the year 1869, after the Pioneer Brewery was up and running, the beer sales were stunted due to the lack of rail transportation. At the time, the product had to be transported to the Lincoln pubs by horse. "It was not till in 1870, when the Burlington Railroad entered the city, that it was possible to expand the trade. The capacity of the brewery was twenty-five barrels a day." Standing in tunnel two looking west toward the staircase, a prominent slope remains. Before steps were installed, this slope would have served as the incline that the brewers used to roll kegs and barrels in and out of the cave from the brewery's cellar. Also in 1870, Lindner would make overnight deliveries of their brew to Lincoln saloons with a team of mules and a wagon. According to Nobbman, these deliveries would have included Lincoln's first beer saloon on the east side of 11th between N and O Streets established by Joseph Hedges in 1868.

I found an article that mentions Ulmer, Andra, the cave, and brewery in a section called "Your Problems by Mary Gordon" in the August 1927 *Lincoln Evening Journal*. William Wilson of 2152 South 56th St. in Normal wrote the following:

> Dear Mary Gordon, a tourist says that he recently visited the Robber's Cave south of the city, perhaps now in the limits. The first summer I was in Lincoln in 1870, I heard about the cave and visited it. A German named Mike (this would have been Michael Ulmer) had a small brewery outside the cave and used the cave to store beer. He would drive into town at night delivering the beer to the saloons with a team of mules and an old farm wagon. Mr. John Hudson who lives on South 10th Street, where the State Hospital turns west and whose father was the homesteader of that quarter section in 1864 told me he knew a man then employed in Whitman's Harness Factory (this would have been Jacob Andra) who helped dig the cave in the sand rock. The late N. C. Brock, a few years before his death wrote an article to *The Journal* saying it was a beer cave.

Ulmer and Lindner dissolved partnership in 1873 at about the time Andra finished the cave system. A local depression that year, along with a drought and grasshopper infestation, surely contributed to the brewery's bankruptcy. According to Tim Wolter, "A messy legal case in 1874 where a bunch of guys named Green sued Ulmer, Linder and some delightful codefendants: Lucy Bennet, Melinda and Marmaduke H. Gilman. The case was no doubt about ownership of the property, brewery, and land." Linder went back to Waukesha and died a few years later. Ulmer died in Lincoln, but not before selling the brewery to John Lutz. Here is McKee's take on the brewery's history from his article "Having a Beer in Lincoln" that appeared in the June 3, 2012 *Lincoln Journal Star*:

> In 1868, Jacob Andra arrived in Lincoln from Lima, Ohio. The next year Michael Aulmer [*sic*] and Andrew Linder bought four acres directly north of the state penitentiary on 14th Street because of the large deposit of sandstone there. Although the sandstone ultimately was mined for construction of both the Capitol and penitentiary, their primary interest was in digging a cave as a cool place to store beer. In April, Aulmer [*sic*] and Linder established [The Pioneer Brewery] and hired Andra to dig a storage cave. For more than three years Andra dug in the extremely soft Dakota Sandstone, ultimately establishing a 5,600-square-foot warehouse cave and a 60-footdeep well. At the height of its production, the brewery was able to turn out 25 barrels of beer per day. The brewery was sold in 1873 to John Lutz, then to Frank Beeser, and finally to Chris Rocke, who subsequently closed the operation and sold the frame building to a widow who dismantled it and moved it to Greenwood.

During an eight-hour interview with Lincoln native Harold J. Moss, Fred Scarborough reveals that while the brewery structure was abandoned, the building was still used as a gambling den, a dance hall or sporting house (a common euphemism for cathouse or brothel), and a hideout for horse thieves (which would explain the 244 horseshoes found and horse stalls mentioned). I wish more information existed describing the building being burned by the Anti-Horse Thief League before the "Widow of Greenwood" used what was left of the lumber to build her barn.

Civil War Veteran John Wesley Scarborough then purchased the property, cave included, in 1906. The 1939 Federal Writer's Project's *Nebraska: A Guide to the Cornhusker State* explains:

> In 1906 when the caverns were being cleared of debris so as to be used as a mushroom garden, stories of hidden treasure brought so many visitors to the place that plans were changed and the cave was kept open for sightseers and picnics.

At the time J. W. Scarborough purchased the property in 1906, the property was 4.2 acres, but the land has since been divided into three lots. The current lot is 1.5 acres. A city of Lincoln comprehensive plan in 2015 reported the cave depth at 62 feet, which is similar to what had been reported in 1937 and 1973, and the cave contained 700 linear feet of tunnels in 1973 when it closed to the public. The land had been in the Scarborough family, in one way or another, for four generations—from 1906 to 1990— beginning with John and his wife Mary, to Fred and his wife Esther, then on to the grandson Edwin Sr. and his wife Agnes, and finally to great-grandson Ed Jr. and his wife Viola.

Utilizing the Cave's Sand

The 1914 *Lincoln Daily Star* interview with Andra included a statement about the removed cave sand being used in the construction of the state capitol building and state penitentiary; however, that comment is up for debate. In a May 15, 2017 email, McKee stated that he had heard, purely apocryphally, that sand, not stone, was used in the construction of the penitentiary, so it is at least conceivable that some sand might have been used in the capitol building's construction. It could mean nothing more than Andra, who had a reputation for being quite the digger, simply worked at the site of either the first or second capitol buildings in Lincoln.

Lincoln's first state capitol building, designed by Chicago architect John Morris, was completed in 1868 through rushed construction and the use of poor materials. Morris designed the capitol with local limestone, which began to deteriorate upon the building's completion (Watkins). Construction on Lincoln's second capitol building began in 1879 and was completed in stages over the next ten years. Is it plausible that Andra worked on the foundation of the "old capitol building" as the *Daily Star* article stated and Scarborough Jr. claimed? That particular building was under construction from late 1867 to late 1868, so it would have been before Andra began extending the cave for Pioneer Brewery in 1869. It could be that Andra labored on the second capitol building because that structure wasn't completed until 1881.

I decided to seek preservation architect Matt Hansen's expertise on the matter. Hansen is the Preservation Architect at the Office of the Capitol Commission. Consider his opinion:

> Like the current capitol, the second Nebraska capitol was constructed in phases during the time period of 1879–1889. In 1879, a west wing was built onto the first capitol. This was followed in 1881 by construction of an identical east wing. In 1883 the legislature approved the removal of the first capitol and its replacement with a new central section, which completed the second capitol. That building was completed and ready for occupancy on January 1, 1889. If Mr. Andra's cave excavations were completed sometime in 1872, in order for that sand to have been used in the construction of any part of the second capitol, that sand would have had to have been stored at least until 1879 when work on the first wing of the second capitol was begun.

While examining possibilities of how Mr. Andra's statement about the excavated cave sand being used for one of the capitols could be true, Mr. Hansen remembered that the contractor for all phases of the second capitol (1879–1889) was a fellow by the name of W. H. B. "Boss" Stout:

> By period accounts, Stout was an interesting person, of questionable intentions by some, but a construction contractor by trade. He was involved in many projects for the state, including construction contracts at the Nebraska State Penitentiary. I do know that he held state contracts for the use of prison labor at various points in time. Having involvement with both the state capitol and the state penitentiary, and being involved in the building trades in Lincoln, Stout would have certainly been aware of the cave and the excavations of sand from it. Because of that, the cave sand could have been a source of material utilized by him in his projects (capitol and penitentiary, among others). I don't know how long Andra's sand pile might have remained at the cave site, but I think it's fair to say that it could have been there for years and served as source of building material for various contractors. Because of that, I don't think it is totally out of the realm of possibility for Stout to have made use of residual sand from the cave excavations when doing his construction on the second capitol during the 1879–1889 time period. We will probably never know for sure unless some account can be found telling of the source of the sand (used for mixing lime putty mortar) used during construction of the second capitol.

In 1985, long-time lawman C. E. Hagstrom donated the aforementioned 1938 issue of the *NSM* to the Nebraska Sheriff's Association. That article also asserts, "sand from this cave has lately been utilized for artistic plastering in some of Lincoln's most costly buildings." Which buildings could the former Saunders Country sheriff and NSA president be referring to? The current capitol building was being constructed in 1932, the Lincoln Benefit Life/Federal Securities Building in 1926, Georgian Place/Hotel Capital/YMCA also in 1926, the Sharp Tower in 1927, and University Towers/Stuart Building in 1929. Mr. Hansen said it best when he responded to my inquiry with, "the 1938 article is tantalizingly vague enough to be frustrating. Without more information on exactly what building [the author] was talking about, we likely may never know."

Post Cards by F. M. Downs

Early photographs of Robber's Cave are scarce. As of 2017, the Nebraska State Historical Society has just seven. The dozens that I've accumulated have come via personal donations. Some of the first images I'd ever seen of the cave, and some of the most widely known photos, are postcards published by the F. M. Downs Company out of Lincoln, Nebraska. When I met Preservation Architect Matt Hansen in July of 2017, I learned that he possesses an extensive collection of postcards, including those of F. M. Downs. One of the Robber's Cave postcards he owns is colored! Mr. Hansen explained that the F. M. Downs post cards were printed and hand-colored in Germany and that minor variations exist due to the human aspect of applying the color. For example, if Hansen's photo were to be seen in person, at the area near the bottom of the entrance, one could notice that an artist added a blue tint, possibly implying the presence of water. "These cards would have been colored by people who had no first-hand knowledge of the scenes they were coloring, so showing water at the entrance is understandable," Hansen points out.

When I'm underground in the sand with a group of guests surrounded by thousands of carvings, we are surrounded by memories. In a way, it is time preserved. Holding an old photo while standing in the exact spot it was taken can be an exciting experience for certain people. I sometimes show guests a few of the old black-and-whites taken from inside the cave over 100 years ago. While positioning the photo in such a way that the actual view from the picture matches the present, I am able to point out how most of the carvings from these old photographs have barely changed. It's as close as I can get to time traveling.

From Open Flames to Lightbulbs

While the Pioneer Brewing Company used the cave from 1869 to 1873, approximately every ten to fifteen feet, small stakes of kerosene-soaked wood were inserted into the ceiling to create a flame that lit portions of the tunnels. Today, several of the charred, wooden stakes remain in their places nestled in small holes that span the cave's ceiling. Often guests will mistake the dark, burnt pieces for bats, and I reassure them that they are merely remnants of an older lighting system.

In trying to pinpoint the exact year the cave became electric lighted, I concluded it was sometime after F. M. Downs photographed the cave in 1908 yet before 1911, which is the year I first found a reference to lights in the cave in *The Valentine Democrat*. According to Don Schaufelberger and Bill Beck's book *The Only State: a History of Public Power in Nebraska*, from 1902 to 1926, the number of municipal electric plants increased from 11 to 282 constituting the largest number of municipally owned light and power plants in the nation. The first time Robber's Cave advertises their electricity is in 1922, which also happens to be the oldest cave advertisement I found. A report on the cave in the December 1948 issue of *Nebraska History* simply states, "Some lights were in the cave at this time. They were mild electric light bulbs, and they existed sporadically thru [*sic*] the cave."

A Geological Perspective

Nebraska State Geologist Dr. R. M. Joeckel and I plan to write more of an academic article about the cave's geology in the future, but for those who are not serious geology enthusiasts, this chapter should suffice. Robber's Cave is located within a bluff of Dakota Sandstone, which is generally formed in terrestrial coastal plains, estuary, and river environments. The water from what is now Salt Creek in Wilderness Park used to reach the base of the sandstone bluff before dams and dikes were built that rerouted the creek. This running water eroded the soft sandstone to form small pocks and crevices in the bluff. Simply put, "what had been a natural, water-eroded fissure in the Dakota Sandstone under Lincoln was expanded with a pick and shovel in 1870 by workers from Pioneer Brewery" (Bartels).

In a 1967 *Lincoln Evening Journal* article the beloved local writer Richard Mezejewski, A.K.A. Dick Mezzy, interviewed Dr. Russel Smith, a geology professor at the University of Nebraska— Lincoln at that time. Mezzy's interview with Dr. Smith provides a nice, simple overview of Dakota Sandstone. The sandstone runs from ground level outcroppings to 100 or more feet in depth, depending on location and the amount of topsoil. "Lincoln is setting above it, and so is the majority of Nebraska, Kansas, Oklahoma, and parts of east Texas. It's all part of an unbroken underground chain of sandstone." Dr. Smith continues:

> The formations can be traced from the Black Hills to the Missouri River, as far south as the east Texas oilfields and into Colorado where the Rocky Mountains break it up. But on the other side of the mountains, the Dakota Sandstone can be found again. Mountain upheaval centuries ago broke up the formations.

A common question that I'm asked on tours is if the cave sustained any damage when Nebraska experienced an earthquake on September 3, 2016. The 5.6 magnitude earthquake happened in north-central Oklahoma, according to the United States Geological Survey, but many Nebraskans sensed swaying. No damage to Robber's Cave could be found. There have been two magnitude 7 earthquakes recorded in Nebraska: November 15, 1877, and March 28, 1964. Considering engineers have deemed Robber's Cave structurally safe, stability of the cave is not an issue, which might be why the city of Lincoln considered it for a fallout shelter on at least two occasions (more on this later).

So why is all the sandstone in Nebraska? This geologic formation composed of sedimentary rocks deposited on the eastern side of the Late Cretaceous Western Interior Seaway (Hayden).

Envision western and central Nebraska covered by the Cretaceous Seaway. The sand that would become the Dakota Formation lay beneath that seaway and was deposited in Eastern Nebraska as that seaway advanced eastward. That sediment eventually became the Dakota Formation.

The aforementioned Gary Soule of the Wisconsin Speleological Society visited Robber's Cave and wrote an excellent article about it for the *NSS News*, which is the national newsletter of the National Speleological Society out of Huntsville, Alabama. When I asked Soule his opinion regarding the natural formation of tunnel number one, his opinion supported Scarborough Jr.'s in that that tunnel number one is indeed a naturally formed passage. Even though he has studied the cave in person, I sent Soule two photos of tunnel number one, also known as Original Council Cave, just to be sure. One photo was circa 1910 before the existence of the archway entrance extension, and the other was taken in the exact same spot as the first photo except in 2017. Soule's response:

> This particular passageway looks very natural to me. I have seen similar wild sandstone caves, and this is a rather usual configuration. Most caves tend to take on the arch effect shown, so this is not at all an unusual shape. Having caved and seen caves for so long, you sort of get a sixth sense on them and this is the case here.

Soule also points out that since Robber's Cave is sandstone, none of the common calcite stalactites and stalagmites or other formations exist in it. Although sandstone caves can indeed have formations, anything like that would have been destroyed during excavations to enlarge the cave.

Once during a tour, I pointed out where the original/natural entrance to the cave used to be and a guest blurted, "There are no natural caves in Nebraska!" This happened before I had contacted Soule, so I decided to look into their claim by querying Dr. Joeckel. Not only is Dr. Joeckel the Associate Director for Conservation and Survey at the University of Nebraska—Lincoln, but he is the Curator of Geology at the Nebraska State Museum, not to mention a professor at UNL's school of Natural Resources and Department of Earth and Atmospheric Sciences. I called Dr. Joeckel to invite him to Robber's Cave, and he eagerly accepted. When I asked if there are any natural caves in Nebraska, he responded with the briefest and most succinct of answers (I'm being a bit sarcastic here):

> Yes, there are natural caves in Nebraska, but none of them were produced by karst processes, that is, the widespread dissolution of limestone or dolostone. All of the surrounding states have true karstic, limestone caves, including Kansas. In fact, one only has to drive to the Manhattan, Kansas, or Kansas City, Missouri, area to see significant karst development (albeit locally). A good question at this point would be: why is there no large-scale limestone karst in Nebraska? Turns out that is a very difficult question to answer, but it doubtless has to do with multiple factors, and I will run through a few off the top of my head: Insufficient time for development; Limestones of the type that could produce good karst are exposed only in limited areas of southeastern Nebraska; Deep burial of limestones by glacial sediments, river sediments, loess, and other surficial materials; Recent history (post 2.5-million-years-ago) of base level and drainage networks; Perhaps, and unfavorable setting in terms of tectonics (this point is a weak one, I'll concede); and other factors. The caves that exist in Nebraska are produced by differential erosion in sandstones, siltstones, and loess deposits, rather than by the wholesale dissolution of limestone or dolostone.

Part of me wishes Dr. Joeckel could have been present with me on that particular tour to answer the ill-tempered guest's question eloquently and immediately. Instead, I bought the geology guru lunch after we explored the cave to examine the different features of each unique tunnel. Speaking of state geologists, one might find it interesting to note that Nebraska's first state geologist, Erwin H. Barbour, actually conducted classes in Robber's Cave! Barbour was assistant paleontologist to the US Geological Survey and taught at the University of Iowa for two years before landing as the head of the Department of Geology for the University of Nebraska in 1891.

The 1869 *Nebraska Statesman* has an interesting description of Robber's Cave that mentions objects taken from the cave walls along the well area. This would be at the west end of the cave below the original entrance. It reads:

> The walls are solid sandstone from which have been taken petrified elk horns, and parts of skeletons of animals [. . .] In one corner, near the entrance a circular pit five feet across opens to a [. . .] dark depth, which in the absence of ropes, we did not dare to descend.

In the early 1900s, one Lincoln resident depicted the lay of the land near the cave on the edge of the Salt River flood plain:

> South, west and a block north and east there were more flats, prone to flooding. Further east was a gentle rise; a block north a fairly steep one. Go east two blocks and there was a rise to the south, up to a sandstone ridge and a knobby bluff, unlike most rolling hills in Nebraska. On weekends and summers when I didn't have a job, I liked to explore on an old fat-tired Schwinn bike that came with our rental, rusting in the garage. Riding up the hills was hard work, but worth it as I loved to explore, either on foot cross-country or on the reconditioned bike. I often went east two blocks to a highway, and turned south up a hill. Near the top was a park with an unusual number of trees for Nebraska; a rolling road crossing it, a few playground items and small basketball court. At the hilltop was a house bearing the sign *Jesse James Hideout*. One had to pay to get in; a small building like an outhouse outside held a light switch and a steep staircase down, down into the bowels of the earth.

The sandstone hill that contains the cave has been mentioned and described in various instances. In a 1930 *Lincoln Star* issue, Dr. Barbour states:

> It is plainly visible where graders cut through it when preparing the road bed several years ago for paving. The strata [are] a deposit of the glacial formation which at one time came down over this country. The nose stopped in the vicinity of the Blue River" (7/23/1930).

The Federal Writer's Project's *Guide to Nebraska* described the varying colors of the cave's sandstone walls in 1939: "The walls scratched with names, initials, and dates, are streaked in ocherous yellow and hematite reds and browns." The sandstone that comprises Robber's Cave is the same type of sandstone one can find at Pioneers' Park beneath Ellis Luis Burman's 1935 sculpture *The Smoke Signal* and north of the Children's Zoo along Antelope Creek and the Billy Wolff Trail. In fact, the feature headline to Judy Harrington's 1960 *Lincoln Evening Journal* article states, "Sandstone Outcrop Makes Antelope Creek Look Like Mountain Stream!" In this article, Dr. Eugene C. Reed, director of the Conservation and Survey Division for the University of Nebraska at the time explained:

The Antelope Creek example and others at Pioneers Park, Robber's Cave, and south and west of the penitentiary are part of a band across Nebraska angling northeast to southwest. This rock, from the surface to 200 feet deep in the Lincoln area, is found wherever erosion or machine has eaten away mantle rock material.

Dr. Reed also maintains that sand and gravel laid down by streams during the Ice Age and deposits from an ancient inland sea contributed to the mantle rock covering. The Pleistocene mantle rock has been completely eroded from many valley sides in and around Lincoln, exposing the bedrock, which consists of Dakota Sandstone at higher elevations and Fuson shale in lower slopes:

Commercially (in the 1960s), sandstone served as a mat under concrete road construction. Hard layers occasionally are used for buildings. Builders of Nebraska's first state capitol even considered using nearby sandstone for facing but settled for magnesia limestone from Beatrice. Lincoln's old city wells were drilled into sandstone, but the water became salty and we finally went to Ashland.

Once, following a public cave tour, a guest who claimed to be friends of the Scarborough family reminisced about how she often camped in the cave as a young girl. She asserted that on several occasions she found egg-shaped stones in the sand. Inside the stone, she explained, was a type of ochre that Native Americans used to mix with animal grease and use for war paint. I asked Scarborough Jr. about such stones and he responded that he didn't know anything about war paint, but at times egg-like stones could indeed be found in the cave sand. "If you shook them, they'd rattle. I broke one open once and found a smaller, dark-orange or brownish pebble inside," Scarborough Jr. recalls.

I decided to seek Dr. Joeckel's expertise once again to learn more about these stones. Dr. Joeckel identified them as hydrous iron oxide (goethite) concretions that probably formed around mud pebbles (once carried by the ancient river), which themselves contained iron oxides. According to *Sedimentology* volume 59, concretions in which a thick rind of iron oxide surrounds a core that contains mud and up to 89 percent void space concretions are fairly abundant in the lowermost Dakota Formation in eastern Nebraska. So what about the guest's claim about the Native American war paint use? Dr. Joeckel helped to clarify that as well:

Elsewhere in the United States, and in other rock strata, the non-politically-correct vernacular term *Indian paint pot* has been applied to concretions like these . . . I seriously question whether or not indigenous Americans actually used the concretions for paint . . . it's probably an example of a story that someone heard . . . second or third hand and applied it to the site.

Even if these *rattlestones* weren't used for war paint, they are valuable capsules of geologic records of the unique soils as they have been transported and deposited into the cave via ancient river channels. Keep in mind that the Dakota Formation is the oldest preserved Mesozoic strata in Nebraska, and the environment at that time was much different than today. "During the time when the Dakota Formation was deposited, the climate was much warmer and eastern Nebraska received about 100 inches [of rain] per year—three times more annual rainfall than today!" Try to envision Nebraska at that time. A coastal plain, an estuary system with meandering rivers. Whenever I'm walking through the tunnels of Robber's Cave, I find it hard to believe that I'm passing through sand delivered by ancient river channels to the eastern side of the Western Interior Seaway—I'll never think of the term Capitol Beach in the same way!

For more geological information, read *The Geology of Robber's Cave* by Erwin H. Barbour found later in the "Souvenir Booklet" chapter (keep in mind that Barbour's info is over 100 years old and could very well be deemed inaccurate today). I still found reading Dr. Barbour's expertise entertaining, even if some of the information might now be considered outdated. Here is an example of Barbour's geology section: "Remember when looking at this rock face that it is an exposure of the great water bearing beds of the Plains, known as the Dakota group of the Cretaceous age . . . In many places it is full of highly interesting leaf impressions."

Not only have I given tours to guests from all parts of the United States, I've had guests from all across the world. A common question is if there are other caves in Nebraska. In addition to caves on private property that won't be mentioned, here are a few other caves of interest in Nebraska:

Indian Cave in Indian Cave State Park—named for the large sandstone cave within the park, this cave borders the Missouri River near Shubert, Nebraska. Indian Cave is the main geologic feature of the area and bears prehistoric Native American petroglyphs of an unknown date and origin.

The Cave at Ash Hollow State Historical Park—for several thousand years, early people camped near Ash Hollow Cave near Lewellen, Nebraska. One of the latest groups identified was the Dismal River People, ancestors of the Plains Apache. Less than 100 years after the Dismal River People left, settlers began to explore the area. Archaeologists have studied the cave and identified several groups of people who used the cave over thousands of years.

Happy Jack Chalk Mine—with more than 6,000 feet of honeycombed caverns, Happy Jack Peak and Chalk Mine features the only publicly accessible chalk room and pillar mine in North America. It is one of only two underground diatomite mines known to have existed in the United States, and the only one that is open to the public.

Taking the Tunnels' Temp

Robber's Cave's natural temperature is consistently 56–58 degrees Fahrenheit. The warmest I've seen the temp rise is 59 degrees, but that was at the end of my giving six or seven consecutive tours of approximately 30 people. The guests' body heat and breath can increase the temperature inside the cave. I found it interesting that in a 1976 *Journal Star* article, Edwin Sr. said that the cave temp remained 68 degrees Fahrenheit year round. The reporter could have misunderstood him, or it could be that in 1976, the airflow in the cave differed then. Nowadays, the temperature changes slightly the closer one moves toward the emergency exit or tunnel three, where the airshaft is left open for the bats.

Rectifying Misconceptions

Undoubtedly I have benefited from the expertise of many researchers on this project. Along with Nobbman, Hansen, McKee, and Zimmer, one source I found to be invaluable was Gary Soule's information about Robber's Cave. As a cave historian from the Wisconsin Speleological Society, Soule produced a historical booklet about the cave for Blue Blood in 2016. Additionally, he published an article on the cave for the National Speleological Society News in February of 2017 called "Nebraska's Historic Robber's Cave." Soule's booklet and article makes reference to the following:

- Native American usage of the cave

- 1862 settlers taking refuge in the cave for an entire winter

- A wagon train using the cave for protection

- The 1863 stone quarry that removed the cap rock

- The cave being publicized as the location of an 1867 duel

- The Pioneer Brewery's usage as well as Jacob Andra's expansion

- Jesse James seeking fresh horses after the 1876 Northfield, Minnesota, Bank Robbery on his way to his mother's in Rulo, Nebraska

- Coxey's Army use of the cave in 1893

- J. W. Scarborough's purchase in 1906, and intent to use for a mushroom garden

- Finding human bones, counterfeit coins and actual silver dollars from 1878 to 1882, a rifle, copper tubing, gambling devices, pocketbooks, a tanning stone, and Indian artifacts

- A lady from Kent, England, visiting Robber's Cave in the early 1900s

- UNL's Union Literary Society's use of the cave in 1912

- Tony Award-winning actress Sandy Dennis's Robber's Cave birthday party in 1952

- The 1968 explosion on the property

- The cave's closure in 1973, as well as its reopening in 1986

Soule provided me a wealth of information about Robber's Cave—all which I found incredibly useful. However, his information did contain a few inaccuracies that I have been able to correct through my interviews with Scarborough Jr. and access to his personal collection of cave photos. First, regarding the coyotes, Soule states, "More likely the real truth is . . . instead of coyotes, she had puppies. So urban legend can sometimes modify reality in strange ways." He's right about urban legends modifying reality, but the Scarboroughs actually did keep coyotes as pets on their property (see the later chapter "Coyotes at the Cave—More Than an Urban Legend").

The second bit of information I'd like to correct is regarding a 1908 post card that shows what Soule calls the natural entrance to the cave with a slightly curved stone retaining wall. This particular photo is actually the secondary entrance to the cave dug by Jacob Andra from the cellar of The Pioneer Brewery. The smaller, original natural entrance is a short distance to the north and features a different shape, the pear or teardrop that is consistent with tunnel number one. With the 1908 photo being taken after the wooden brewery structure had been removed, the stone wall he references is actually a remaining section of the brewery's foundation.

Scarborough Jr. described to me during one of our interviews how he and his grandpa attempted to fill in this section of the brewery foundation with sand and junked auto parts. Scarborough's admission to filling the foundation with auto parts explains why guests have described being able to see frames of cars protruding from the ground while driving past the property in the 1960s and 1970s.

I appreciate that Soule notes in his *NSS News* article that most of the early history on this cave, including up to when the brewers took over in 1869, may well just be folklore, yet he included it all in the name of completeness.

Do the Tunnels Extend to the Penitentiary or Regional Center?

When writer L. C. Oberlies visited J. W. Scarborough at the cave in the summer of 1906, Scarborough explained that "These [caves] have long been known as the Penitentiary Caves although there is no connection between them and our penal institution."

So what is the origin of such rumors? In the late 1900s, visitors would have been met by walls of stone and brick at the west ends of tunnels two and tunnel three. These bricked barriers inspired rumors as to what was on the other side and beyond, and they are mentioned in Boye's *The Guide to the Ghosts of Lincoln*. Urban legends developed that had the tunnels extending and connecting with the Nebraska State Penitentiary and the Lincoln Regional Center. So exactly what was on the other side of the walls? The answer: the cellar of the old Pioneer Brewery.

The Pioneer Brewery's cellar was described as having three tunnels radiating from it. One was walled off with stone sometime after 1931 but before 1947. Before that, a wooden door led from the far west end of tunnel two into the area where the Pioneer Brewery's cellar had been. The wooden door can be seen at the back of a photo of the May 1932 Cooties group. Later, a wall of stone replaced the wooden door.

Were There Other Entrances?

Every once in a while, a guest on a tour will slowly approach me with this look on their face that conveys they know something that no one else knows. "You know, the real entrance to this place is on the other side of 10th street, right?" The simple answer is, not a chance. The first original or natural tunnel of the cave stops at its east end, the second tunnel stops at its east end, and the third tunnel stops at its east end. The obstructions are not manmade barriers either; it's where the cave tunnel simply ends. For some time, tunnels two and three were stoned up at their west ends, but, as previously explained, on the other side of those two walls one would not find a secret tunnel to the Regional Center or State Penitentiary. Again, one would find themselves in the cellar of the old Pioneer Brewery.

The 1920 Lincoln City Directories listed Robber's Cave at 3300 South 11th Street, but by 1966 its address was 3243 South 10th Street. A Robber's Cave ad in *The Lincoln Star* from 1923 reads, "Entrance at 3213 So. 11th Street." These varying addresses might have added to the confusion. There is no actual cave entrance north of the Scarborough property; these references merely describe the entrance to the Scarborough property.

Approaching from the north and heading south, one would pass Van Dorn Park on the right and stop at about 10th and High Street where the Scarborough's mailbox stood. This is where a dirt path angled in a southwesterly direction leading to their property. The dirt path would turn to mud when wet and caused many automobiles to high center before paved, but at its end, one would see the Scarborough's house complete with sunporch, coyote pens, and an aviary at the back of the home with lily ponds. There was a windmill cistern covered in stones at the base, a row of mulberry trees to the north, and a concrete path that led up to the cave's entrance, which was a hut or shack that angled into the ground to the west.

Are the Legends of Native American Use True?

Between 1825 and 1892, eighteen separate treaties between American Indian tribes and the US government for land in Nebraska were negotiated. By the 1850s the Pawnee, Omaha, Oto-Missouri, Ponca, Lakota, and Cheyenne were the main Great Plains tribes living in the Nebraska Territory. What is known to most as tunnel number one has been labeled Pawnee Council Cave and Original Council Cave.

To be clear, I know of no claims that Native Americans lived in Robber's Cave, but according to legend, a short distance north of the cave, which today would be approximately 13th and Arapahoe or 14th and High Streets, now Arapahoe Gardens in Indian Village, local Indians utilized the promontory to hold trials for chiefs and high-ranking persons. It is said that those found guilty were to be buried in disgrace at a low area in the bluff, which logically could have been through the small, naturally-formed, original entrance to the cave. Also, there are claims that Pawnee medicine men held religious rites there (8/15/1976). It is important to note that the Indian rites that were supposed to have been held in the cave, though possible, remain unauthenticated.

This being the case, I thought to ask someone who had a strong interest and knowledge in American Indian history and culture. With the help of UNL Professor and author Joe Starita, I contacted Dr. David Wishart, a historical geographer at the University of Nebraska—Lincoln's

School of Natural Resources. Dr. Wishart has published several books on the Great Plains Indians, but when I asked him about American Indian use of Robber's Cave, he responded, "The local Indians here were the Otoe-Missouria. This was likely too far southeast for the Pawnee. I know nothing about Indian use of the cave."

I had known from the maps at the Nebraska History Museum that Lancaster Country primarily was Otoe or Oto-Missouria territory, but I wasn't sure if the Pawnee came into the area to hunt, given that they were principally hunters. So I again sought Jim McKee's input:

> The Pawnee could have come into Lancaster County; their land was considerably to the west and central part of the state. There is no evidence that can be proven that the Pawnee used the cave for ceremonies at any time [. . .] The cave was actually more of a pock originally and only through later working was made into a cave so its actual use by the Indians is probably apocryphal. The trinkets supposedly found in the cave were termed Indian trinkets, but I've never seen any corroboration of their origin. Why it was called the Pawnee Council Cave is probably not factual (2/28/2017).

Tales describing Native use of the bluff have existed since the cave first became known, but the 1939 Federal Writer's Project's *Guide to Nebraska* certainly added to the lore of the location. "In Pawnee legend it was in the Nahurac spirits cave that medicine men held mystic sacred rites, and neophytes were proven and initiated. And after the Indian scare of 1862, settlers lived in it [the cave] all winter." Another reason Natives could have used the cave at one time was for its sandstone, which was a popular rock used by tribes in the mortar and pestle design. Some American Indians created sandstone molds for silver-casting or to sharpen and sand tools.

Once, I gave a private tour to a gentleman of Ponca and Omaha heritage. He stated immediately upon entering the cave that he sensed the location was definitely used by Native Americans. He felt the cave could have been used for a sweat lodge or a ceremony, but as a member of the Omaha, he couldn't offer specifics on the Otoe-Missouria as they hold different customs. The gentleman explained that many Native Americans view caves as the womb of the earth, and for a tribe to know of the existence of a cave, yet not use it in some manner, would have been unlikely, although they would have left after temporarily using the space, rather than claiming the area or naming the cave. When this guest noticed the many small holes that still exist in the tunnel's walls, he mentioned the possibility of natives ceremoniously placing bones into them.

The only reference to bones in the cave I had known occurred when a few were found in 1906 while the first generation of Scarboroughs cleaned the cave in preparation for their mushroom garden. But after finding such interesting contents such as a tanning stone, arrowheads, rifles, counterfeit coins, gambling devices, and copper tubing, they decided to display the items and open the cave to the public. I looked into the prevalence of cave burials and learned from *National Geographic* that burial customs varied widely from tribe to tribe. Native Americans disposed of their dead in a variety of ways. While some practiced secondary bone burial, other tribes often deposited their dead in caves or in fissures of rocks. With a little help from the Nebraska State Historical Society's Highway Archeology Program Manager Rob Bozell and archaeologist Nolan Johnson, we've determined that if there was indeed Native use of the cave, it would have been by the Central Plains tradition people. "There are some Central Plains tradition sites not far from the cave so we know those folks were in the area," explained Johnson.

If only photos or sketches of the arrowheads that J. W. Scarborough found still existed, experts would likely be able to determine which Plains Indians used the cave, but unfortunately, like many of the objects excavated from the cave, they're long gone. Scarborough Jr. contacted Judi gaiashkibos (last name purposefully lowercased), Executive Director for the Nebraska Commission on Indian Affairs, because he wanted to give her the box of Native American items that had been passed on to him from his grandfather Fred, who received them from his father, J. W. Scarborough.

I eventually learned what happened to that box of items with the help of former Nebraska State Senator Colby Coash. Coash, a former coworker of mine who represented the 27th Nebraska legislative district, was the chairman of the State-Tribal Relations committee, and he invited Ms. gaiashkibos and her assistant to the cave for a tour. After I gave them a tour, Ms. gaiashkibos explained that she discarded the items Scarborough Jr. gave her because they didn't strike her as significant art or pottery.

During my next visit with Scarborough Jr., I asked what was included in the box that he gave the Indian Commission, and he described the objects that had been in possession of his grandfather Fred, an avid collector of Native artifacts, for many years. Fred Scarborough's collections included beadwork, arrowheads, an old photo of a chief, and an object that Scarborough Jr. described as follows: "It wasn't a tomahawk but it had a long handle. And fastened to the handle was a pinkish-colored stone, like an elongated football. If someone were hit by it, it'd put them down," he said. There were other objects, but vandals stole much of them from the display case that used to be be near the Scarborough's sunporch on the cave property, so Scarborough Jr. began keeping items inside on the nights when guests rented the cave. Unfortunately, I've come to the conclusion that any opportunity to examine Native items found in the cave has come and gone.

Logically, as the original temperature-controlled environment, open caves have been homes to people and animals for thousands of years. They offer shelter from weather and danger, and we have learned much about our ancestors by studying their contents: what they ate, their tools and burial practices. Unlike some caves that have existed for thousands of years, Robber's Cave in its current form has existed for nearly 150 years. Undoubtedly, the tunnels have seen many undocumented uses. Being mostly manmade, who knows what has all happened in the smaller, natural cavern before Jacob Andra began to extend it in 1869. If only the walls could talk, right?

Was Robber's Cave a Station for the Underground Railroad?

Another question I often receive while giving tours is whether or not Robber's Cave was ever a station along the Underground Railroad, the informal network of routes that led slaves north to free states. Professor, historian, and filmmaker Henry Louis Gates Jr. contends, "Few institutions [. . .] have attracted more attention recently from teachers, students, museum curators and the tourism industry than the Underground Railroad [. . .] but in the zeal to tell the story of this great institution, legend and lore have sometimes overwhelmed historical facts." The same can certainly be said for Robber's Cave.

The actual phrase Underground Railroad first appeared in *The Liberator* on October 14, 1842, but it did not become common until the mid-1840s. The original tunnel of Robber's Cave wasn't much of a cave until 1869, although settlers are said to have used the concealed space in 1862 for protection either from a harsh winter or an Indian attack. Gates also points out, "Since the end of the 19th century, many Americans—especially in New England and the Midwest—have either fabricated stories about the exploits of their ancestors or simply repeated tales they have heard."

First, I'll address the important question: were slaves owned in Nebraska? The answer is yes. According to the Mayhew Cabin's education and history page, "In the 1855 Territorial Census, six slaves were listed in Otoe County owned by residents of Nebraska City. The 1860 Federal Census showed that of the 3,953,761 slaves in America at the time, fifteen were in Nebraska Territory. The only known slave auction in Nebraska took place at Nebraska City in December 1860." The slaves attempting to flee would usually travel south across the Ohio River to the North via a vast system that actually stretched from Maine to the territories of Nebraska and Kansas.

One common misconception is that this railroad was physically underground. At certain points, subterranean spaces were used, but the *underground* adjective comes from the route's secretive aspect. "It led through woods, over fields, and across rivers, often operating under the cover of darkness. Escaping slaves followed the North Star or were directed to a specific safe house, or station, across the borders into freedom." Brave men and women, known as conductors, were willing to risk their own safety by offering temporary shelter. The refugees hid in cellars, attics, closets, and even secret rooms and tunnels. So did a famous Harriet Tubman-like conductor assist in or near southeast Nebraska in the mid-1800s? Actually, yes: James Henry Lane.

An associate director for the Nebraska State Historical Society David Bristow explains in his article "Lane's Army" published in *The Iowan* in 1997 that Lane was a Mexican War hero and former Congressman from Indiana, as well as a savvy political opportunist and a master of publicity. A Democrat whose political career had floundered after he voted for the Kansas–Nebraska Act, Lane emerged in Kansas as an anti-slavery leader. In 1856, the same year he was elected to the US Senate, he established a trail that dodged Missouri River steamboats (the boats could have been targets for proslavery Missourians). This trail would come to be known as the Lane Trail, and it actually crossed the Missouri River into Nebraska City, Nebraska, before heading south into Kansas after approximately 50 miles. Interestingly, Lane's chimneys, which were piles of stones, could be discovered on hilltops through Richardson, Nemaha, and Otoe counties.

Although Lane's Army of the North, as his collaborators would come to be known, did in fact aid many along a small portion of the Underground Railroad in Nebraska, Robber's Cave in Lincoln was not included along this route. A map of the Lane Trail clearly shows that Lincoln lies west of Nebraska's Underground Railroad depots, which include Little Nemaha, Camp Creek, and Nebraska City. There are countless ways this myth might have originated, but my guess is that the rumors connecting Robber's Cave to the Underground Railroad most likely developed from Fred Scarborough's story (detailed in his 1938 interview with Moss) of how his great-grandfather, who lived in Orleans County, New York, west of Rochester, was killed in 1860 "in his own yard, upon his return from delivering a group of runaway slaves to the next depot near Keokuk, Iowa. All it would have taken for the seeds of a runaway slave story to be planted was for Fred Scarborough to recount his great-grandfather's tale to a few people in Lincoln. It doesn't take much to form false presumptions, especially when people desire a story that simply isn't there.

Since Robber's Cave features 5,600 square feet of cave and 500 feet of linear tunnels, it is not surprising why active imaginations in the past have placed the cave along the path of the Underground Railroad. If interested in learning more about Lane, I highly recommend David Bristow's 1997 article from *The Iowan* titled "Lane's Army," and McKee's 2009 article from *The Journal Star* titled, "Lane and his Once-Famous Trail to Freedom."

Coxey's Army Quarters in the Cave

The cave's constant temperature would have made it a logical location for wintering quarters. In his book *Remember When* Jim McKee maintains that the cave is "well documented as an 1893–1894 wintering site for Coxey's Army." Gary Soule's Robber's Cave article in the *NSS News* also mentions Coxey's Army quartering in Robber's Cave on their way east. By the time Coxey's Army quartered in the cave during the winter of 1893, the cave would have been enlarged by Andra.

Coxeyites organized themselves into regiments and traveled across the country from as far west as Oregon to join businessman Jacob S. Coxey. Coxey led this group of unemployed men on a march to Washington, D.C. for the purpose of persuading Congress to authorize a vast program of public works that would provide jobs for the unemployed:

> He proposed a Good Roads Bill, a Federal project to help the unemployed and to give the poor the work that they needed, while also helping to maintain and improve America's infrastructure. Coxey's idea was radically ahead of its time—four decades ahead of FDR's New Deal programs. But Coxey had faith in his plan, declaring, "Congress takes two years to vote on anything . . . millions of people are hungry and cannot wait two years to eat" (Grinspan).

Although an estimated 20,000 joined the march at some point, many never reached D.C. as the participants were ridiculed in the press (or they could have been tired of marching across the country). Of the several groups that had set out for the US Capital, only about 500 arrived in Washington on May 1, 1894. Despite the publicity Coxey's Army received, the journey had no impact on public policy.

Robber's Cave as a Jesse James Hideout

Some of the most frequently asked questions before, during, and after tours have to do with the renowned outlaw Jesse James. Soule references a 1966 article from *Visiting American Caves* that states, "Since the time Jesse James holed up in the cave for three days after robbing the Northfield Bank, it has been known by its present name." When *Journal Star* writer Peter Salter interviewed me about this book, I gave him permission to print my phone number and email address along with the front-page article so that people could contact me and share stories about the cave. A secretary would have been handy as my voicemail and email inbox immediately filled with numerous Jesse-James-slept-in-my-grandpa's-barn tales. I enjoyed listening to all of the stories. Many contributors were certain that their accounts were fact; others were not so sure.

Not meaning to be a killjoy, yet wanting to retain credibility, I am sure to attach the terms "unsubstantiated and folklore" to this subject when giving tours. Fred Scarborough mentioned in a 1938 interview that he remembers locals mistakenly spotting James in the vicinity of the cave:

> Frank Rawlins, who drove a hack for The White Elephant Livery Barn in Lincoln, used to drive a Mr. Howard out here often. Some thought this Mr. Howard was Jesse James! [. . .] When we cleaned the cave we found an old carving, "A thief and a coward was Mr. Howard, but he laid as Jesse James in his grave."

This carving is a reference to a line from the 19th century American folk song about James first recorded by Bently Ball in 1919. Here is the actual lyric:

> But that dirty little coward
> That shot Mr. Howard
> Has laid poor Jesse in his grave

Of the thousands of carvings in the cave, I admit I have not found this one yet. Since this book is not intended to be a biography of James, (more than 500 books have been written about him, along with a dozen motion pictures), I'll focus mostly on the larger-than-life legend's connection to Nebraska. According to *Journal Star* writer Joe Duggan, the truth behind James's

Nebraska exploits can be "as elusive as James was after he robbed a bank." In a February 5, 1939, *Lincoln Sunday Journal and Star* article, it reads:

> The legends that have sprung up concerning the bandit were as thick as dandelions and he must have had the ability to be in a hundred different places simultaneously if all the several million people who saw him are to be believed.

Although James's criminal exploits transpired in Missouri, Iowa, and Minnesota, he never claimed a job in Nebraska. Even in 1939 the superintendent of the Nebraska Historical Society A. E. Sheldon stated, "I don't think Jesse James ever operated in Nebraska." Simply put, there are connections between James and Nebraska that can be verified, while others cannot.

Historians agree that James did indeed step foot in Nebraska repeatedly during his criminal career as he was quite familiar and comfortable with Nebraska, but whether he ever spent time in Robber's Cave is another story. McKee's May 31, 2009 article in the *Lincoln Journal Star* describes James's Nebraska connection in detail. As an eighteen-year-old Confederate sympathizer in Missouri, James joined Quantrill's Raiders who rode with guerrilla fighters and ambushed Union sympathizers. Toward the end of the Civil War, as the South weakened, Union troops were ordered west to subdue secessionists. With Quantrill's Raiders being one of the targets, these soldiers attacked the home of Zerelda Samuels, James's mother. She then fled from her home near Kearney, Missouri, to Rulo, Nebraska.

As the Kansas City Public Library's *Civil War on the Western Border* explains, once the Civil War ended, Jesse and his brother Frank accepted amnesty by surrendering at Lexington, Missouri. While in Lexington on May 15, 1865, Union troops, who were eager to avenge President Lincoln's death, severely wounded Jesse in the chest with .36 caliber bullet for being an amnesty seeker. James's brother Frank, with the help of a local farmer, whisked James to an uncle's, then eventually to Rulo, Nebraska, where he recovered with the help of Dr. Samuels, his mother's husband at the time, and a cousin, Zee Mimms, with whom James would marry in 1874 and later have two children. An interview with James historian Jim Beckner explained that Frank James turned himself in to Governor Thomas T. Crittenden in Jefferson City, Missouri, six months after Jesse's death.

The story that I hear mentioned most is that Jesse and Frank James hid in Robber's Cave after being badly wounded during the botched Northfield Bank robbery attempt. A brief account of the Great Escape as it has come to be known is given by writer Johnny Boggs in *True West Magazine*:

> Around 2 P.M. on Thursday, September 7, 1876, Frank James, Bob Younger, and Charlie Pitts walked into the First National Bank on Division Street [Northfield, Minnesota]. Clell Miller and Cole Younger rode up and dismounted . . . When the plan went to hell, Jesse James, Jim Younger and Bill Chadwell galloped in from Mill Square, guns blazing. Roughly seven minutes later, the surviving robbers—most if not all of them wounded—galloped out of town on five horses . . . They had managed to ride off with $26.60.

Boggs describes the gang separating near what is now Minneopa Falls State Park near Mankato, Minnesota, and after Frank and Jesse rode off, the Youngers were overtaken by a posse from Madelia at Hanska Slough near La Salle. Boggs continues:

> But the most mythic Jesse James story is found in eastern South Dakota near the town of Garretson. A 20-foot long foot bridge spans a 30-foot deep gorge. The spot is known as

Devil's Gulch. The story is that Jesse James leaped the gulch on horseback as a posse closed in.

From there, they escaped farther south into Dakota Territory or Sioux City, Iowa, before eventually settling around Nashville, Tennessee. James actually rented a home at 711 Fatherland Street in Nashville until 1881 under the alias J. D. Howard. Most historians doubt the jump happened as the span is too great, but as Mark Steil of Minnesota Public Radio said, "Even if the physical leap did not occur here, a psychic leap did. It's folk stories like this that freed James from the shackles of reality and propelled him into the heart of American mythology."

Shortly before the raid at Northfield, Jesse James did visit Nebraska City banker Logan Enyart (also a former Confederate officer from Missouri) who convinced James to pose for a portrait at the Walbaum Studio in 1875. Allegedly, this portrait resulted in a well-known daguerreotype of the desperado. The *Nebraska State Journal* reported that in 1939 this portrait was used in an issue of *Life* magazine. Nemaha County Sherriff Dave Plasters of Brownville, Nebraska, married one of James's cousins and the two (James and Plasters) were said to be close friends. Census and genealogy records verify that James had cousins in Jefferson, Thayer, Buffalo, Custer, and Webster counties. James even wanted to buy land in south-central Nebraska. On March 2, 1882, he responded to an ad in the *Lincoln Journal* using a pseudonym Thomas Howard. The 160-acre property was on the south edge of Franklin County, and James wrote to the owner who lived in Lincoln indicating that he planned to travel to Nebraska to inspect the land (10/18/2007).

Did the best-known bad man in all of America have a desire to settle down and become respectable? Some historians believe so, but we'll never know for sure, as one of his young recruits, twenty-oneyear-old Bob Ford, shot James on April 3, 1882, for a $10,000 bounty as James turned to adjust a picture on the wall of his home in St. Joseph, Missouri. As the wandering musician Billy Gashade's late-1800s song states, "Robert Ford came along like a thief in the night, and laid poor Jesse in his grave." Jesse, his wife, mother, stepfather, and half-brother are all buried in their family's plot at Mount Olivet Cemetery in Kearney, Missouri.

Two other stories place James east of Lincoln and just south of downtown. The first is from Jerry Fisher, who called me in response to Peter Salter's May 2017 article in *The Lincoln Journal Star*:

In 1933, we purchased the farm ground at 134th and East O Street. We built Crooked Creek Golf Course and opened in 1995. There was an abandoned farm on the property, which we tore down. One day an old cowboy walked into the clubhouse looking around, and when I asked if I could help him, he had an interesting story for me. His grandparents had homesteaded the land and lived in the farmhouse. The cowboy told me that one day the James Gang stopped and asked his grandmother if they could water their horses in the creek. Jesse gave his grandmother a five-dollar gold piece before they left. I am sure they passed through this area.

Even former cave owner Ed Scarborough Jr. had what he called "second-hand information" from his grandfather, Fred. He recounted the following tale during one of our interviews:

Alba Brown was a barber and a doctor and later on an undertaker. He had a funeral parlor on Ninth Street across from the old power plant on the southwest corner. [Scarborough Jr. could be referring to Alba Brown's mortuary on South 11th Street.] He was to have treated Jesse James for a gunshot wound with Frank. They later got fresh horses from the barn at the old cave place and rode off to Rulo to rest at their mother's house before going on to Missouri.

When I read this account to James historian, Jim Beckner, and asked what he thought of its validity, his response was, "I believe it—it sounds exactly right to me."

A well-respected source to find answers in Jesse James subject matter is award-winning American biographer T. J. Styles. Stiles now lives in Berkley, but was born and raised in Foley, Minnesota, and actually graduated from Carleton College in Northfield with Distinction in History. His book about Cornelius Vanderbilt won a National Book Award in 2009, and in 2010 the same book won the Pulitzer Prize for Biography/Autobiography. Furthermore, his book *Custer's Trials: A Life on the Frontier of a New America* received the 2016 Pulitzer Prize for History! I decided to ask Mr. Stiles if he thought Jesse James had hidden in Lincoln's Robber's Cave. His response:

I'm afraid probably not. The James brothers did not like caves. They had lots of supporters who put them up in houses, and now and then they slept in barns. I've never read any original sources that placed them in caves.

According to Emmett Hoctor, a historical researcher from Plattsmouth, Nebraska, "Jesse always chose to stay in the finest hotels; he didn't dwell in caves. He shook hands with detectives who were looking for him. He would say, 'I hope you find him.'"

McKee agrees that there are facts in the James connection to Nebraska, but his presence at the cave is not one of them, as stated in his May 31, 2009 *Journal Star* article:

It is true that Jesse's mother, Zerelda Samuels, taught school at Decatur in 1862, and that his brother Frank married Anni Ralson in Omaha in June of 1874. Frank also drove a stagecoach once from Arbor Lodge in a parade and judged a horse show. He was not however involved in the 1877 Union Pacific train robbery at Big Springs, nor was he ever at Robber's Cave in Lincoln after visiting his mother at Rulo—though he is the robber who gave it his name.

I read the statements of Styles, Hoctor, and McKee to Mr. Beckner during our interview because I was curious to hear what his response would be. Up to that point, I had convinced myself that the James brothers never used the cave, but Beckner's response forced me to reconsider once again:

They're mostly right; they (Frank and Jesse) didn't need to hide in caves because they had friends and family all over. And most of the time, hiding out in a cave would have been a dumb idea . . . smoke, only one way out, but if Frank and Jesse were both wounded like they were after Northfield, those are not normal circumstances, and that is not a normal cave (Robber's Cave). They could ride right into it, there was a water source, an airshaft for the smoke, and a second way out. They were very comfortable in Nebraska and it makes a lot of sense to me that they stopped there [the cave] on their way south to get closer to Rulo.

I believe one reason why many have attached James's name to the cave in Lincoln is simply because his name is attached to basically all Robber's Caves throughout the Midwest. There is another Robber's Cave on the bank of the Missouri River near Macy, Nebraska, where Jesse and Frank supposedly hid. That particular Robber's Cave, now known as the Hole in the Rock, is part of the Hole in the Rock Recreation Area and Big Elk Park. This also happens to be where, according to another legend, Jesse rode his horse off of a 100-foot chalk cliff called Maiden's Leap and swam away!

Another such account locates the James brothers in 1867 hiding out in a Robber's Cave, also known as Cave Springs, in Missouri. If one were to attend one of Richmond, Missouri's, 1867 bank robbery reenactments during Outlaw Days, one might hear musician David Knopf, who is also the news editor for the Richmond News, perform his song "Robber's Cave," which takes a few liberties with the historical record. According to Knopf's song, Jesse and the boys were reported to have ridden west out of town and headed to Robber's Cave.

In addition to Missouri and Nebraska, Oklahoma also contains a Robbers Cave (although it's spelled differently—no apostrophe). Four miles north of Wilburton, Oklahoma, near Lake Carlton in the Sans Bois Mountains is Robbers Cave State Park. Today there are 8,000 acres, three lakes, and plenty of tourists, but the area was once a rugged southeast Oklahoma wilderness that, *allegedly*, Jesse James and the Younger Gang escaped to in order to gain a few days of rest. Some even say that James hid out in Oklahoma's Wichita, also known as Ouachita, Mountains, which claim to have sheltered many outlaws. Apparently, the heavily forested area is lined with hidden caverns and is known to have concealed everyone from the James brothers, the Youngers, the Dalton Gang, the Rufus Buck Gang, and Belle Starr. As you can see, when someone mentions Robber's Cave and Jesse James in the same sentence, there is much to sort through if veracity is desired.

Local Historian Dale Nobbman informed me of a James connection with the small village of Washington, Nebraska. What's unique about this version is that the James gang is on their way to Northfield. In the town's centennial celebration book, *The History of Washington, Nebraska: A Struggle for Survival, 1887 to 1976*, a section reads "Jessie James Slept Here":

In 1876, on their way to Northfield, Minnesota, the Jesse James gang spent the night in a barn on the Fritz Bergman farm just a fourth of a mile east of the present town. Jesse and Frank James, along with Cole Younger and his two brothers Bob and Jim, and a man named Charlie Pitts asked to sleep in the hay loft of the barn. They told the family not to leave the place that night, and posted a guard. The next morning, Mrs. Bergman fed them breakfast, and they left. The family wasn't sure who it was until later; but they were very frightened. This was verified by Fritz Bergman's daughter, Mrs. Amanda Paasch, of Elkhorn. It is interesting to note that the barn is still standing today.

Nobbman's take on the matter is as follows:

After leaving Lincoln and traveling one day to the future Washington area, the Bergmann farm would have made a perfect place to stay the first night and lay low. Washington is still a small town nestled into a low area completely surrounded by hills. Even today you would never know the town is there from a mile or two away if it weren't for a sign along Highway 36 pointing the way to Washington. The Lincoln to Washington—and virtual straight-as-an-arrow route aiming right towards Northfield—seems as plausible and more likely than any other possibility I have read. I never took much stock in the James Gang at Robber's Cave in Lincoln folklore, but I've almost convinced myself it's a real possibility!

So the question remains: did Jesse James ever set foot in Lincoln's Robber's Cave? After questioning historians who claim he did, and some that assert he did not, my conclusion is that he probably did not; however, after interviewing Beckner on the matter, I almost changed my mind (but only hard evidence could do that for me). The James brothers were comfortable in Nebraska, and they were definitely in the Lincoln area—that is one truth we do know. It's not out of the realm of possibility that after being injured at Northfield, Frank and Jesse took cover in or near the cave as they worked their way south to Rulo. Again, Beckner made an interesting point: being injured created abnormal circumstances, and Robber's Cave is an abnormal cave.

Therefore, I find nothing wrong with mentioning the James legend to add entertainment or mystique to those who visit Robber's Cave, as long as it's introduced as legend or folklore. As Blue Blood Brewing Company's President and Co-Founder Brian Podwinski once stated regarding the what draws visitors back to the cave, "There are so many stories, [. . .] and maybe they're not all true, but at the same time we can't say for certain they're not true" (8/27/2015). It is fun to speculate about the possible link between the James Gang and Robber's Cave. Tie in a few facts with the folklore, and one can certainly weave a seemingly credible case.

Jonathan Roth makes an important point in his book with Mary Jane Nielsen *Lincoln Looks Back*, "We've always been of the opinion, that under more than a few sets of circumstances, a legend can be a good thing." Whether or not James ever stepped foot in Robber's Cave, we'll most likely never know, but the fact remains: he is the outlaw the cave is named for.

Vigilante Groups and Horses at the Cave

During Moss's 1938 interview, Fred Scarborough mentions stalls and describes some of the objects found in the cave:

> The first cavern in the cave was fixed with 16 stalls. In cleaning out this cavern, we found 244 old rusty horseshoes. Everything was screened and we had a bushel basket of broken knife blades, buckles, bayonets, and other things.

I had no prior knowledge of horses in the cave, or of the Anti Horse Thief League for that matter, before Fred Scarborough referenced them during his 1938 interview. In the age before the automobile horse theft was a more common and serious offense. To combat the problem, Major David McKee of Clark County, Missouri, and a group of his friends formed the Anti Horse Thief Association or A.H.T.A. in 1853. (This group is not to be confused with the National Horse Thief Detective Association or State Horse Thief Detective Association.)

According to Mark Boardman, a writer for *True West Magazine*, the A.H.T.A. was an important citizen-based crime fighting outfit in the Old West. After starting in the late-1850s, it spread to many states and territories and included a national constitution and bylaws. Membership worked to prevent theft of livestock and more. They denied being vigilantes.

The A.H.T.A. grew and spread to many states reaching its membership peak of 50,000 in 1916. They were organized into jurisdictions with the Kansas Jurisdiction governing Kansas, Nebraska and all territory north, south and west not otherwise districted. American sociologist, historian, and educator Frank Wilson Blackmar describes the group in his 1912 book with a wonderfully long-winded title, *Kansas: a cyclopedia of state history, embracing events, institutions, industries, counties, cities, towns, prominent persons, etc.*:

> The Anti Horse Thief Association is in no sense a vigilance committee, and the organization has never found it necessary to adopt the mysterious methods of 'Regulators,' 'White Caps' or kindred organizations. Its deeds are done in the broad open light of day.

Blackmar's statement causes Fred Scarborough's mentioning of White Caps setting fire to the brewery all the more intriguing. Author Chris McCormick describes whitecapping as a violent, lawless movement among farmers that occurred specifically in the United States during the late 19th century and was originally a ritualized form of enforcing community standards, appropriate behavior, and traditional rights. By the mid-1870s there were numerous groups like this showing up in the Midwest, and it is possible that Scarborough confused the A.H.T.A. with another group that actually did carry out vigilante justice against horse thieves such as the State Horse Detective Association.

With brothels being referred to as sporting houses, dance halls, and gambling houses, the old dance hall that Scarborough references would have been not only a likely target for the A.H.T.A., but also for White Caps who, at times, acted as morality enforcers. Two of the more serious crimes in Nebraska at that time were horse and cattle theft, as these were among the most valuable items a settler was apt to possess.

Furthermore, additional references to horses in the cave and the Anti Horse Thief Association can be found in the *1938 NSM* article. The article mentions the visible indications of the horse stalls that still existed at the time in the larger passageways. "That cannot be questioned as Sam Melick, who was then a member of a vigilante organization or Anti Horse Thief Association during the year 1879, entered the cave and cut five stolen horses loose."

In addition to cutting loose horses from Robber's Cave, Melick had no shortage of suspenseful moments on horseback once he joined law enforcement. On August 23, 1884, Melick was transporting a rape suspect, Luciano Padillo, from the jail to a homestead in the southwest portion of the county in order to obtain an eyewitness and to avoid a lynch mob. Melick's strategy was leaked and he was confronted by "a mob of some fifty masked riders" who hanged Padillo along the timber near Cheese Creek. The incident is recorded in detail as Lancaster County Law Enforcement history. Melick went on to become deputy sheriff under Sheriff Grant Ensign during the years 1880 to 1882, and then served as sheriff of Lancaster Country from 1884 to 1888. Following an outbreak at the penitentiary in which three convicts killed Warden James Delhanty, Melick became the acting warden.

The 1938 *Nebraska Sheriff's Magazine* article also mentions that in addition to the 244 horseshoes found, parts of bridle bits and harness buckles had been cached in a small cavity that led off from one of the main hallways. This could have been the "question mark," "robber's roost," "fat man's misery," or the spot where the fireplace would eventually sit as these three are the only cavities that offshoot from main tunnels. The article continues, "There are now people living in the vicinity of Seward and York who recall their parents recovering stolen horses found at the Lincoln Cave."

Moreover, on the subject of horses in and or near the cave, one of the objects found buried deep in the cave's sand actually coincides with hammering horseshoes. Several objects that were excavated from the cave, mostly rusted antique auto parts, are displayed today along the ledge in the barrel room. I recently conducted O.C.C. Preservation Architect Matt Hansen on a tour, and he noticed that one of the rusted pieces was similar to a leg vise or post vise. After a bit of research, he found that the mechanism is probably a foot-operated leg vise:

> These were used by someone who did a lot of work forging horseshoes and needed repeated quick access to a vise for forging without having to tighten and loosen the vise jaws by hand. A piece like this would be very convenient for hammering on a horseshoe and then putting it back in the fire to get hot again before hammering some more until it reached the desired shape.

In the 1938 Moss interview, Fred Scarborough mentions the Anti Horse Thief League burning down an old dance hall and sporting house, which stood on the cave.

Will Robber's Cave Become a Nationally Registered Historic Landmark?

To be clear, Robber's Cave as of 2017, is not listed on the National Register of Historic Places in Nebraska. Certain comments printed by Vi Scarborough in the 1980s intrigued me, so I asked her husband, Scarborough Jr., and historic preservation planner Ed Zimmer what happened with the idea. Regarding listing the property on the National Register of Historic Places, the Scarboroughs were interested, but Mr. Zimmer had a different interpretation of the property and the nomination never moved forward. In a July 15, 2017 email from Mr. Zimmer, he states:

> National Register of Historic Places require a very specific nomination process including a thorough description; discussion and defense of a property's 'integrity' of design, materials, location, etc.; and a well-documented statement of significance in predefined areas of history. I thought there was a reasonable chance for a successful nomination based on the cave's excavation by Andra for Pioneer Brewery and subsequent reuse as a recreational site. I even thought there was a means to introduce the legends by describing the cave as a source of folklore described by scholars such as Louisa Pound. However, the 'Pawnee Council Cave' and Jesse James hideout stories did not appear to me to have the documentation for those to be the basis of the Cave's National Register significance, and there my 'impression of the site differed' from that of the Scarborough family's as I recall.

Not only did the Scarborough family try to have the cave named as a historical landmark, but Kent Seacrest asserted that Ridge Development looked into the possibility too. (Ridge Development Company owned the cave after the Scarborough family). Nothing came of the idea. "It may be another piece of Lincoln's culture going by the wayside like drive in movie theaters and Cool Crest Miniature Golf" (Reist).

Depending on Blue Blood Brewing Company's interest, I would be willing to pursue a Robber's Cave nomination in the future. In an email from Mr. McKee, he explains, "I have strong doubts about the use by the Pawnee and/or Jesse James but I don't think either would affect the nomination potential."

In an attempt to counter a few opinions that Robber's Cave contains little to no significance, I'd like to reference a two-year study that was undertaken in the 1970s in order to determine alternate corridors for the proposed freeway system aimed at relieving the traffic in downtown Lincoln, Nebraska. The planners were to consider the impact on the following "historic and archeologic [sic] landmarks" deemed the most important by the State Historical Society. The list of landmarks included Robber's Cave, along with other historically significant locations: the Prey Farmstead, the Krull House, pioneer buildings near Roca, pioneer graves, John Cadman's house and his stagecoach station site, Old City Hall, the Tyler House, and the Hudson cabin, just to name a few. The fact that the planners at that time considered the cave an historic site in Lancaster County says something about its significance. "Items that serve as natural and historical landmarks anchor mankind to legacies of the past. They are milestones of nature's or man's achievements," and I believe Robber's Cave to be one of them.

In August of 1925, the *Lincoln Star* published a list of "Interesting Spots to Please Visitors" and besides the beautiful homes, the new capitol building, the state fairgrounds, Capitol Beach, the University's city campus and farm campus, Robber's Cave was featured as attractive and worthy of inspection (8/30/1925). Robber's Cave truly is a unique local landmark that links many to their past.

Deciphering Fact from Fiction

I own every single book by historian James L. McKee. Moreover, I thoroughly enjoyed attending his history of Lincoln classes. I combed through all of his books that make mention of Robber's Cave in an attempt to separate the fact from fiction. The following are undocumented uses of Robber's Cave according to McKee's book *Remember When . . . Memories of Lincoln*: Before and during the eighteenth and nineteenth centuries, the cave was once used by local American Indians—some say for a sweat lodge or as a burial ground, others say for a meeting or trial site. Jesse James spent three nights in the cave after the Northfield Bank Robbery on his way to his mother's in Rulo, Nebraska.

On the other hand, the following cave uses are those listed as confirmed according to the same text *Remember When . . . Memories of Lincoln*: As early as 1862, settlers fled to the cave during an Indian attack. The first recorded event at the cave was a duel held there in 1867. The cave was an 1893–1894 wintering site for Coxey's Army. It became a commercial picnic site in 1906 charging 25 cents for admission. When the cave was cleaned out, the new owners found copper still tubing, counterfeit coins and numerous Indian relics (McKee 42).

Coyotes at the Cave: More Than an Urban Legend

Whenever I mention the coyotes that the Scarborough family kept in cages or pens on the property, I'm often met with looks of surprise or bewilderment. Some claim that the Scarboroughs never kept coyotes; that their presence on the property was merely an urban legend (as previously mentioned in the "Rectifying Misconceptions" chapter). I can assure you that the Scarboroughs did indeed keep coyotes. Scarborough Jr. gave me photos of them and provided their names.

A 1925 *Lincoln Evening Journal* article describes Esther and a young Edwin Scarborough capturing a coyote pup, Jack, in Colorado. Mrs. Scarborough thought about having the pup mounted, but instead gave Jack to Fire Station No. 1 to become the station's third mascot. Fireman Petey Gross was Jack's official keeper. "Jack was not overly pleased with his prospects for existence in the future when he was led into the station at the end of a stout chain" (7/6/1925). For what it's worth, the two mascots preceding Jack were Alec the garter snake and Jim the crow.

The family had other coyotes as well. Scarborough Jr. came in possession of two young coyotes after their mother was killed in a coyote hunt southeast of Lincoln. He raised the two and named them Minnie and Seymore. He commented about how they were beautiful animals and they didn't stink like dogs. My inquiring what happened to the two coyotes conjured up a bad memory for Scarborough Jr. He explained that his Grandma Esther became really angry with him once and let them loose. Seymour was shot and killed in nearby Van Dorn Park, but later he found Minnie trotting along south of College View. He called out, "Minnie!" and she stopped what she was doing, turned and looked, but then kept on running along. That was the last Scarborough Jr. saw of her.

Early Opinions of the Cave

Often the term *Robber's Cave* conjures images of loot and a gang of thieves. Many caves of this type have been discovered around the United States—and around the world for that matter. For example, in 1919 four men found the loot of a gang of railway thieves in the mountain side at Thorold, Ontario, including expensive silks, tapestries, and velvets. The find was deemed a treasure trove and readers in Lincoln could enjoy the exciting story in the *Lincoln Evening Journal* under the headline, "Explore a Robber's Cave." During the late nineteenth century and early twentieth century, the Midwest was no exception to stories such as these, therefore, it's enjoyable to learn what many thought were the cave's origins before Jacob Andra put pick axe to sandstone for nearly four years.

Before 1919, uncertainty surrounded the cave's origin. L. C. Oberlies of *The State Journal* wrote in 1906, "An antiquated stone foundation of unknown age built by some old master hand in operative masonry, stands not far away, and a secret passage way has been found leading from the basement of this old dwelling into one tunnel of the cave." This reference of a stone foundation and secret passage either refers to a remaining wall from the Pioneer Brewery's foundation (the old brewery cellar had an entrance to the tunnel two) or the stone wall with arch built that is now the south wall of Blue Blood's barrel room (the arch now leads guests into the first tunnel).

To be honest, many initial descriptions of the cave are downright humorous. Here's one in particular from an April 1898 *Nebraska State Journal*:

> It was in the largest vault that the most singular discovery was made. In a corner, and on the floor were found implements of industry, which from their appearance had evidently been used in the construction of this singular work—a work of art originally, for although the lapse of time had erased some, there were still other marks of the tools of the artisan perceptible along the [. . .] chamber and passage. The tools were there—the result of their use was there—but the workmen were gone—and where? The Toltec and the Aztec builded [*sic*] vast temples for ages, but their ruins have been the habitations of birds and beasts. The builders of the Ohio and Mississippi mounds and fortifications are known only by the remains of their ancient labors. The aborigines have left on inscription rocks, records of their history—but alast [*sic*] who can read them? But those who delved in the rock, and left the shapely caverns we have just described—who were they? Was their work a retreat from ferocious enemies—a defence [*sic*]—a domicile or a prison? The builders were gone—no written record remains—and ages may not tell when nor how nor why their work was done. They invite examination, and the learned in antiquities may trace their origin and purpose.

In December 1913, someone wrote to *The Lincoln Star's* "Dear Minerva" section and asked the following:

QUESTION, "Dear Minerva—Will you please tell me who made the so-called Robber's Cave? I have reference to the one located between Lincoln and the penitentiary." —Curious.

ANSWER – "There is a difference of opinion as to who made this cave and no one really knows whether it is artificial or natural or a combination of natural and artificial means. In a booklet edited by the present owner of the cave, Mr. Scarborough [this would have been J. W.], a paragraph on its origin reads: 'As to the origin of the cave in detail, there are those who believe at some remote date, the earth at this place was disturbed by earthquake or gaseous upheaval that left crevices in the stone, either entirely open or in loose condition, and that the crevices have been opened up by natural or artificial means or both. This theory is supported by the fact that in places there is comparatively loose sand, while slag like or cinder formations are found suggesting volcanic heat. Others believe that the lowland along the creek and reaching up to the mouth of the cave has been an inland sea or lake; that the waves lashing back against the elevated shore had washed the softer parts away leaving cavities in the hill, the cave thus originating. This theory is supported by the lay of the land and the fact that the receding lake was still here at the time of the early settlement of the country'" (12/30/1913).

This wasn't the first time volcanic heat had been mentioned in the cave's formation. From a geological point of view there is much to study in the caves. Again, a reference to Oberlies 1906 article, "The dips and various strata shown are very interesting if not remarkable. There is evidence of volcanic action in the iron slag-like chunks of moulten [*sic*] metal."

I'm sure Fred Scarborough, who would have owned the cave at the time of the Oberlies article, would have known about the Pioneer Brewery Company and Andra's enlargement of the cave. I wonder what Jacob Andra, a hardworking horse collar maker that lived on nearby Rose Street would have thought having his daily work compared to that of the Aztecs, Toltecs, North American Mound Builders, and aborigines!

Another one of my favorite explanations is from Jerome Schamp, sometimes Shamp, who served in the state legislature in the 1880s. Jerome happened to be a nephew to Peter Schamp, historian Dale Nobbman's great-great-grandfather who settled in Lincoln in 1862. Schamp's explanation was printed in *The Lincoln Star* in August of 1917:

> One disclosure made by Mr. Shamp [*sic*] is as to the origin of the well-known Robber's Cave south of the city. In 1869 a young man came to this country and settled about where Eleventh and High Streets are now. Beer was scarce in these parts at that time—too scarce to suit the youth. He dug a hole in the ground and put the beer in it. As his business grew, the hole grew, until it became quite large.

Dr. Wesley Queen's Thoughts

If you haven't heard of Dr. Wesley Queen, he seemed like quite the man who had an opinion on everything. *The Journal Star* in 1914 described him as Lancaster County's only Union represented soldier in the Civil War and founder of the first Sunday School and sanitarium in the vicinity. Apparently he was Lancaster's first physician and was even appointed by President Lincoln to be Lancaster County's first postmaster. He walked to what is now Lancaster County in 1860 from northern Iowa and saw the first Fourth of July celebration in Lancaster, which took place on Yankee Hill. He also mentioned helping to build the first house constructed in Lincoln in 1864 on the north side between 16th and 17th and O Street. According to *The Lincoln Daily Star* the stone for this home was obtained in the vicinity of the cave near the penitentiary and asylum (11/1/1914).

Some of the stories about Dr. Queen seem quite outlandish, like his Indian Scare of 1864 encounter. Jim McKee asserted in a June 19, 2017 email that "some, even many of Dr. Queen's firsts may be true, but it is hard to sort out the fact from the fiction." So keep in mind that Dr. Queen's *expertise* regarding the formation of Robber's Cave could be a bit off. First in 1908, in a letter to the Nebraska State Historical Society, Queen posited that "the pioneers enlarged Robber's Cave in the winter of 1863 to get protection from cold, stormy weather," and about six years later, in the same November 1914 *Lincoln Daily Star* article, Dr. Queen made a similar claim that due to there being little wood on the creeks, part of the Robber's Cave was dug as a necessity to have some place to spend the cruel winters.

Folklorist Louis Pound's Take on "Lincoln Cave"

Here is an experience that most bibliophiles can relate to: one day while reorganizing my personal library I came across the book *Selected Writings of Louise Pound*. I had kept the book in a certain spot for some reason, but of course I couldn't remember exactly why. Well, it became clear when I thumbed through the pages and browsed the table of contents. Pound dedicated a section on what was known at the time as "Lincoln Cave" in a chapter entitled "Nebraska Cave Lore," which she read in part before the Western Folklore Conference at the University of Denver in 1948. Pound references a two-sided sign that read "Notorious Old Cave" on one side and "Robbers' Cave" on the other. Even though the 1939 Federal Writer's Project's *Guide* mentions nothing of the cave for storage by brewers, Pound acknowledges that in 1869 two brewers (these would have been Ulmer and Lindner) hired a laborer (this would have been Andra) to enlarge the cave for storing beer in the old-world fashion: "In 1873 the brewers became bankrupt in the financial collapse and the cave was given up." She points out that the information in the 1939 FWP's *Guide* likely came from the present owners of the place, and she dismisses much of the cave's lore seemingly because her parents had no knowledge of Indians or settlers using the cave. For example, "As for the robbers . . ., their presence is very doubtful; their origin probably commercial. Members of the Pound family were all on hand then and never heard of them."

Pound was a prolific scholar, professor, and writer, and I surely respect her opinion, but just because her prestigious family had no knowledge of crime at the cave doesn't quite disprove its existence. Pound goes on to discount the presence of horse-thieves: "Horses could not well be concealed in or outside the cave." On the contrary, deputy sheriff Sam Melick cut five stolen horses loose from the cave in 1879. Pound might not have known about the 16 horse stalls in the cave, or the 244 horseshoes later found there. She might not have known about the horse barn that stood just a few hundred feet south of the cave, or about the Anti Horse Thieve League setting fire to the barn (or perhaps the abandoned brewery as one theory has it) in 1885.

Pound declares that such illegal activity could not have existed so close to such a vibrant city as Lincoln, " . . . so near the thriving Lincoln of those days, with its growing university, the presence of horse thieves and robbers . . . would have been known." Pound asserts, "My father was a judge and, of all persons, would have been likely to hear of their operations. Dwellers . . . never reported robbers in the neighborhood."

Are we to assume that if a crime isn't reported or a judge doesn't know about it, it never happened? I don't intend to be overly critical of Pound, but I find some of the reasons to her assertions a bit condescending and naive. However, I am glad that I came across her excellent book, as Pound's account of "Lincoln Cave" is helpful in that it captures what a very knowledgeable and well-respected professor and citizen knew of the cave in the 1940s: she felt that Indian knowledge and utilization of the cave was possible but improbable; the cave had never been one of the five *loci* recognized as sacred by the Pawnee; and last, Coxey's Army, never quartered there (although McKee would beg to differ). McKee states in his book *Remember When*, "It is . . . well documented as an 1893–1894 wintering site for Coxey's Army." All things considered, I find it pleasing to know that the venerable Louis Pound stated that the cave was worth visiting, and I appreciate how she felt about the cave's various legends being inevitable, but to her, "not regrettable."

The Souvenir Booklet

(circa 1910)

In 1910 J. W. Scarborough published the *Souvenir Booklet of Robbers' Cave*, which today can be read at the Nebraska State Historical Society. On the cover the reader is instructed to "Take Pen. Car to High Street" (Lincoln featured street cars for nearly 64 years beginning in 1881 when horses pulled the cars. The street cars operated until 1945).

As I describe the content of the booklet, please keep in mind that it was written more than 100 years ago and, regarding specific geography, what the writer may have claimed as fact then, might not be completely true, or could have been since proven inaccurate.

The tiny, 100-year-old manuscript includes a layout of the cave's tunnels referred to as the "Ground Plan of The Cave." Before opening up to black-and-white photos, the booklet reads, "There is more than 500 lineal feet of tunnel, divided into five main rooms, with smaller niches or get-ways, as they are called now. There is over 5,600 feet of floor space."

One of the photos depicts seven people standing near the brewers' entrance to the cave, and it reads, "Turf, Loess Soil and Sub-Soil, Glacial Drift, Sioux Quartzite, Dakota Formation, Stratification, False Bedding." The question is posed, "What is THE CAVE?" and by the aid of illustration and descriptions, "the author hopes to adequately convince the most skeptical that it is worthy of their time and attention."

The little volume begins with three paragraphs that describe the Dakota Sandstone underlying the eastern slope of the Rocky Mountains. The sandstone varies in depth from a few feet to several hundred feet and varies in thickness almost as much as in depth. Lincoln, Nebraska, features an outcropping of this stone in which the cave is located. The many colors of sandstone are described:

> The heavier drifts of iron ore, intermingled with sand, make a very hard and impenetrable substance. In some places the water seems to have flowed through underneath the more hardened strata and left the sand loose with small cavities or fissures . . . The ground over the cave lies high and is slightly, and has at one time been timbered, evidences still remaining. The indications are that it was used as a camping ground or signal station by the Indians many years ago, and there is a tradition that at one time the place was called Pawnee Council Cave, and that it was a place of resort or rather of holding court. Thus when a chief was to be dealt with, this was one of the places of trial, and if found guilty of certain crimes

such as cowardice, he was executed and buried in a low and obscure place. Some of the old pioneers, visiting here now, tell us that there are Indian graves here, but no trace of them has been found.

The next paragraph of the booklet provides an idea of what many thought of the cave's origins before Jacob Andra explained how he enlarged it for the Pioneer Brewery in his 1914 interview with *The Daily News*. I showed the booklet's explanation of the cave's origin to Nebraska State Geologist Matt Joeckel over lunch one day, and he received a good chuckle while reading some of the explanations:

> As to the origin of the cave, in detail, there are those who believe that at some remote date the earth at this place was disturbed by earthquake or gaseous upheaval that left crevices in the stone, either entirely open or in loose condition, and that the crevices have been opened up by natural or artificial means, or both.

The author lists the support for this theory as the presence of comparatively loose sand, along with slag-like or cindery formations suggesting volcanic heat. One paragraph asserts:

> Some of the cavities may have been enlarged by wild animals at a prehistoric date, or the Indians may have enlarged them, since the relics found in the walls of the cave prove that Indians inhabited parts of the place at least. When white men came, the place was enlarged to meet the demands of their lawless purposes.

The explanation included in the booklet that is closest to being accurate is the following:

> Others believe that the low land along the creek [. . .] reaching up to the mouth of the cave had been an inland sea or lake; that the waves lashing back against the elevated shore had washed the softer parts away leaving cavities in the hill, the cave thus originating.

The author lists support for this theory as "the lay of the land" and the fact that "the receding lake was still here at the time of the early settlement."

Then, the author references the brewery: "At one time the cave probably was used to harbor an illicit still and about the time of the founding of Lincoln, beer was manufactured in large quantities." The author goes on to provide us a description of what the property might have been like after the brewery was abandoned:

> In years later the place was allowed to go uncared for and, unclaimed and as no man's land, it became a rendezvous for lawlessness, and is reputed to have been perhaps the toughest place in the whole country.

The next statement is what indicates to me that the booklet was published in 1910. J. W. Scarborough purchased the property in 1906 and points out, "The debris and wastes accumulated in past years [. . .] has been removed in the last four years at the expense of great labor." A man named Chris Rocke owned the cave prior to J. W. Scarborough and evidence leads one to conclude that he left the cave property in shambles. The author then describes what he found while removing debris from the cave:

In removing the debris accumulated in the cave, a number of articles, some natural and some from the arts, have been found that are of great interest to visitors, such as an old flint lock rifle so badly decayed that only those acquainted with such weapons should be able to identify it.

In the 1930s, Scarborough Jr. found an 1873 Winchester Model rifle south of the cave in the charred ruins of what he called "the old horse barn." What's so special about an 1873 Winchester Model? Designed for the more powerful 44–40 cartridge, this particular model was the most popular lever-action center fire rifle that Winchester ever produced. After cleaning the antique gun considerably, he was able to notice that the rifle contained a low serial number. Scarborough Jr. mounted the rifle on an old piece of wood with barbed wire and a hangman's noose and even included on the display board a few of the old coins found buried in the cave sand. He sold it to a gentleman named Dick Headley. Scarborough Jr. doesn't remember the exact price, but he said he made a "pretty penny off it." Nowadays, early 1873 Winchester Models with a low serial numbers have sold for $1,500.00 to $7,000.00 at auctions!

Other items found in Robber's Cave by J. W. Scarborough: copper tubing from an illicit still, a number of silver dollars dating from 1878 to 1882 (some counterfeit, some not) gambling devices, pocket books, a tanning stone, Indian pottery, arrowheads, iron nodules, and concretionary forms. "Most of these are on exhibition at the cave," the booklet states. Scarborough Jr. mentioned that into the 1960s he exhibited items in a display case located near the sun porch, but vandals eventually broke the glass and stole the contents. To this day Scarborough Jr. still becomes angry while recounting some of these memories—understandably so. During our interviews, he could get quite worked up about thieves and vandals to the point that I'd decide to move on to another subject.

The booklet then recounts an elderly guest's claim that she had made several attempts to see the cave but always found it occupied by such "objectionable characters" that she did not enter. From this guest I found the first reference made to the "shooting in a duel manner of two men around 1867. This has been verified by others who came later and stated that the affair was not publicly known and the few who were eye witnesses were afraid to tell what they saw." This duel, if it ever happened, would have occurred about two years before the brewery was built.

Following mention of the 1867 duel, Scarborough describes six different "characters that came alone and in a cautious way between November 1906 and April 1909." These characters remind me of the many guests that return to the cave, admit to breaking in, and offer to the other guests their comments describing their one-of-a-kind knowledge of the cave. "Each grew quite confidential and told some very interesting things; but there can be no doubt that such as they told actually occurred."

I find the wording interesting—if the mysterious guest grew "quite confidential" when telling their tale, it must've been true, right? Now, here is some of what the six cautious characters divulged: One man said he had been in the cave hundreds of times and had won many a dollar at craps and poker. But now, for the first time, he realized that there was a world of beauty and study in the various colored walls of the cave. This guest also claimed to have witnessed and known of several occurrences, but would only tell of them after assurance that they would not be made public. He said that there were relics in or near the cave, and that he knew a man that was later shot during an express holdup. He also knew a man who could get some facts about the affair if that man wasn't doing time.

Not all of the visitors' recollections in *A Souvenir Booklet of Robbers' Cave* are dark. "There are humorous stories of pranks of various kinds" by those "who on learning that the place is now under civil management and kept clean and respectable, come and enjoy an hour of retrospective and real sight-seeing." Enjoy the following example of one such prank:

> Some students got into a mix-up and concluded to punish one of their number. The victim was blindfolded, conducted to a remote place in the cave, ordered to sit down and remain quiet or suffer violence at the hands of his captors. Having been roughly handled on the way, and not knowing where he was, the prisoner remained quiet for some time, but finally concluded to remove the hoodwink and see why his captors were so quiet. The darkness was so intense that he could see nothing, and not being acquainted with the place, he groped about in the cave until the next forenoon, when he discovered a ray of light which led him to liberty.

I've heard many accounts such as this from guests that visited the cave while attending college in Lincoln. The booklet explains such uses by college students in a very early-twentieth century manner. "The cave has been used by Greek Letter Societies of the State University for many years when impressing the weighty ties of fraternalism upon recruits."

By this point, Robber's Cave had also become a favorite location for "ghost parties and winter parties" organized by various societies, universities, and churches. In the spring of 1907, a lady from Kent, England, visited the cave and explained to J. W. Scarborough that she learned of Robber's Cave in an English magazine article that described the popular attraction!

Also mentioned in the booklet is a Native American belief that anyone who remained secluded in a cave overnight and had a dream should go four nights in succession in the same manner. Should that person's dream remain the same for four nights, then the dream would come true (only Pawnee traditional history is mentioned in this particular paragraph).

A Souvenir Booklet of Robbers' Cave wouldn't be complete without a mention of Jesse James of course:

> Was Jesse James in the cave? [. . .] Those who associated with Jesse are not numerous in Lincoln; a few however, say positively that Jesse was here at one time for some days, others shake their heads and say, "I doubt it." Scarborough then makes quite the claim: "But after four years of careful investigation and search for truth in the matter, the writer is forced by preponderance of evidence to conclude that Jesse was here, and safely lodged within the confines of the cave for more than three days, sometime soon after the Northfield Bank robbery. The one who tells us most, adds positively that Jesse James was one of the best-hearted men he ever knew." How helpful would it be to know what the writer's "careful investigation" entailed and what the "preponderance of evidence" actually was, as well as the identity of "the one who tells us most."

Unfortunately, J. W. Scarborough omits such information in the pamphlet. The wording of the next paragraph promoting the cave also entertains:

> For many years the cave has been attracting attention. Numerous efforts have been made to make it a resort, but none of those interested in such efforts seem to have thought of making it a clean, respectable, sight-seeing, instructive, law-abiding place, fit for the best of society [. . .] where any lady could go at any time. The present management has only that

object in view—to make the place clean morally and physically, and to see that each customer goes away satisfied [. . .] Only those who fail to avail themselves of the opportunity are the losers [. . .] So you are requested to give no heed to those who through ignorance, prejudice, superstition or egotism, may ridicule the idea of any cave in a prairie country. It is here; come and see it.

The final two sections of the booklet are "The Geology of the Cave" and "What the People Say." Keep in mind that Professor Erwin H. Barbour's geological explanation is based on early-twentieth century information—not to say that it is all incorrect—but I've included it more as a period snapshot. For anyone interested in science, or if anyone might like to know how the cave's geology was explained around 1910, here it is:

> It is a boast of this state that her inexhaustible soil and Loess subsoil is so thick that rock exposures are generally concealed from view. Accordingly, a sandstone exposure in the suburbs of Lincoln has unusual significance to those who are in any way interested in natural phenomena, and the more so because of Robber's Cave which is entered from its face. Since coming to Lincoln, the undersigned, has visited this cave many times and has conducted many classes thither, and does not hesitate to recommend the cave to the general public as well as to the student. The sandstone bluff exposed at the cave is stained yellow, or brown in places, with that form of iron ore known as limonite. The bedding planes run in horizontal lines and are very readily distinguished between which occurs the false bedding or cross bedding which looks like tipped strata. Remember when looking at this rock face that it is an exposure of the great water bearing beds of the Plains, known as the Dakota group of the Cretaceous age. It is from this same bed that the excellent water, which supplies Lincoln, is drawn. In places this ferruginous sandstone is very poorly consolidated, elsewhere it is sufficiently compact for building purposes, and in many places it is full of highly interesting leaf impressions. In the State Museum there are nearly 6,000 such petrified leaves collected from the Dakota Formation. Overlying the ocherous sandstone may be seen purplish boulders of Sioux quartzite of glacial age, and above and overlying all, the buff subsoil of this region known as Loess, or Bluff deposit. Accordingly, one sees three formations at this spot. Adults and youths alike must enjoy a visit to the cave and cannot fail to benefit by the simple geology revealed there.

Last, we arrive at the "What the People Say" section, which is a collection of testimonials by somewhat prominent citizens that serve to convince the reader that visiting the cave is worth their time. Enjoy a few of their accounts:

> *I have visited The Caves under the guidance of my friend, J. W. Scarborough, and was much interested in the rare sand formation and tints—as well as in the history of these underground passages, with the stories of Indian, Hunter, Moonshiner, and Robber who have in turn utilized and enlarged the cavern recesses. The place is well worth a visit by student, antiquarian and pleasure seeker.*—Chas. M. Shepherd

Charles M. Shepherd would go on to officiate J. W. Scarborough's funeral service in 1922 at Wyuka Cemetery in Lincoln, Nebraska. Also, I found it humorous that Shepherd once filed a complaint in July of 1902 in Nebraska City to the Judge of Otoe County because a group of teenagers were unlawfully engaged in the game commonly called "baseball" on the first day of the week, commonly called Sunday, contrary to the form of the statutes in such cases made and provided against the peace and dignity of the state of Nebraska. I wonder, what would Mr. Shepherd have thought about the unlawful activities that would eventually take place in the cave by pleasure seekers in the years to come?

To Whom It May Concern:

> *The caves just south of the city are interesting because of the varied and beautiful sand formation, the interesting history connected with them, and because they are so large and different from the other sights in this locality. As the charge for single admission and for picnic parties is very reasonable they are well worth visiting.*—Roscoe C. Ozman, (City Clerk for Lincoln in 1910).

Indian inspector E. C. Kemble involved with the Ponca Trail of Tears in 1877, had a few brief comments on the cave as well:

> *Local or visiting schools will always find the Cave an interesting place to visit from an educational standpoint and for a pleasure trip as well. The friable Dakota Sandstone is beautiful in its colorings and shows cross bedding and other features very distinctly.*—E. C. Kemble

Kemble met with Ponca leaders to make arrangements for them to visit the Indian Territory and select a site for a new reservation. During the scouting mission to the Osage Reservation, Standing Bear and the other tribal leaders informed Kemble they wanted to return home, but Kemble refused to honor their request according to nebraskastudies.org. Kemble would go on to be the nominee for Lancaster County superintendent in 1914.

> *I have visited the Cave frequently with classes, instructing them about the Dakota Formation, which Professor Barbour has so well described. This sandstone exposure and Cave are exceptional for this locality and should be better known, both by Lincoln people and visitors from over the state. The Cave is greatly improved by having been cleaned out and well kept. Being personally acquainted with the present owner, Mr. Scarborough, I assure Nebraskans that a visit to the Cave is well worth while [sic]. Here one learns something of the intensely interesting legends and history of the Cave and sees geological structure in a way never to forget.*—G. E. Condra

George E. Condra served as director of the Conservation and Survey Division (CSD) at the University of Nebraska from 1921 to 1954.

> *I have visited the Cave at Lincoln and was shown through it. I was surprised at the size and peculiar construction. It is very interesting and no one who can go should miss the opportunity of going through it. He will be well paid for his time.*—J. D. M. Buckner

Reverend J. D. M. Bucker (1859 to 1941) is buried in Aurora, Nebraska. He served on the Conference Board of Examiners in 1907 for the 47th Nebraska Annual Conference held at Trinity Church in Lincoln.

Advertising "Lincoln's First Tourist Attraction"

While meeting with senior museum curator Laura Mooney at the Nebraska State Historical Society to look at a few Robber's Cave objects, Ms. Mooney showed me an advertisement from the Broadside Collection that read at the top, "The Caves, The Sandstone Caves, The Robbers Caves." The small poster states:

> Now open for admission to the public. Don't fail to visit this mysterious artificial wonder about which tradition tells so much. If you've been there go again. Many people, thinking they were all through it years ago, find they had seen only a small part. Over 400 ft. of tunnel and shaft, some 30,000 cubic ft. of stone removed. Why? When? What for? What has been done all these years! Standing with their gaping mouths wide open, they still refuse to reveal any of their secrets lest they bring a shudder to even the hardest nerves.

I found that searching for old Robber's Cave advertisements is not only educational, but quite entertaining. In an August 6, 1933 edition of *The Lincoln Star*, just below notices for unclaimed diamonds at 11th and P Street and a 35-cent fried chicken dinner at Ryman's Café, I found a description of the enrollment at the Epworth League Institute, which described an outing to Robber's Cave. Cave advertisements could be found not only next to postings for Beach Blanket Bingo at the Starview Outdoor Theatre, but alongside Capitol Beach amusement ads and the 84th and O drive-in as well. How about, "Dr. Farrington's Dentistry at 1130 O St. The Most Beautiful False Teeth in the World!"

Robber's Cave ads could be found posted alongside Hardy's Furniture ads in the 1940s, and in the 1960s, I found a cave ad surrounded by, "John Wayne and Rita Hayworth in *Circus World*!" Not to mention "Snooker Bowl at 48th and Dudley" and "Georgi Griffith direct from Las Vegas at the East Hills Supper Club"—all snapshots of a Lincoln entertainment scene from bygone eras.

The Scarboroughs published many cave ads during their years of ownership. Through these ads, the cave took on various nicknames and descriptions, some quite amusing. Throw grammar rules out the window and take a look at how depictions of the cave transformed through the generations—even the address changed a few times!

1915   *"Robbers' Cave—for winter picnics." The contact phone number: F3445*

1922   *One of the Sights of Nebraska: The Robbers' Cave. Open Every Day.*

A Maze—A Labyrinth. Seven hundred feet of wonder winding passages and small pathways, stately galleries and cozy picnic rooms. Older than the town of Lincoln. Pronounced a historical and geological wonder by instructors of the State University. Always open—Clean—Well Lighted. Robber's Cave.

We use this space to let you know, that though the wind may blow and blow, the mercury creeps down to O, and all outdoors be white with snow, you want a good time then just go . . . to Robber's Cave.

Robber's Cave. 3200 So. 11th St. F2618. A network [sic] of historic caverns. Deep in colored Dakota Sandstone. Open every afternoon and evening. Special rates to picnic parties. Fred Scarborough, Mgr.

A LABYRINTH. Can you imagine? Winding Passages. Connecting Caverns. Deep in the sandstone. Robber's Cave. 3213 South 11th. Fireplace for picnics.

1923   *Why the Name Robber's Cave? We will explain that and more when you visit the place. The caves are electric lighted throughout. Open every day, Noon to 11 P.M. Entrance at 3213 So. 11th St.*

The Coolest Place. We have it ready for you today. It's deep underground—but no matter. It's solid as the rock of Gibraltar. Re-enforced with stratified iron ore, the formation is interesting to study, then the caverns and connections. And the history of the different places. Cool? Yes, you can see your breath. Robber's Cave.

The Old Rendezvous. Where nature began and outlaws finished a hidden refuge of gigantic caverns with connecting passages. But times have changed. Today the cave is all electric lighted, kept clean and ready for visitors or parties. Open Every Day. Noon to Eleven.

SOME WONDER—Enough to visit Robber's Cave. They see 5,000 cubic yards of caverns. 700 feet of underground passages hidden in a bluff of Dakota Sandstone. They hear its history—how, when and why. Then they call it "Some Wonder." Always Open. Electric Lighted.

Robber's Cave: Hidden in a Bluff of Sandstone. Used by Indians, Pioneers and Outlaws—We Explain the Geology and History. Always Open. Electric Lighted.

Entertain Lincoln Visitors by showing something different from their sights at home. Interesting and instructive; our place is really unique. A refuge, an old rendezvous hidden in a sandstone bluff. Robber's Cave, 3213 So. 11th St.

Robber's Cave, 3213 So. 11th St. Seven hundred feet of cave. Unique geologic exposition. Interesting and instructive. Nature started—man finished. Here before the town of Lincoln. Used by Indians, Pioneers, Outlaws. Now kept clean, electric lighted. Open every day until 11:00 P.M.

Have You Seen the Mysterious ROBBERS' CAVE? Open 7 A.M. until midnight. Electric lighted, competent guides. 2½ miles south of O on Eleventh Street. Take Pen or Lancaster car to High Street. Always Same Price—28 cents.

HAVING A PARTY? Plan it for . . . ROBBER'S CAVE 3243 South 10th, 3 floors, open 7 days a week. 10 A.M. to 10 P.M. 30 ft. picnic table—grill your steaks or hot dogs right here! FOR PARTY ROOM RENTAL call F2618.

A LASTING GIFT—Thrill the family. Let them hear 200 canaries. Females 75 cents. Robber's Cave F2618.

Mysterious Robber's Cave: 3213 South Eleventh St. These old caves are connected with Lincoln's earliest history in the beautifully colored sandstone walls. Seven hundred feet of adventurous thrill and geologic wonder. Electric lighted, Nature Cooled.

1924

Amusements: Robber's Cave. F2618. 3200 So. 11th.

[Note the gap in advertisements during the Great Depression (the financial and industrial slump of 1929 and subsequent years). I found no ads from 1924 until 1965. The Scarboroughs still had the cave open during this time and many citizens visited as depicted in the chapter "A Timeline of Social Use"]

1965

Attention Church Groups! Have your annual picnic in the cool, comfort of Robber's Cave. 3245 South 10th 3 Floors. OPEN 7 DAYS A WEEK.

Fair Visitors, while in Lincoln Visit Historical ROBBER'S CAVE. 3243 South 10th 3 Floors. Open 7 days a week. 10 A.M. to 11 P.M.

Businessmen's Clubs—Women's Clubs—Student Organizations. MAKE YOUR RESERVATIONS FOR YOUR CLUB'S PARTY at ROBBERS CAVE. 3243 South 10th St.

1966

Have your office or store party at Robber's Cave. 3 Levels. 3243 South 10th.

It's ROBBER'S CAVE for JR-HIGH PARTIES. BIRTHDAY PARTIES. SCOUT MEETINGS.
Plan yours now at Robber's Cave.

School & Church Groups—Plan Your Meetings and Parties at ROBBER'S CAVE. 3243 South 10th 3 Floors. 30 ft. picnic table—grill your steaks or hot dogs right here!

Attention School Groups. While in Lincoln plan a tour of ROBBER'S CAVE. 3 Levels. 3243 South 10th.

Attention Tourists. While in Lincoln plan a tour of ROBBER'S CAVE. 3 FLOORS. OPEN 7 DAYS A WEEK. 10 A.M. to 10 P M.—3243 South 10th. 30 ft. picnic table—grill your steaks or hot dogs right here!

Rana and Donald Schreiber of Lincoln donated an interesting piece of the cave's marketing from 1987. At the time the Scarboroughs distributed the ad, adult admission cost $3.00 and children 4–11 cost $2.00, the Party Room for birthdays, picnics, etc., cost $10.00/hour plus admission, and cave rentals were $150.00/evening plus $100.00 damage—cleanup deposit. The family did not permit Friday evening rentals. The heading of the ad reads, "Lincoln's First Tourist Attraction" and then provides a brief history of the cave. This piece written by Vi Scarborough includes several accurate, along with a few inaccurate statements in an attempt to boost business:

> In Pawnee Legend, it was a spirit cave where councils were held. After the Indian Wars, 1860 to 1890, the Indians were moved south to reservations. In 1863, a stone quarry here destroyed the original entrance. In 1869, brewers from Wisconsin hired a laborer to dig out the tunnels to store their product. The Pioneer Brewery failed in 1873. From this time on, the cave was a meeting place for gamblers, horse traders, outlaws, and the like. The James Boys were here in September 1876 seeking remounts after the bank robbery in Northfield, Minnesota. A few members of Coxey's Army stayed here in the winter of 1893. In 1906, a story of a treasure box found in the cave by John Scarborough printed in *The Sate Journal* brought so many visitors to the cave that it was kept open for sightseers and picnics.

> There are 14 shades of sandstone . . . A few artifacts that have survived over the years include some old coins, iron pick head, old lantern, rifle, and miscellaneous small items. Geological specimens are displayed along with photographs and documents from the Nebraska Historical Society and the US Geological Survey. We have a photograph of Jesse James taken in Nebraska City and a copy of a letter he wrote dated March 2, 1882, to Mr. J. D. Calhoun, a land agent in Lincoln, inquiring about some property he was interested in buying. He signed the letter with his alias—Thomas Howard, 1918 Lafayette Street., St. Joseph, Missouri. Jesse James' mother lived in Rulo, Nebraska, with her second husband, a doctor, after Jesse's father, a minister, was killed.

Mrs. Scarborough concludes with, "Robber's Cave will be in the national register of historic places sometime this year. Mr. Ed Zimmer of the City Planning Office is currently working on this." (More on the national register topic can be found in the chapter entitled "Will Robber's Cave Become a Nationally Registered Historic Landmark?")

Roads to Robber's Cave

Before 1930, the Scarborough's mailbox was at 3000 So. 11th St.—where 11th Street ended at High Street. At that mailbox, a dirt road, more of a path, began and proceeded southwest to the front of the Scarborough's property where J. W.'s original house sat just next to the family's larger farmhouse. Their windmill and water tank stood just south of the farmhouse.

That dirt path that led from the mailbox to the house crossed diagonally with what would become 10th street in the late 1940s. When dry, the dirt paths were used as an experiment in March of 1926. At the suggestion of property owners along the thoroughfare, the city council chose 9th Street from South to High Street to be graveled. The curbing and guttering were to be constructed the same as if the street were paved. Commissioner Duncan suggested that the street be graveled through to its junction with the Burlington right of way south of Robber's Cave and from the Southeast to Ponca Street, which at the time were Lincoln's new city limits. The decision aimed to help farmers who marketed livestock and farmed and raised poultry in the wholesale and industrial districts of Lincoln. It would also mean a more direct route for tourists.

By 1958, the Lincoln city telephone directory listed Robber's Cave at a new address: 3245 South 10th Street. Also at this time, a large rectangular Robber's Cave billboard stood high on a pole complete with a mounted arrow, and the display directed passersby to the cave.

Grain Elevators—The White Curtains to the West

Oftentimes on tours, guests will inquire if the elevators to the west have had any effect on the cave or property. In fact, one guest claimed to have fallen in the 1950s while working on one of the towering grain bins. He landed on the rails and broke both of his legs. During a 1972 Lincoln High class reunion, a guest approached me after the group's tour to tell me quite the somber story. He had grown up near 13th and High Street and a childhood friend of his who worked on the elevators fell to his death. He even pointed to the specific elevator where the tragedy occurred.

On lighter notes, can you imagine how gorgeous the sunsets must have been from the cave property before 1949? "Oh, you should have seen those sunsets… just beautiful!" Ed Jr. lamented during one of our conversations. Atop the sandstone bluff overlooking a rolling valley that stretched to Salt Creek and what is now Wilderness Park, the Scarboroughs, along with their many visiting guests, could enjoy the descending glow of Nebraska sunsets for many years. Framed photos of these vivid twilights still hang in the hallway of Ed Scarborough Jr.'s house. These picturesque evenings lasted until Robert Puelz, the district manager of the Equity Union Grain Company in Kansas City, Missouri, appeared before the Lincoln City Council in August of 1949 to announce that a 1,000,000-bushel grain elevator would be erected just west of the cave. He explained that many sites had been tested, but the Calvert Street location proved to be the only that could sustain the size of grain tanks the company planned to build.

"Upon a motion by Tom Pansing, the council suspended the rules and passed on second reading an ordinance amending the property regulation map to allow for construction to start immediately. The area will be zoned to the new classification, commercial C." Interestingly, Pansing moved that the ordinance be read a third time as the necessary votes were not forthcoming. Pansing and Arthur Weaver were the only ones voting to make the zoning change on this third reading" (8/29/1949). Oddly enough, Mayor Miles and Councilman John Comstock were not present.

On March 3, 1950, the superintendent of construction William Siebert of Denver, Colorado, reported to *The Lincoln Star* that construction was ahead of schedule on the new elevator being built by the Equity Union Grain Company of Kansas City, Missouri. Construction began September of 1949 and costs were running below estimates (original estimates were $625,000.00–$825,000.00). Seibert described the elevator as one of the most modern grain elevators in this part of the country.

Plans called for the eventual enlargement of the structure to the point where it would hold 3,000,000 bushels of grain. It would have two 12,000-bushel legs or elevators, which would be able to carry 24,000 bushels of grain an hour to bins at the top of the structure. Contractors on the project were Chalmers and Borton Co. of Hutchinson, Kansas.

Blue Blood Brewing Company Leases Space Above Robber's Cave

Three friends from the Lincoln Police Department founded Blue Blood Brewing Company in December 2011. The friends each shared a love for craft beer and the Lincoln community. President and co-founder, Brian Podwinski, sustained an injury in a training accident that forced him into early retirement, and since he and his team of investors have pour their hearts and souls into the brewery. Blue Blood Brewing Company aspires to bring people together and support the community as well as their fellow officers. From their shield-shaped logo and police department patch-trading system, to the thin blue line American flags displayed, a support for law enforcement is conveyed throughout Blue Blood's brewery and tap room. Not to mention, police, emergency responders, and military personnel all receive a discount at Blue Blood. One of the brewery's unique tributes is whenever an officer is killed in the line of duty anywhere in the country, Blue Blood reserves a seat at the bar to honor that fallen officer. A toast to his or her life and mission is usually given as well.

During an episode of *Pints and Politics* in April 2016, host Dan Parsons asked Podwinski how he transitioned from a policeman to a brewer. Podwinski explained that after his injury, he had to leave the department and retired in 2006. After a short stint working for the Nebraska Emergency Management Agency, he began home brewing. "Really, it became logical that the brewery was the next step to take." He knew he wanted something different than government life, so he talked to friends, worked together to prepare their business plans, convinced their spouses it was a good idea, and opened Blue Blood in December 2011.

Parson's then asked Podwinski to comment on his initial experiences with Robber's Cave:

It [the cave] really didn't impact me growing up. It was closed by that time. It's kind of funny when I talk to my friends from Lincoln High, nobody really ever went there. But the Southeast kids, that was more where they lived in that area, they went there all the time. When I was an officer, it was already concreted over, so we never really had to be called out there. We had heard that at one point a church wanted to buy it and use it, but I think everybody was scared of the cave itself and didn't understand what they could and couldn't do around it, which now I understand why. It was a very interesting process to build around that thing, but ultimately it scared people off in not knowing much about it. It's not like there are documents providing all of the information and engineering behind it. This was a guy and pick axe. It has held up extremely well through construction and we couldn't be happier right now [. . .]

It was a rundown lot in the middle of town with weeds everywhere. Even aside from the historical nature of the property, it sat vacant for 21 or 22 years I believe. So this is something we've been very lucky to work with the city on. It's been surreal to see how things have come together.

The first day we opened May 4 of last year (2015) we were sitting here at 11 o'clock when we unlocked the doors, and we all kind of look at each other and were like, "OK, is somebody going to come in?" And since then we've had thousands of people through, it's great! We wondered if it would start to slow down after people relived their memories, but the tours haven't slowed down. The support, the curiosity, I truly hope we're doing the city a favor in the sense that it gives another thing to do when businesses come here. We host so many business events here.

During this same episode, Parsons asked Mayor Beutler what he thought about the cave's rejuvenation from the City of Lincoln's standpoint:

This is absolutely a great investment from the city's point of view. There are a whole number of connections here that start to build on one another. First of all, for the people of the city that grew up here or lived here all their lives, Robber's Cave is a significant piece of history. I think almost every high school kid in the city back when it was open experienced Robber's Cave. So it was good from the historical perspective to preserve that piece, and it adds a flavor of color to the whole experience. I'm glad we did it—I'm glad we could help.

Utilizing the Property and Surrounding Space

Construction on the property began after engineers deemed the cavern structurally sound. But the building of a 12,000-square-foot brewery, tasting room, and restaurant stalled with the discovery of bats (learn more about the bats in the chapter "A Bat Cave in Lincoln, Nebraska?"). Construction resumed after the bats left in the spring of 2016, and Blue Blood Brewery began serving food and hosting concerts and events at its current site in May 2016.

One of the brewery's most popular events is when the University of Nebraska's Pep Band performs at Blue Blood each Friday before a Cornhusker football home game. This tradition began years ago at Grandmother's Restaurant in Lincoln, and since Grandmother's closed, Blue Blood is proudly carrying on the tradition.

The Yard is the open-air event space directly above Robber's Cave on the south side of the Blue Blood's brewhouse and restaurant. Podwinski had a stage constructed in 2017 as a concert venue and entertainment space. This open-air space has even been used for wedding rehearsal dinners.

On May 5th and 6th of 2017, in celebration of Blue Blood Brewery's first anniversary at the Robber's Cave location, the Kris Lager Band with Evan Bartels and The Stoney Lonesomes played above the cave on the outdoor stage, (Kris Lager would later perform sessions inside the cave in the fall of 2017), followed by Josh Hoyer and Soul Colossal with Stonebelly. Blue Blood continues to host concerts and events in The Yard: Portland, Oregon's, The Talbott Brothers with Bernardus filmed a promo in the cave and performed at Blue Blood in the summer of 2017. Them Coulee Boys with Ragged Company, Lazerwolfe, A Ferocious Jungle Cat, Ro Hempel and Cornerstone Dub are just a few of the many bands that have performed in The Yard above the cave.

In addition to a pinball tournament, beer Olympics, and trivia night, Blue Blood has hosted New Year's Eve prime rib dinners, Valentine's date nights, and even TV show auditions! In August of 2017, talented locals turned out for the Lincoln Idol Auditions held in Blue Blood's Barrel Room (located at the cave's entrance) in an attempt to earn a pass for the "*American Idol* Bus Stop" in Omaha.

Blue Blood's Brew Pub is also very pet friendly as they've teamed up with Beer Paws, which makes dog treats using spent grain from craft beer. Each time guests buy a pint of beer, their dog can enjoy a free Beer Paw from the biscuit dispenser. Robber's Cave even has its own blend of coffee created by The Mill, a small-batch craft coffee roaster, espresso bar and teahouse located in Lincoln since 1975.

Furthermore, Blue Blood created Battle of the Badges, which challenges first responders to bring together the community, friends, and family members in a friendly competition to save and sustain lives through blood donation. Here are a few of the other events Blue Blood has held at Robber's Cave: Beer, Brats, and Bats, Suds and Stogies, a rally in opposition to a certain provision in LB632 (A.K.A. the Kill the Bill party), Yoga in the Yard, and Joggers and Lagers. Dan Parsons, a public relations expert and political advisor, hosted an episode of his radio show *Pints and Politics* from Blue Blood on two occasions, one of which included Lincoln Mayor Chris Beutler as a guest.

In August of 2017 Robbers Cave LLC allowed Lincoln Fire and Rescue to utilize the cave's unique environment and distinct conditions for training exercises. Captain Grant Collings found practicing in the cave's narrow and slick places to be invaluable.

School Fieldtrips Return

Much in the way that Robbers Cave LLC brought a brewery back to the cave after 146 years, I wanted to be a part of bringing fieldtrips back to the cave. Today, I can proudly say that on February 21, 2017, I welcomed a group of eleven students from Our Redeemer Lutheran School in Staplehurst, Nebraska, to the cave marking the first school fieldtrip at Robber's Cave since the 1980s. My daughter Brooklyn, as usual, was my sidekick as we shared information with the students about the cave's legends, geology, and bats.

Later that summer, Brooklyn and I gave more tours of the cave for summer camps and school field trips. What a joy it has been to provide young kids the experience of descending into the cool tunnels to peek into the "bat cave" or the "question mark." Their faces light up in wonder as they step through the sand and marvel at the hearts, faces, peace signs, and initials, carved into the soft sandstone. And you can't beat the cave's constant 55-degree temperature during a steamy Nebraska summer.

Scarborough Jr.'s stepson, Scott Maybin, brought me an April 28, 1986 issue of EdLines, a newsletter for Lincoln Public Schools employees. An article described a writing contest, which resulted in a fieldtrip for Belmont Elementary students. Vi Scarborough had placed a newspaper ad offering a free visit to whichever school could write ten letters that listed ten reasons for reopening the cave. The Scarboroughs were so pleased they invited the entire class! Belmont fifth grade teacher Jeanne Gaston, along with parent volunteers, descended into the cave to roam, run, and crawl through what the article described to be a product of "Nebraska's glacial age near the southwest edge of the city." Old bullets and quarters were the treasures found in the cave by students that day. "They had a chance to let their imaginations drift back to the time when the Plains Indians used the caves . . . when robbers and cutthroats hung about."

Trick-or-Treating and the Robber's Cave Film Series

Countless "Hallowe'en" parties (as they used to be called) have been held in Robber's Cave through the years. In the 1920s, Spanish War veterans held annual Halloween parties at the cave in which guests roasted hotdogs over the fire, and then ghost stories were told while the ladies served donuts and coffee. Robber's Cave has once again become a busy location for Halloween activities and other holidays as well.

In October of 2016, Blue Blood Brewing Company welcomed a few hundred children to trickor-treat through the tunnels of Robber's Cave. Games, candy, and fun were had by many at the free event, and the children who wore costumes even received a free dinner! Once the youngsters finished having their fun, I gave lights-out lantern tours through the darkened cave for the adults. Traversing the tunnels in darkness reminded me of H. P. Lovecraft's short story "The Beast and the Cave."

Chilly weather, wind, rain, and even a little snow didn't deter kids and parents from returning to the cave in 2017 as trick-or-treating attendance skyrocketed to over two thousand! Automobiles filled Blue Blood's main parking lots, the overflow lot, and even lined the street all the way to Van Dorn Park. Some even parked on the grass. The line of costumed kids snaked from the cave's entrance, up the barrel room's staircase, through the brewery, up the restaurant's staircase, out Blue Blood's front doors, and then extended outside and down the sidewalk! Trick-or-treating at Robber's Cave seems to have the makings of a new Lincoln tradition. Fall events added in 2017 included an Oktoberfest celebration, Pints and Pumpkins (a carving competition), and a Howl 'O' Ween doggy costume contest.

In the 1960s, films were often shown in Robber's Cave for events such as senior parties and class trips. Blue Blood Brewing Company revamped this idea by showing suspense and horror films in the cave in the spirit of Halloween. Guests brought lawn chairs and blankets to view Stanley Kubrick's *The Shining* and Wes Craven's *A Nightmare on Elm Street*. The incredible attendance led to the creation of the Robber's Cave Film Series, which began with Steven Spielberg's *The Goonies* in November of 2017. For the holidays, Blue Blood screened *National Lampoon's Christmas Vacation, Elf, Home Alone,* and *The Nightmare Before Christmas* in the cave. In addition to a brewery returning to the cave and school field trips making their way back for tours, the film series is just one more way Robber's Cave has come full circle!

Blessing the Cave

One could claim with a reasonable amount of certainty that the majority of activities that have taken place in the tunnels of Robber's Cave have occurred with the intent of innocent, good-natured fun. However, it is an unfortunate yet inevitable fact that there have been a number of guests whose memories of the cave are not pleasant ones to say the least. Considering the age of the cave and the sheer number of visitors, the Ku Klux Klan's usage, accidents and injuries, and even the many owners—some quite colorful—it is logical to assume that the cave has seen its share of seedy behavior. For these and several other reasons many have recommended that the cave be blessed.

I know of a few occasions on which Robber's Cave received blessings: twelve Lincoln priests performed one in the summer of 2016, and the other was a Native American smudging ceremony during the summer of 2017. Father Michael Zimmer comments, " . . . Robber's Cave with a nefarious background now, all of a sudden, is going to be a place of entertainment, of joy, of people gathering together. It's been blessed and now it's this place where good things can take place." Not that good times hadn't been had in the cave before. Some might find it quite interesting that the priests blessed more than just the cave, they also blessed the brewery and beer! "There is literally a blessing specifically for beer, because of monastic tradition," explains Father Zimmer" (8/5/2016).

Alan Boye's *A Guide to the Ghosts of Lincoln*—The Robber's Cave Chapter

As I mentioned earlier, I often read Alan Boye's *A Guide to the Ghosts of Lincoln* (Saltillo Press) as a youngster. "When we were kids, as early as I can remember until my teen years, Robber's Cave was always a great destination," Boye remembers in a July 20, 2000 *Lincoln Journal Star* article by Margaret Reist. Although the book is not a serious historical source, countless guests to the cave remember Boye's book as well, and much of their initial knowledge of the cave, although sensationalized, came from Boye's book. The first edition from 1983 had three printings through 1984. Then the second edition released in 1987 had three printings through 1994. A copy of the first edition/second printing (that I still happen to have) included illustrations that Boye had drawn as well. It is an entertaining book, but the reader should keep in mind that the content has been embellished and should not be read as a factual text.

In Boye's chapter on Robber's Cave he describes "a vast series of catacombs, with a labyrinth of tunnels that run for miles underground . . . the tunnels at one time were claimed to connect the State Hospital with the Penitentiary." That's exciting to imagine but simply not true. Further examples of Boye's hyperbolic descriptions include getting past "the old woman with the snarling coyotes that gave any brave soul trepidations," the description of the well as "a massive underground hole that plunged two hundred vertical feet into darkness," the account of the bats "a seething mass of dark fur," and the moisture on the walls illustrated as "constantly dripping water the color of blood."

The book also mentions Jesse James hiding in the "robber's roost" chamber during his trips through Nebraska, as well as the Underground Railroad using the mysterious cave to lead slaves from the South, also a misconception. Boye recommends placing one's ear to the stoned-off wall and the end of a tunnel in order to hear faraway voices:

> It was through these tunnels that inmates from the Penitentiary escaped. It was through these tunnels [. . .] that patients from the State Hospital attempted their escapes [. . .]

Perhaps one day a new entrance will appear in the sandstone and open to reveal the secrets of the dark underworld.

Well, the entrance was reopened in 2015, and I'm not sure dark secrets of the underworld were found, but a lot of old cans, glass bottles, rusted tools, car parts, rotted picnic tables, trash, batteries, candles, and graffiti definitely were. Nonetheless, I thank Mr. Boye for writing the book that piqued so many youngsters' curiosity about the cave.

A Chilling Overnight in Robber's Cave

*Please keep in mind that the intent of this section is not to convince readers to believe in ghosts.

On October 22, 2016, local radio station KX 96.9 performed an overnight ghost hunt at Robber's Cave. Cheryl Ann Fletcher, a world-renowned physic medium of 45 years, along with J. P. and Lauren, Paul Durban, Gordon Kyhn, filmmaker Mark Fletcher, and special guest Kelly Garagiola spent the night in Robber's Cave with Blue Blood's marketing coordinator at the time, Jullia Grossman. Their findings included drastic temperature decreases (usually the temperature increases slightly with people in cave), a flashlight being "messed with" near the well, and the presence of orbs. One orb in particular reportedly caused Miss Fletcher to become ill. Also, Miss Fletcher stated her left arm felt "really hot," and she was heard stating on video, "The murderer is down here." Someone, possibly named Kevin, made someone put their hands together and hanged them (in the well). Although a few in the cave that night could see their breath, some could not. Last, someone noticed what appeared to be a set of eyes above J. P.'s head.

Fletcher also mentioned the spirit of a young girl who followed Grossman through the cave because she was familiar with her. Fletcher also felt the presence of a man who overdosed in tunnel two in the 1960s. On another occasion, one psychic heard women crying or weeping in the cave.

On nearly every tour I'm asked what I think about the cave's ghost stories. I've seen a few strange photos that are quite interesting, but I've never seen anything in the cave that has frightened me, although others have. Here is my final thought on the ghosts of Robber's Cave: to those really wanting to see ghosts in the cave, simply think of them in a different way—as a memory floating alongside the present. If you do so, you'll begin to see them everywhere.

A Ghost Story

During one of my first trips to the NSHS to research the cave in 2005, I came across a story about Robber's Cave in a November 1894 edition of *The Courier*. The headline read "A Ghost Story" and began with: "Down south of Lincoln, perhaps a half a mile this side of the penitentiary, there is an old cave."

The narrator speculates about the cave's origin claiming robbers dug it, counterfeiters burrowed into it to make bogus money, or it could have been a cellar where beer was kept in great vats (now we're getting somewhere). Although many "grown people in the city" had no idea the cave existed, countless gangs of boys often visited looking for adventure. "It is just such a place as the heroes in many a dime novel inhabit," the narrator writes. The landscape was much different then, desolate, with nearby fields of dead sunflowers and dry cornfields.

Once inside the cave, the young narrator sets the scene for his story by mentioning the "gothic-roofed" tunnel and the "hieroglyphiced" walls. One carving read: "Though your sins be as Scarlet [*sic*], they shall be white as Snow [*sic*]." The narrator then describes the bleakness of the area:

> The place has not been inhabited for a long time save by bats and tramps. It is a paradise for tramps. The railroad is but a step below the mouth of the cave, and the Weary Willies and the Dusty Petes always find a welcome awaiting them in the side of the old hill. [. . .] And so the old place shelters many a ragged and friendless man, the wrecks of life that float hither and thither, till they find a narrow home at last in the ground where no policeman cries, "Move on!"

After this nineteenth century exposition, the narrator claims the cave was known to be haunted by a sobbing, young woman. The narrator's friend recounts how he visited the cave alone on a windy, moonlit night to catch a glimpse of the ghost. He arrived at 11 o'clock, lit a candle, and entered the cave. After a bat flew past his face, he nearly fell into the well. Eventually, he spread his blankets at the back of a tunnel and planned to fall asleep, but he couldn't. He simply lay at the back of the tunnel amongst the big vats that lined the walls. The piles of grain sacks, kegs, and bottles filled the dark shadows as he watched the "glimmering mouth of the cave."

Then a man entered the tunnel with a light, followed by other men carrying a shapeless mass. The boy tried not to scream as he noticed the mass was a woman with long hair. He watched the men climb a ladder and drop the body over the edge of a vat. He could hear gurgling along with a smothered cry within the "wooden walls of the great tub."

The friends' exciting tale provoked the narrator to stay a night at the cave as well. On a gloomy night in November, the narrator and his friend returned to the cave with blankets prepared to spend a night. "We chatted a while after we had got [*sic*] into our blankets and at last were in dreamland." After sleeping a short while, the two youngsters were awoken by a sound at the mouth of the cave. They became horrified when a "shapeless mass" entered the cave, groaned, and fell to the floor. The friends could only remain in the dark and hold their breath. They never went back to sleep, and after a long night of remaining silent and still, daylight began driving out the shadows:

> We were able to see that the monster that had entered the cave and frightened us so fearfully was an old, white cow seeking shelter from the outside storm. We took up our blankets without saying a word and went home.

> The two friends didn't look in each other's eyes for hours, and they never mentioned the cave again.

A Bat Cave in Lincoln, Nebraska?

In January of 2015, the following experts visited Robber's Cave to assist with identifying the cave's bats: Dr. Patricia Freeman, professor emeritus/curator with the School of Natural Resources and the University of Nebraska State Museum, Michael Fritz, a zoologist with the Nebraska Natural Heritage Program, and retired biologist Cliff Lemen. These three specialists have served to monitor Robber's Cave's bat population, which consists of three species: tri-colored, big brown, and northern long-eared bats. Bob Harms, a biologist with the US Fish and Wildlife Service, confirmed Lemen's findings. Harms also offered advice to Podwinski regarding how to protect the bats since in April of 2015, the northern long-eared bat became a federally threatened species due to a fungal disease: the white-nose syndrome.

Once during a Lincoln Public Schools fall break, my daughter and I explored the Happy Jack Chalk Mine near Scotia, Nebraska, (it's one of the focal mines being monitored by the Nebraska WhiteNose Syndrome Project). While there, I learned more about the white-nose syndrome, or WNS. WNS is a novel fungal pathogen killing millions of hibernating bats in eastern North America. The syndrome has been spreading westward in North America since its discovery in 2006, and as of 2017 it has reached Nebraska's Cass County. WNS causes death to certain hibernating species when the bat's natural immunity is suppressed during winter months.

Why are these bats so important to us? According to the National Wildlife Health Center, a decline in bat population can have substantial impacts on the environment and agriculture since they eat the insects that damage crops and spread disease. Consumption of insects by bats can save farmers billions of dollars in pest control services annually.

In the spring of 2016, Dr. Freeman and her team captured about 65 bats in Robber's Cave. At 55-degrees year round, the cave provides the consistent low temperature that hibernating bats seek. The cave also features three airshafts that provide tight holes, slits, and crevices where the Northerns like to have their pups.

Many Nebraskans are familiar with big browns as they are common in older neighborhoods. As one of the larger bats, this versatile species hasn't just been found in Robber's Cave but in houses, churches, and barns. Memorial Stadium in Lincoln, Nebraska, is not only famous for housing one of the most storied college football programs in the country but for its significant brown bat population as well.

Tricolored bats are mostly on the eastern side of Nebraska, and their numbers are drastically decreasing due to WNS. Dr. Freeman explained that the Northerns are probably all short-distance migrators and that all three species can be distinguished by their echolocation calls, at least in Nebraska.

Discovering federally protected bats caused Manzitto Bros. to delay construction and alter some of his plans for the cave—but not much as he explained in a recent *Lincoln Journal Star* interview: "Having the bat cave hasn't deterred tours or special events from happening, but a designated bat habitat has been constructed in tunnel number three." The airshaft (formerly the fireplace) is left open so the bats can come and go as they please. Manzitto installed mesh netting in the tunnel to protect the bats, as well as nocturnal lighting, which gives the tunnel a soft, red glow.

In fact, on May 20, 2016, Blue Blood hosted the Beer, Brats, and Bats Fundraiser, which not only offered the first public tours of the cave, but also raised $8,500.00 for the Pioneers Park Nature Center! Blue Blood provided the brats and beer while presenters educated guests about the bats. I attended the event with my wife and because this was the first time in many years that the public was allowed to legally tour the cave, there was a definite buzz in the atmosphere created by the many eager guests excited to either return to the cave or see it for the first time.

There are many misconceptions about bats in general, and the approximately 65 bats that call Robber's Cave home are no exception. When I first read about Robber's Cave, I envisioned them to be more like how they're described in *The Guide to the Ghosts of Lincoln*: "High in the cistern ceiling a seething mass of dark fur meant a hundred bats were awake and preparing to fly." This description, although perfect for a ghost book, isn't quite the case. Many guests are eager to spot a few bats while touring the cave, and often one or two can be found suspended from the cave ceiling or hiding in one of the many small holes and crevices in the sandstone walls. Most guests particularly enjoy spotting a bat or two as they fly from tunnel to tunnel, others shriek.

Robber's Cave as a Filming Location

The fact that a few movie scenes have been filmed in Robber's Cave should come as no surprise. In 1966, a group of "Uni High Girls" filmed a horror movie at the cave, which was viewed at a Halloween party at the Roberts Party room hosted by Deborah Jo Rachwal and Lou Ann Black. This party room was likely the old Roberts Dairy building at about 59th and South Street, formerly used by the YMCA and then as a meeting hall. Their guests included Susan Coffey, Sharon Nicholls, Anita Rech, Cindy Rachwal, Gayle Peterson, Peggy Evans, Audrey Hartmann, Patricia Hurlbert, Crystin Moore, Bonnie Packet, Nancy Pickering, Jolene West, Lydia Scherbak, Susan Taylor, and Sandy Kettlehutt. The *Lincoln Evening Journal* article described the viewing of this horror film as a highlight of the evening.

Justin Ferguson of Lincoln, Nebraska, wrote and directed the horror movie *Meathook Massacre II* at Robber's Cave in 2017. Ishma Valenti, also of Lincoln, Nebraska, wrote and directed an independent film entitled *Free*, a historical drama about the role of Nebraska in the Underground Railroad, which features a scene shot in the cave. Interestingly, both films include Blue Blood's partner Colby Coash.

During an interview with Scarborough Jr., I learned of something many might find creepy about the cave property. Years ago, near the row of mulberry trees that he planted along the north side of his home (which still exist), Scarborough Jr. plotted a small section of land where he frequently buried animal heads. I realize that this might seem strange to most, but Scarborough Jr. is an avid collector of skulls. He used to bury badger, coyote, and even the rare prairie dog heads in this plot. After a few months, he'd exhume the skulls in order to add them to his collection or display them.

Photos

Jim McKee and Arthur Duerschner said it best in their book *Lincoln: A Photographic History*, "Photographs provide accurate and permanent records of history without time blurring emotion and errors exaggerated through retelling." With that, I hope you'll enjoy the many Robber's Cave photographs I have accumulated.

(Several of these photos are excellent quality given their age, while others are simply snapshots of old Polaroids, slides, or glass plates. If the image quality happens to be low, please consider their age.)

291

THE UNITED STATES OF AMERICA,

To all to whom these Presents shall come, Greeting:

WHEREAS, In pursuance of the Act of Congress, approved March 3, 1855, entitled "An Act in addition to certain Acts granting Bounty Land to certain Officers and Soldiers who have been engaged in the military service of the United States," there has been deposited in the GENERAL LAND OFFICE, Warrant No. *92803* for *160* acres, in favor of *Harriet Green formerly widow of Roswell Huntington, Private Captain Bishop's Company 31st Regiment U.S. Infantry War 1812*

with evidence that the same has been duly located upon *the North East quarter of Section Two in Township Nine of Range Six East in the District of Lands subject to sale at Nebraska City Nebraska containing One Hundred and Fifty-five acres and twenty one Hundreds of an acre*

according to the Official Plat of the Survey of said Lands returned to the **GENERAL LAND OFFICE** by the SURVEYOR GENERAL *the said Warrant having been assigned by the said Harriet Green To said Daniel Low, Andrew Cochran and W.W. Chipman in whose favor said tract has been located* NOW KNOW YE, That there is therefore granted by the UNITED STATES unto the said *Daniel Low, Andrew Cochran and W.W. Chipman as assignees as aforesaid and to their heirs*

the tract of Land above described: TO HAVE AND TO HOLD the said tract of Land, with the appurtenances thereof, unto the said *Daniel Low, Andrew Cochran and W.W. Chipman as assignees as aforesaid and to their*

heirs and assigns forever.

In testimony whereof, I, *Abraham Lincoln* PRESIDENT OF THE UNITED STATES OF AMERICA, have caused these Letters to be made Patent, and the SEAL OF THE GENERAL LAND OFFICE to be hereunto affixed.

GIVEN under my hand, at the CITY OF WASHINGTON, the *Sixteenth* day of *December* in the year of our Lord one thousand eight hundred and *Sixty four*, and of the INDEPENDENCE OF THE UNITED STATES the *eighty-ninth*.

BY THE PRESIDENT: *Abraham Lincoln*

By *Edw. D. Neill* Sec'y.

J.N. Granger, Recorder of the General Land Office.

This land grant dated December 16, 1864, shows Harriet Green's 160 acres being assigned to Low, Cochran, and Chipman. Green was the widow of War of 1812 veteran Roswell Huntington.

Photo courtesy of Joel Green
Document courtesy of Dale Nobbman

This is one of the oldest, if not the oldest, photos of Robber's Cave as the bluff is completely bare. The original/natural entrance can be seen at the left, and the Pioneer Brewery's cellar would eventually be atop the opening at the right. Dale Nobbman dated this photo as early as 1865 when Low, Cochran, and Chipman were planning to start a quarrying business. Perhaps the man pictured is a geological surveyor with a chisel or hammer taking samples.

Photo courtesy of the Nebraska State Historical Society (RG2158-962)

This photo was likely captured in the summer of 1865 when Low, Cochran, and Chipman came to Lincoln to see what they had inherited from Harriet (Green) Huntington. Four from this group of seven are believed to be Daniel and Evelina Low, Ellen and William Chipman.

Photo courtesy of the Nebraska State Historical Society. This image has been transposed to accurately depict the original photo as it is backwards in the cave's souvenir booklet.

Founded in 1869 by Michael Ulmer from Hastings, Minnesota, and Andrew Lindner from near Waukesha, Wisconsin, the Pioneer Brewery operated from 1869 to 1873—at one point they produced 25 barrels a day. The Pioneer Brewery was the first brewery in Lincoln, Nebraska. This photo was taken facing northeast.

Photo courtesy of Ed Scarborough Jr.

This is an excellent view of the cave's west entrance. It corroborates perfectly with the map of the cave showing the exact location of the Pioneer Brewery's foundation. This entrance provided access from the brewery's cellar and is now the cave's emergency exit.

Photo courtesy of the Nebraska State Historical Society (RG2133-12-368)

Jacob Andra in his earlier years (1880s). Not only was Andra a renowned digger, he served as an officer in the Harmonic Musical Society.

Photo courtesy of Dale Nobbman

Jacob Andra, the German horse collar maker from Lima, Ohio, spent three and a half years (1869–1873) digging the cave for the Pioneer Brewery, including the well.

Photo courtesy of Joel Green

Jesse Woodson James at age seventeen photographed wearing his Quantrill's Raiders uniform. Quantrill's Raiders were pro-Confederate partisan guerillas, A.K.A. Bushwhackers, who fought in the American Civil War.

Public Domain | Photo authenticated courtesy of Eric F. James, the James Family Preservation Trust co-founder, archivist, and genealogist.

This photograph is from the Library of Congress, reproduction number LC-USZ62-3854. According to the LOC, it was taken May 22, 1882, although it has been claimed that it was taken as early as 1875 in Nebraska City, Nebraska; however, Eric F. James pointed out that there is no date attached to this particular photo and the only inscription stated "wedding photo." Jesse's uncle Rev. William Henry James performed the wedding on April 24, 1874, at the home of the bride's sister, Lucy Frances Mimms Browder in Jackson County, Missouri.

Public Domain | Photo authenticated by Eric F. James, the James Family Preservation Trust co-founder, archivist, and genealogist.

The F.M. Downs display at the Nebraska State Fair. Downs photographed Robber's Cave shortly after J. W. Scarborough opened it to the public in 1906.

Photo courtesy of Matt Hansen

This photo appeared in the 1908 Robber's Cave souvenir booklet above the caption, "A small party on their way through the cave."

Photo courtesy of the Nebraska State Historical Society

One of the covers of the souvenir booklet that J. W. Scarborough produced shortly after he opened the cave to the public around 1908.

Photo courtesy of the Nebraska State Historical Society

The cover of a second edition of the Robber's Cave souvenir booklet.

Photo courtesy of Ed Scarborough Jr.

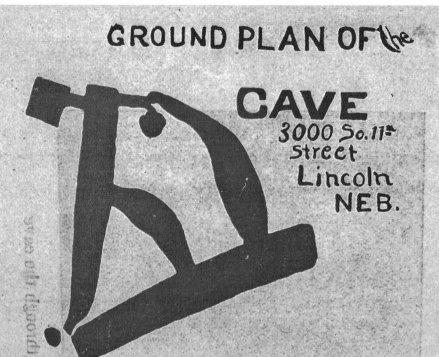

There is more than 500 lineal feet of tunnel, divided into five main rooms, with smaller nitches or getways, as they are called now.
There is over 5600 feet of floor space.

A ground plan of the cave from the souvenir booklet.

Photo courtesy of the Nebraska State Historical Society

Robbers' Cave

Near South Eleventh
and High Street

The Cave is a very interesting place and was undoubtedly a mysterious Robbers' Cave long after I worked there, over forty years ago. I will assure anyone that he will not regret a visit to The Cave.
Jacob Andra

Take
**Penitentiary or Lancaster
Car to High Street**

See the place. It is worth while.

OVER

Mel Goddard kindly donated this old Robber's Cave business card when he returned to the tunnels for a tour in 2017.

Photo courtesy of Mel Goddard

ROBBERS'

**C
A
V
E**

Take Pen or
Lancaster Car
to High Street

Phone F-2618

A visit to The Cave is well worth while. Here one learns something of the geological structure in a way never to forget. *G. E. Condra*

One sees three formations at this spot. Adults and youths alike must enjoy a visit to The Cave and cannot fail to benefit by the simple geology revealed there. *Prof. E. H. Barbour*

I have visited The Cave. The place is well worth a visit by student, antiquarian and pleasure seeker. *Dr. Chas M. Shepherd*

Mr. Dick Veta says he was at The Cave in 1853. No one knew its origin.

Dr. Wesley Queen, in a letter to the State Historical Society, says that the pioneers enlarged Robbers' Cave in the winter of 1863 to get protection from cold, stormy weather.

OVER

The back of the business card donated by Mel Goddard.

Photo courtesy of Mel Goddard

Pictured are Charles, Josephine, Nellie, and Mable Sauler holding little Wilma. This is the only image I've seen that shows this crude entrance, which would be near the cave's emergency exit today. The photo's date is difficult to determine. One historian thought pre Pioneer Brewery, while another suggested 1936-38 judging by bright, flowered dresses that became popular at the end of the Depression years.

Photo courtesy of Jim McKee

Den mother Carrie Looschen–Luther and her Girl Scout troup enjoy a fire just outside of Robber's Cave in 1920.

Photo courtesy of Mary Toren

Hidden in a Bluff
of Dakota Sandstone

—50,000 Cubic yards of cavity.
—700 feet long—greatest depth 74 feet.
—Largest room 112 feet long.
—Used by Indians, Pioneers, Outlaws.

ROBBERS' CAVE

Whose history and geological wonders make it one of Nebraska's wonders.

Always Open
Clean, Well Lighted

3200 So. 11th.   Lancaster car to High Street.

This ad from a 1923 issue of The Lincoln Star calls the cave a "geological wonder" and is one of the very few that includes street car directions.

Photo courtesy of Joel Green

In 1922, Fred Scarborough installed a flat slab to serve as a dance floor in cross tunnel two in front of the "questions mark." Although large pieces have been broken off by vandals, the floor can be seen today.

Photo courtesy of Joel Green

The Scarboroughs installed a flat slab dance floor and began advertising it in 1922. Pictured is a portion of the dance floor in 2018.

Photo courtesy of Joel Green

Ku Klux Klan activity in the Capital City peaked from 1924 to about 1929. A 1965 Journal Star article stated that three Klan leaders from Indiana set up headquarters in the Fraternity Building in Lincoln, now the Sharp Building, and leased Robber's Cave for initiation purposes.

Photo courtesy of Joel Green

On May 21, 1932, the Nebraska and Des Moines chapters of the Military Order of the Cootie surprised Arthur D. Dodds on his birthday and "After the Des Moines chapters had partaken of a chicken dinner at the home of Mr. Dodds, 3411 Cable St., they joined the Lincoln group at Robber's Cave." Founded in New York City in 1920, the MOC provides social and entertainment programs to members of the VFW to this day.

Photo courtesy of the Nebraska State Historical Society (RG2183-1932-521-2)

Esther was known to many as the "Bird Lady" or the "Canary Doctor." Here she is in her aviary in November of 1942.

Photo courtesy of the Lincoln Journal Star

The College View school paper photographed a Halloween Party at Robber's Cave in 1949. Pictured are Eunice Grant, Everett Fisher, Leo Herber, Claudine Huber, Joan Sharp, and Ed Perry. Also in attendance but not pictured were Bonnie Syfert, Richard Swena, Marvin Gunter, and Evelyn Hansen.

Photo courtesy of Dale Nobbman

Wayne Copes, a high-scoring point guard for Palmyra's basketball team in 1952, raises his glass of Gatorade, no doubt, at a Robber's Cave party in July of 1957.

Photo courtesy of Martha Brown

Another July 1957 party scene in tunnel three. Note the metal chimney in the background.

Photo courtesy of Martha Brown

Roasting wienies at the fire pit in tunnel three, now known as the Bat Cave, in July 1957. The cylindrical metal chimney is gone and there is now a wooden ladder leading out of the airshaft.

Photo courtesy of Martha Brown

This University of Nebraska track and field athlete takes a break from training in this scene from a July 1957 Robber's Cave party.

Photo courtesy of Martha Brown

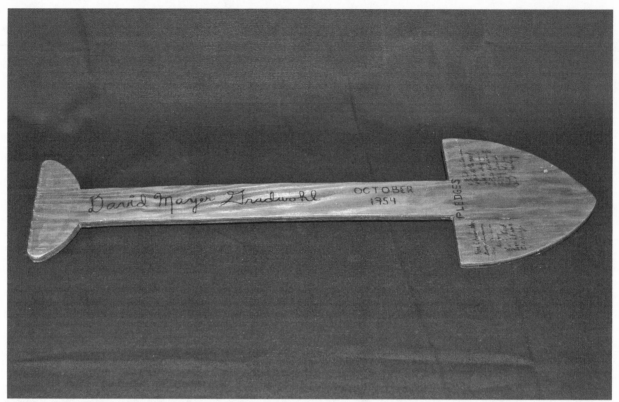

This fraternity paddle used in Robber's Cave in October of 1954 is signed by David M. Gradwohl and pledges. Imagine being blindfolded, having to crawl beneath the display cases at Morril Hall, only to end up at Robber's Cave. Read who all signed the paddle in the Initiations, Rituals, and Ceremonies at Robber's Cave chapter.

Photo courtesy of the Nebraska State Historical Society (9044-8)

Matt Norsworthy discovered two beautiful glass slide photographs in his father's collection. James Norsworthy, a longtime Lincoln photographer, captured this 1950s party scene in tunnel three. Note the pointed gun, the pipe, and fire burning in the background.

Photo courtesy of Matt Norsworthy

The second of two glass slide photographs from James Norsworthy's collection captures this photogenic 1950s couple.

Photo courtesy of Matt Norsworthy

Although we'll probably never know why, Chris Christensen, a biology major form Montrose, Iowa, seems to be the center of attention in this Union College senior class party scene at Robber's Cave from 1960 published in Union College's Golden Cords yearbook.

Photo courtesy of Dale Nobbman/the Union College Golden Cords 1960 Yearbook

One of the Scarborough's coyotes with the base of the family's windmill visible in background.

Photo courtesy of Ed Scarborough Jr.

Esther Scarborough in the late 1940s or early 1950s with Minnie on her lap.

Photo courtesy of Ed Scarborough Jr.

Esther Scarborough created a sand bottle (left) using the many different shades of Robber's Cave sand. A visitor in the 1980s gave a souvenir bottle (right) to the Scarborough family and stated it had been purchased in the early 1900s from the Robber's Cave gift shop.

Photo courtesy of Gwyneth Roberts/Lincoln Journal Star

Located at the east end of tunnel two, this ledge would have been directly behind the wooden stage and was often used as the drummer's chair when bands played.

Photo courtesy of Joel Green

Sheriff Merle Karnopp, pictured in 1971, led a crackdown on the increasingly out-of-hand cave parties in the 1950s and 1960s. Karnopp graduated from the FBI academy in 1948 and is well-known for his role in arresting serial killer Charles Starkweather.

Photo courtesy of Maurine LeBlanc

This photo was once thought to be of Robber's Cave; however, Matt Hansen found the original article from August 19, 1954, explaining that it's in North Omaha. In the summer of 2019, Omaha historian Michaela Armetta and I located it near Hummel Park.

Photo courtesy of Dave Kennedy/Lincoln Journal Star

The cave's entrance as it appeared on November 29, 1970. To the north of the door is the roof of what once was Fred Scarborough's exotic and tropical fish shop, which became a garage and store room after the fish store closed after WWII when Fred had trouble importing his rare fish.

Photo courtesy of Lincoln Journal Star

Vi Scarborough, Ed Scarborough Jr., and Scott Maybin walk just south of the cave entrance in 1986—a rare look at the back of the entrance structure and adjacent fish shop/store room/garage.

Photo courtesy of Jim Burnett Omaha World Herald

The Scarborough residence on March 26, 1976.

Photo courtesy of Scott Maybin

The greenhouse at the south side of the Scarborough residence, pictured here on April 8, 1977, at one time was Esther Scarborough's aviary.

Photo courtesy of Scott Maybin

A snow-covered Scarborough house looking west in 1950 before they removed their windmill/water tank.

Photo courtesy of Ed Scarborough Jr.

While Fritz Yeany burned weeds on the property, a fire spread on July 2, 1968. The blaze ignited gunpowder stored in Fred Scarborough's "old fish room," and the explosion destroyed Scarborough Sr.'s antique vehicles and damaged the south side of the house.

Photo courtesy of the Lincoln Journal Star

This is the one-and-only photo of the Scarborough family's smokehouse that sat atop tunnel three's airshaft. The small building, pictured here in 1976, is where many kids attempted to enter the cave by lowering themselves into what is now the "bat cave." Now, there is a small, wood-framed structure in its place for the bats to come and go. A young Scott Maybin is planting an Easter egg atop the stone marker.

Photo courtesy of Scott Maybin

Scott Maybin seen in tunnel one from beneath the entrance arch.

Photo courtesy of Jim Burnett Omaha World Herald

Scott Maybin stands at the west end of tunnel one, the original entrance to the cave. Quarrying in the late 1800s destroyed the cap rock.
Photo courtesy of Jim Burnett Omaha World Herald

Ed Jr. and Scott Maybin in tunnel one in 1986.

Photo courtesy of Harald Dreimanis

Tunnel one looking west in 2018.

Photo courtesy of Joel Green

Tunnel one circa 1908 depicting two men sitting at the eastern terminus of the first tunnel.

Photo courtesy of the Nebraska State Historical Society (RG2133-12-369)

Facing east from tunnel one in 2015.

Photo courtesy of Brian Podwinski

Cross tunnel one circa 1908 looking north. Notice the white dog sitting on the landing facing the gentleman with his lantern.

Photo courtesy of the Nebraska State Historical Society (RG2133-12-371)

Scott Maybin stands at the top of cross tunnel one in 1986.

Photo courtesy of Jim Burnett Omaha World Herald

When the Nebraska Cornhusker football team held "huge" parties following the Spring Games of the 1960s, this tunnel, cross tunnel one, would be "lined with kegs" remembers a former Husker.

Photo courtesy of Joel Green

Scott Maybin and his mother Vi Scarborough in 1986. This photo conveys the many shades of Dakota sandstone, and it's the only photo that shows the small stage at the east end of tunnel two.

Photo courtesy of the Lincoln Journal Star

Tunnel two looking east in 2018.

Photo courtesy of Joel Green

Scott Maybin in 1986 points to a carving from December 13, 1901.

Photo courtesy of Jim Burnett Omaha World Herald

Scott Maybin points out the same carving in 2018.

Photo courtesy of Joel Green

Scott Maybin stands at the entrance to tunnel three in 1986.

Photo courtesy of Jim Burnett Omaha World Herald

Scott Maybin stands at tunnel three's entrance in 2018.

Photo courtesy of Joel Green

This F. M. Downs 1908 photo provides a view of tunnel two looking east from what would now be the top of a staircase.

Photo courtesy of the Nebraska State Historical Society (RG2133-12-370)

Before reopening in 1986, Ed Scarborough Jr. installed railings and relocated sand with the help of his stepson Scott Maybin. Here are Scarborough Jr. and Maybin in tunnel two facing west.

Photo courtesy of Jim Burnett Omaha World Herald

I purchased this photo from Mr. Wendt at Bluestem Books in Lincoln, Nebraska. It's of the University of Nebraska—Lincoln's Palladian Party circa 1910. Notice most in attendance are holding candles.

Photo courtesy of Joel Green

An often recreated scene during holiday parties, company parties, and class reunions, this early 1900s photograph captured twelve men at the east end of tunnel two engaged in what appears to be a dice game.

Photo courtesy of the Nebraska State Historical Society

The east end of tunnel two in 2018.

Photo courtesy of Joel Green

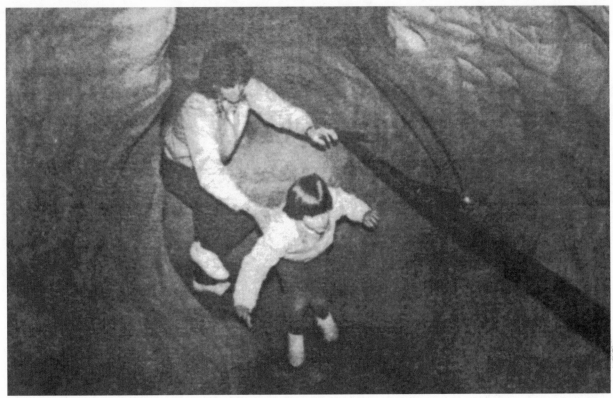

A Belmont student and parent volunteer ascend steps from well area in April of 1986.

Photo courtesy of Scott Maybin

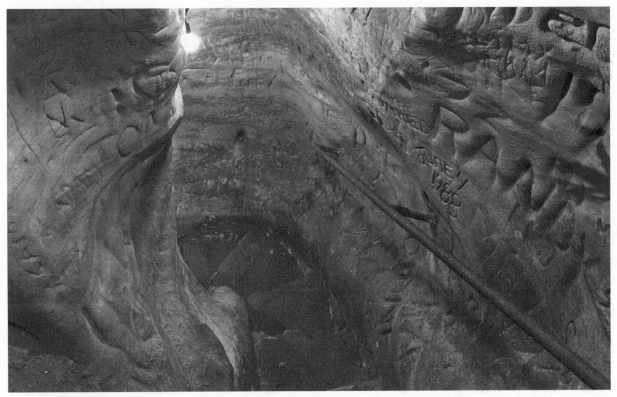

Steps to the well in 2018.

Photo courtesy of Joel Green

Ed Jr. in the winding stairwell that leads to the bottom of the well.

Photo courtesy of Jim Burnett Omaha World Herald

Due to safety concerns, Ed Scarborough Jr. installed these bars from the back window of his Capitol Shooting Supply business. Before, just a single, horizontal rail was in place to prevent mishaps. Many accidents and injuries occurred by people falling into the well, leading to a few lawsuits.

Photo courtesy of Joel Green

The University of Nebraska Union Literary Society poses for a photo in tunnel two near fat man's misery in 1912. Membership included the likes of Willa and Elsie Cather (not known to be present in this photograph), Louise, Olivia and Roscoe Pound, and Rufus Lyman.

Photo courtesy of the Lincoln Journal Star

Vi Scarborough and her son Scott Maybin in April of 1986. Note the west end of tunnel two is stoned up—the source of many rumors that the cave connected to the Nebraska State Penitentiary.

Photo courtesy of the Lincoln Journal Star

Tunnel two looking west in 2018.

Photo courtesy of Joel Green

"Fat man's misery" looking east. The steps at the east end of this tunnel lead into tunnel two.

Photo courtesy of Joel Green

"Fat man's misery" looking west. This path leads to the bottom of the well.

Photo courtesy of Joel Green

This tight tunnel used to continue deeper, curved to the right, then led back into the bottom of the well making a complete circle.

Photo courtesy of Joel Green

Looking up from the bottom of the well (approximately 50 feet deep today). The Pioneer Brewery utilized the well, initially 62 feet deep, as their water source for the lagering process.

Photo courtesy of Joel Green

Scott Maybin explained that this ladder had to have been placed into tunnel three's airshaft sometime after the Scarboroughs moved in 1989. This spot had been the fire pit/fireplace, and the shaft led up into the Scarboroughs' smokehouse. Today, this shaft is the bats' entrance and exit to the cave.

Photo courtesy of Eric Gregory/Lincoln Journal Star

Remnants of the dance floor can still be found in cross tunnel two, also the location of the "question mark."

Photo courtesy of Joel Green

Cross tunnel two (then considered tunnel four) circa 1908 looking north. Notice the African American gentleman sitting at the left and the "question mark" entrance visible to the right.

Photo courtesy of the Nebraska State Historical Society (RG2133-12-372)

Tunnel three was known to many as the lunchroom as it featured a fireplace and picnic table. This tunnel is now known as the "bat cave" as it is meshed off to protect the bats and features nocturnal lighting. (The tunnel was labeled tunnel five at the time of this photo, circa 1908.)

Photo courtesy of the Nebraska State Historical Society (RG2133-12-373)

This airshaft, labeled blowhole on the wooden map, can be found in a cross tunnel at the east end of the cave. Several guests recall entering Robber's Cave by sliding down a pole through this particular chute.

Photo courtesy of Joel Green

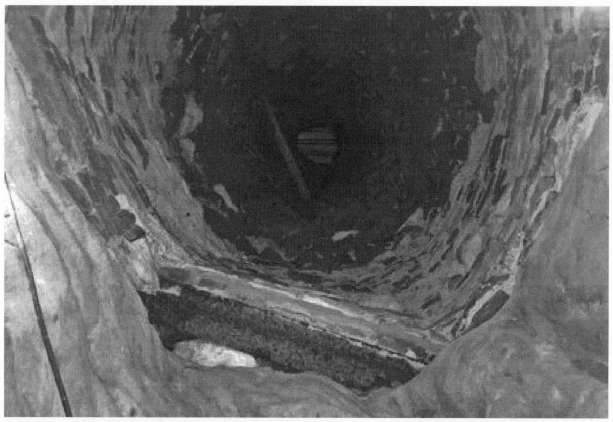

Looking up the airshaft from the bottom of what is labeled the "Blowhole" on the map. Brewers needed ventilation shafts such as this to maintain temperature.

Photo courtesy of Joel Green

Cross tunnel number one leads south into tunnel two. This location reads "sink hole" on the cave map.

Photo courtesy of Pixel Bakery

Fred Scarborough teaching his grandson, young Ed Jr., to drive on the cave property in the 1930s.

Photo courtesy of Ed Scarborough Jr.

Twenty-one-year old Ed Jr. in his 1932 Ford Roadster just before heading to Burbank, California, to work for the American, global, aerospace company Lockheed Martin. He spent two years building the Roadster on the cave property.

Photo courtesy of Ed Scarborough Jr.

Esther Belle Stevens Newnom remarried Fred C. Scarborough on March 18, 1914, in Sidney, Nebraska, and the two adopted and raised Edwin as a Scarborough.

Photo courtesy of Ed Scarborough Jr.

Fred Scarborough operated an exotic and tropical fish shop partly connected to the north side of the cave until WWII prevented him from importing his fish. The entrance to this shop was through a door at the landing between the two flights of stairs in the cave's main entrance stairwell.

Photo courtesy of the Lincoln Journal Star

Fred was a sergeant in the *Third Nebraska Infantry* during the Spanish War. The colonel happened to be William Jennings Bryan, who would become a Nebraska, orator and three-time Presidential candidate.

Photo courtesy of Ed Scarborough Jr.

Edwin Scarborough Sr. flew in the Army Air Corp.

Photo courtesy of Ed Scarborough Jr.

Ed Senior next to Agnes holding their son Ed Jr. Agnes and Ed Sr. divorced and she moved to California in 1948. This photo was taken in their front yard on the cave property.

Photo courtesy of Ed Scarborough Jr.

Ed Scarborough Sr., left, and Ed Scarborough Jr., right, stand in front of Ed Jr.'s 1943 Boeing Stearman in 1964 at the Lincoln Air Force Base.

Photo courtesy of Ed Scarborough Jr.

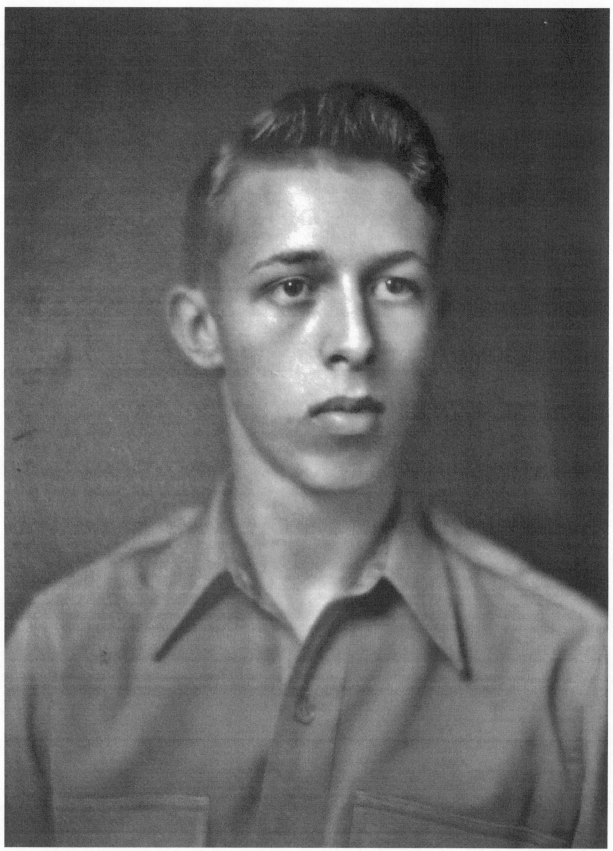

Ed Scarborough Jr. at sixteen years old.

Photo courtesy of Ed Scarborough Jr.

The 1873 Winchester Model rifle that Scarborough Jr. found in the 1930s amidst the burnt remains of what he called the "old horse barn" off of the south side of the cave. With its low serial number, he made quite a bit of money when he sold it to Dick Hedley.

Photo courtesy of Ed Scarborough Jr.

Capitol Shooting Supply, Scarborough Jr.'s gun shop, pictured in 1955. Also pictured is 1955 Ford Station Wagon Ed Jr. owned for 52 years.

Photo courtesy of Ed Scarborough Jr.

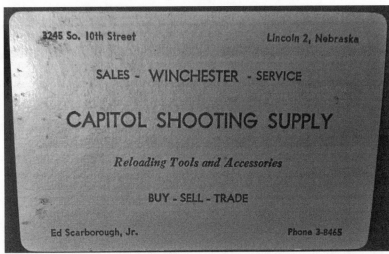

Ed Scarborough Jr. had a gun shop, Capitol Shooting Supply, just east of his house. He also had a private shooting range in Robber's Cave in the 1970s.

Photo courtesy of Joel Green

John Wesley Scarborough's grave in Lincoln's Wyuka Cemetery. J. W. was the first of four generations of Scarboroughs to own the cave property.

Photo courtesy of Joel Green

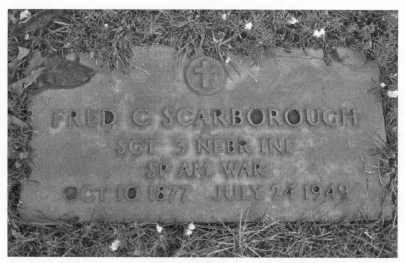

Fred C. Scarborough's headstone in Lincoln, Nebraska. Fred passed away at his home on the cave property, as did his father J. W. Scarborough.

Photo courtesy of Joel Green

Ed Sr.'s headstone in Lincoln, Nebraska, indicating he was a flight officer during WWII.

Photo courtesy of Joel Green

Ed Scarborough Jr. accepted my invitation to meet with Dale Nobbman and me on March 15, 2017. We conversed about the cave and looked over many photos during a two and a half hour recorded interview.

Photo courtesy of Dale Nobbman

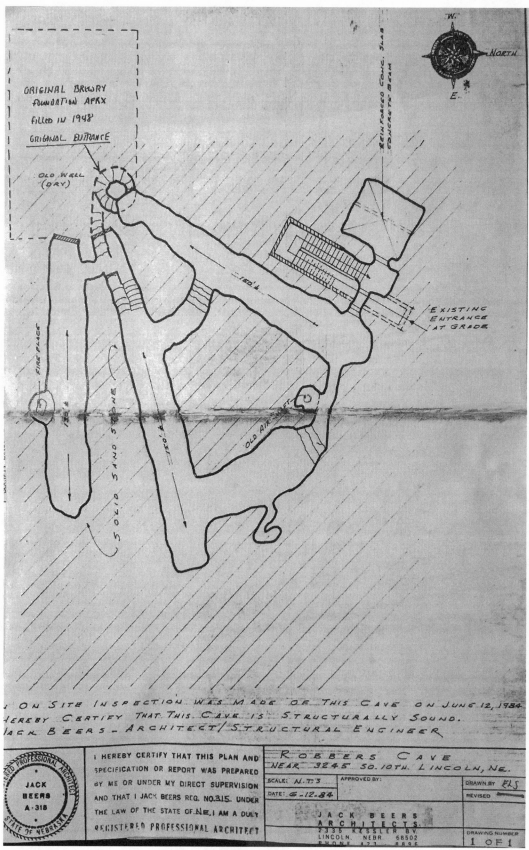

In order to reopen the cave in the mid 1980s, Ed Scarborough Jr. contacted Jack Beers Architects to inspect the cave. The firm certified the cave to be structurally sound in June of 1984.

Photo courtesy of Joel Green
Document Courtesy of Ed Scarborough Jr.

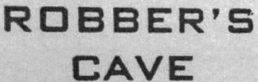

ROBBER'S CAVE

LINCOLN'S "FIRST" TOURIST ATTRACTION

A BRIEF HISTORY OF ROBBER'S CAVE

A 1986 Robber's Cave ad made quite a claim—Lincoln's "First" Tourist Attraction. The cave is older than the city of Lincoln, lending some truth to the assertion.

Photo courtesy of Rana and Donald Schreiber

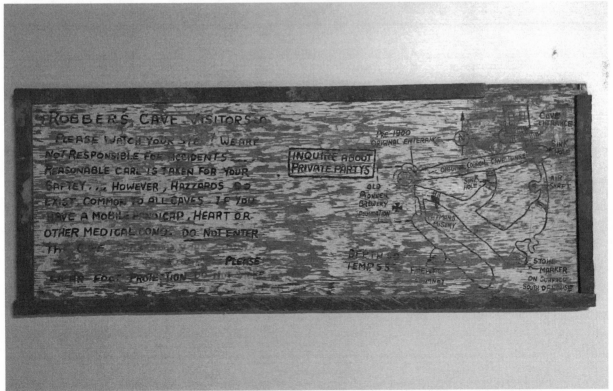

Ed Jr. hand painted this wooden sign/map and displayed it in 1986 for the cave's reopening. In the early 1990s, Frosty Chapman plucked it from a rubbish heap and kept it in his garage for many years. He kindly returned it to be displayed once again near the cave's entrance.

Photo courtesy of Joel Green

Willard – Phi Kappa Tau – Nebraska Wesleyan University, Date Dash, January 23, 1989.

Photo courtesy of an anonymous cave tour guest

Willard – Phi Kappa Tau – Nebraska Wesleyan University, Date Dash, January 23, 1989.

Photo courtesy of an anonymous cave tour guest

Willard – Phi Kappa Tau – Nebraska Wesleyan University, Robber's Cave Bash, March 26, 1988.

Photo courtesy of an anonymous cave tour guest

Three youngsters cool off in Robber's Cave in August 1955.

Photo courtesy of Kent Griffith

A handsome gang of eight poses just outside the cave's entrance in August 1959. (Note the cursive warning just inside the door.)

Photo courtesy of Kent Griffith

This west entrance once led from the Pioneer Brewery's cellar into the cave. It is now the cave's emergency exit.

File courtesy of Blue Blood Brewing Company

What once was a room for birthday parties with a picnic table and firepit is now the primary entrance for cave tours.

File courtesy of Blue Blood Brewing Company

Tunnel one looking west in 2015 before lights were installed.

Photo courtesy of Blue Blood Brewing Company

The west end of tunnel one seen as it looked in 2015. To the right, there are stairs that lead down to the well area.

Photo courtesy of Blue Blood Brewing Company

The cave's entrance as it looked on March 26, 1976.

Photo courtesy of Scott Maybin

What used to be the cave's entrance as it looked in 2005.

Photo courtesy of Joel Green

The cave's entrance stairwell as it looked in 2015.

Photo courtesy of Blue Blood Brewing Company

After being closed to the public for thirteen years, Cindy Schultz of Owosso, Michigan, and Shar Frye of Holt, Michigan, were two of the first visitors to the refurbished Robber's Cave. Schultz and Frye were in Lincoln for a wedding and are pictured ascending the stairwell in April of 1986.

Photo Courtesy of the Lincoln Journal Star

A view from the bottom of the entrance stairwell in 2015.

Photo courtesy of Blue Blood Brewing Company

Founded in 2011, Blue Blood Brewing Company leased space above Robber's Cave from May 4, 2016, to May 15, 2019.

Photo courtesy of Joel Green

Found items from the cave on display.

Photo courtesy of Joel Green

With the aid of Preservation Architect Matt Hansen, we were able to determine this mechanism found in the cave to be a foot-operated leg vise used for forging horseshoes.

Photo courtesy of Joel Green

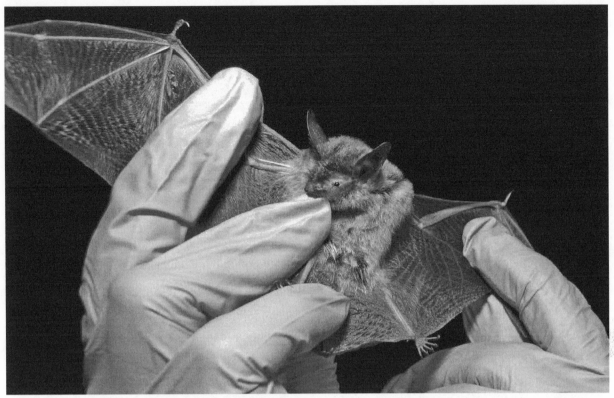

A northern long-eared bat in 2015. Approximately 55-60 bats hibernate in Robber's Cave from fall to spring.

Photo courtesy of Pete Pattavina

Zoologist Michael Fritz and retired biologist Cliff Lemen have served to monitor Robber's Cave's bat population, which consists of three species: tri-colored, big brown, and northern long-eared bats.

Photo courtesy of Joel Green

Left to right: Cavett's childhood friend Freddy, Joel Green, Cavett's wife Martha Rogers, and Dick Cavett in February of 2017.

Photo courtesy of Jamie Schack

Cavett and Green discuss something in tunnel two—the subject probably had to do with Mark Twain or Marlon Brando.

Photo courtesy of Jamie Schack

Cavett inspects the "question mark" tunnel. Now what could I have done in there?

Photo courtesy of Jamie Schack

In the summer of 2016, twelve Lincoln priests were invited to tour and bless Robber's Cave.

Photo courtesy of Cathy Bender, Southern Nebraska Register

Matthew Braunsroth proposes to Annie Kobold in July of 2017 at the entrance to Robber's Cave. The couple shared a love for Robber's Cave and the history behind the location.

Photo courtesy of Jordan Lambrecht

Cave Sessions features local and nationally known musicians, giving them an intimate setting to play their music and tell their story. Pictured is Kris Lager based out of Omaha, Nebraska.

Photo courtesy of Jordan Lambrecht

Tunnel two prepared for the Robber's Cave Film Series.

Photo courtesy of Joel Green

On Halloween night 2017, the line to visit Robber's Cave snaked all the way around toward Van Dorn Park!

Photo courtesy of Joel Green

Easton Schack, Brooklyn Green, and Logan Schack were three of the two thousand trick-or-treaters who braved the cold, rain, and wind to visit Robber's Cave on Halloween night in 2017.

Photo courtesy of Joel Green

The Robber's Cave Pep Band performs two sets on the Fridays before the Nebraska Cornhusker football team's home games.
Photo courtesy of Blue Blood Brewing Company

The Pep Band has performed in the cave, on the brewery floor, in the restaurant, as well as onstage in the Yard.

Photo courtesy of Blue Blood Brewing Company

When Grandmother's Restaurant closed in 2016, Robber's Cave carried on the tradition of the Pep Band's Friday night performances.

Photo courtesy of Blue Blood Brewing Company

The Yard just south of Blue Blood Brewery's restaurant. Much of Robber's Cave is directly beneath the Yard.

Photo courtesy of Blue Blood Brewing Company

Brooklyn Green began giving tours of Robber's Cave with her dad at age five. When she puts on her Vala's Pumpkin Patch hardhat, she means business! Stay tuned for Brooklyn's children's book about Robber's Cave.

Photo courtesy of Joel Green

Joel Green during a private tour in 2017. Green is always quick to share a photo in order to compliment his many stories during tours.

Photo courtesy of Amanda Remmenga

Nostalgic Tales and Random Recollections

Life is filled with so many fond moments, why not write them down? I've enjoyed listening to people reflect on their Robber's Cave memories so much that, even if their stories don't always add up factually, I feel compelled to preserve them. American writer Anais Nin once said, "We write to taste life twice, in the moment and in retrospect." So while you enjoy these short memories I've collected, I urge you to keep in mind another quote from local author John Roth: ". . . try to temper criticism with the knowledge that one's personal memories (especially the memories of those who have lived the longest) shouldn't always be impeded by a voice of dissent, armed with factual information." Just enjoy them, however the individual remembered the account.

In general, many cave recollections that guests have shared with me are very similar to Randy Carlson's. He remembers Esther Scarborough sitting on the porch collecting 25 cents to enter the cave in the early 1960s. He would follow a narrow concrete sidewalk to the cave's entrance. "Playing in the cave as a kid was a blast!" he remembers. Here is another local's particular recollection:

> At the hilltop was a house bearing the sign, "Jesse James Hideout." One had to pay to get in, a small building like an outhouse outside held a light switch and a steep staircase down, down into the bowels of the earth . . . the owner of the bluff and entrance would charge less when a group of us kids would get together to explore, with a flashlight in case the lights went off. A large main room was well lit and furnished with picnic tables, a barbeque carved into the side with a cast iron grill, a smoke-hole above giving a little light; the rest of the extensive cave was dark.

A Nebraska Jaycee Hall-of-Famer Reminisces about the Cave and a Pot of Chili

Marlen Luff was born in 1937 at about 17th and Calvert Street in Lincoln. He shared the following story with me, which struck a chord since I walk through the cave so often with my young child:

When I was eight years old, my daddy took me to the cave. It was a great experience that I still remember. I was scared to death but Daddy held my hand and I felt safe. In 1948, the neighborhood gang rode our fancy and not so fancy bikes to the cave and had so much fun. Did Jesse James stay in the cave? Well certainly, everyone knew that, a hero to my generation! As early as 1947, there were paths that were blocked off rumored to lead to the penitentiary. We believed that escaped convicts would use these cave tunnels in order to escape to greater places in Lincoln and beyond, never to be seen again. I remember fat man's squeeze and the bat cave. My mother would tell us to protect our hair because the bats would get into our hair, oh my!

As I grew older, I made many trips to the cave, took girlfriends to the cave, and had parties at the cave. In the later days, it was a party place when I was at UNL and later as a Lincoln Jaycee. It was a grand place to get away from the world's problems. My last visit was in about 1968 or 69, the Lincoln Jaycees had a giant party at the cave—probably 50 or 60 people. My friend, Ron Hoffman, and I were in charge of making and delivering a huge pot of chili to serve everyone. Everything went well, the chili was done, and it took two of us to handle this huge pot. We stepped down the stairs, hearing the rock 'n' roll music, and as we approached the last step, one of us tripped and down we fell . . . along with all the chili that took hours to prepare! I'm sure that there must still be remains of the chili on the soft sandstone floor. The party went on, but without our famous chili. That's my story, and I'm sticking to it. I shall return to the cave.

Marlen Luff of Lincoln/Falls City, Nebraska, and the late Cal Robinson of North Platte were inducted into the Nebraska Jaycee Hall of Fame in 2013.

Union College Packs the Cave for Class Parties

On a Saturday night in March of 1950, one hundred students left Union College in two large city buses bound for Robber's Cave. When they arrived, a warm fire had already been prepared for them. After exploring the tunnels, three short films were shown inside the cave providing plenty of laughs. Hot chocolate and donuts where served. Then, a Mr. Beaven read to the students their class president's letter, told ghost stories, and after hollering "all aboard" they headed back to campus on the buses. Faculty members Elder and Mr. Gordon, Mr. and Mrs. Beaven, Mr. and Mrs. Pete Roehl, and Mr. and Mrs. Hohensee (3/3/1950).

Later in 1970, Union College had more class parties in the cave. Highlights included Roadrunner cartoons and W. C. Fields films, group games, door prizes, and hot dogs (11/13/1970).

A Texan Visits the Canary Doctor, the Cave, and the Gun Collection

Originally from Texas, Ray Storey came to Nebraska to attend Union College. He met Esther Scarborough in 1955 when she had him work on her cabinets. Since then, he referred to her as the "canary doctor." After showing him the cave, she had one more item to flaunt: an extensive gun collection! Ray had thought that Esther lived alone with all of those guns to protect her, but I explained to him that what he saw was most likely Fred Scarborough's massive gun collection he kept in the basement of the farm house. Who knows, maybe the guns belonged to Fred *and* Esther.

Saved by the Coyotes

Ten-year-old Jeff Walter had recently moved to Connie Road from 40th and Sheridan Boulevard when two kids from the neighborhood took him and his older brother to the cave in the 1960s. After playing in the cave for quite a while, Jeff remembers the lights flashing on and off. The boys didn't know what that meant, so they continued to play and a little while later they flashed again . . . and again. The boys continued to play. Sure enough, the lights went out.

Jeff and his thirteen-year-old brother were locked in the cave in complete darkness for over an hour, and they remember being "scared shitless." Eventually they found the stairs and climbed the top where a bit of light shown through the bottom of the door. They banged and hollered at the door, but to no avail. Finally, Mrs. Scarborough must've noticed her pet coyotes whining and whimpering (they had to have heard or sensed the terrified boys behind the door). She finally came and unlocked the door, releasing the boys into daylight.

Junior High Girls Have a Shocking Experience at Robber's Cave

A woman shared the following story with me after her tour in 2017. She and two of her junior high girlfriends visited the cave in the 1960s. She remembers the tunnels being much darker than they are now. The three girls held hands as they slowly passed through the shadows. The girl in the front reached up for a light switch, but she actually grabbed a livewire! The current quickly jolted through and zapped all three girls surely creating an electrifying cave experience for them.

The Bat's Belfry . . . and a Protruding Model T

Lincolnite Bob Luebbe shared the following story with me in June of 2017. While visiting a cousin that lived at 11th and Van Dorn Street in Lincoln, he checked out Robber's Cave with his wife in the 1960s. In tunnel number three (currently the bat habitat), which Luebbe referred to as the "bat's belfry," a bat flew past and became stuck in his wife's hair!

Luebbe also remembers being able to see the frame of a 1914 Model T Ford jutting from the ground when driving past the cave property. That frame likely came from when Scarborough Jr. and his dad, Ed Sr., filled in the old brewery foundation with antique car parts that were ruined in the infamous explosion that damaged the home while the Yeanys rented the property from the Scarboroughs in 1965.

A Former Cornhusker Recounts Wife's Unwholesome Experience

A couple visiting the cave in June 2017 gave me additional information on a private tour about the airshaft that is labeled the "blowhole" on the old wooden map. The gentleman had a difficult time maneuvering through the cave with his bad knees, but he toughed it out—after all, he had played football for the Cornhuskers in the 1950s. He recounted a story that typifies being at the wrong place at the wrong time.

His wife had been standing at the bottom of that airshaft at the same time someone above the cave decided to relieve themselves down the chute. The solids struck the poor woman on the top of the head. Talk about being at the wrong place at the wrong time! I thanked her for returning to the cave after such an unwholesome experience years ago. Laughs were had, and she had a good attitude about the whole situation, although I got the sense that she wasn't too happy that her husband decided to share that particular memory on the tour.

Juvenile Spelunkers Risk Lives in Summer of 1965

This next story came to me after I gave tours for another Lincoln High School class reunion, but I must grant a request for anonymity. After the reunion's tour, a guest from the group led me to the specific location near the grain bins where in 1965 as twelve-year-olds he and a friend began to dig a tunnel with the intent of reaching the cave. They found an isolated spot and began to burrow into the bluff. Secluded by tall bins, the slope, and surrounding trees, the juvenile spelunkers dug their secret passage day by day. For weeks on end they continuing to dig even though portions repeatedly collapsed on them! The brave diggers had burrowed an astounding 15 feet into the bluff when a fairly significant cave-in finally frightened them enough to stop. The Scarboroughs found out what the boys were up to and placed two large downed trees on their sides to block the front of the hole. Andy Dufresne from *Shawshank Redemption* would have been proud.

Rockin' Out in Robber's Cave

In the 1970s and 1980s, long before Blue Blood erected a performance stage in the Yard area, bands performed inside the cave. One heavy metal band in particular, Cross, played in the cave in the early 1970s. Mike Weigert, a former member of the band, toured Robber's Cave with me in December of 2017. During the tour, Weigert described being dropped off at the cave as a youth about every other day during summers, and when he became a bit older, he played for the band Cross during huge cave parties. Weigert explained that the amplifiers and speakers he and his band members carried into the cave were unnecessary due to the tunnels' natural acoustics. On one unfortunate occasion, Weigert remembered losing grip on an amplifier and watching it tumble down the main entrance staircase (the steep steps caused many issues over the years). Weigert also recalled how smoky the cave became during parties of the 1960s and 1970s. The thick clouds of cigarette and at times marijuana smoke created a perpetual haze in the crowded cave. Weigert even pointed out that regardless the band playing, the drummer always sat on the ledge at the east end of tunnel number two as the flat stone spot made the perfect drummer's chair!

Stealing Hearts in Robber's Cave

Sixty Years of Marriage Began with Cave Halloween Party as First Date

Claudine and Leo Herber met the autumn of 1949 at Union College in Lincoln, Nebraska. Not many couples have photos from their first date, but Claudine and Leo happened to be an exception. They considered themselves a serious couple after the first date!

Ultimately, Claudine and Leo were married at the College View SDA church in Lincoln on August 27, 1950. In 2010, they celebrated 60 years together. Not only have they remained committed to each other, Dr. Herber and Claudine remained committed to Union College as the two proud 1952 graduates funded the Herber Student Missionary Endowment. What a couple!

Robber's Cave Sets the Stage for Unique Proposal

Matthew Braunsroth and Annie Kobold had been dating for five years. The couple shared a love for Blue Blood Brewery, Robber's Cave, and the history behind the location—my kind of folks. Matthew thought proposing to Annie would be a great way to add yet another story to the cave's history. He wanted to go bigger than just kneeling and proposing. So he spent a week planning, organizing, and eventually executing a unique proposal in July of 2017.

Matthew told Annie that he had to bartend on July 24, 2017, at Blue Blood, but instead he used that time to prepare his unique proposal. Once he reached the brewery, his brother/best man stood ready to help along with Annie's best friends. They suspended lights down the staircase to the barrel room and placed candles on the steps. Smaller candles were elegantly set on the barrels along the walls, ledge, and original cave entrance steps—the scene resembled a fairy tale. Once everything was in place, all Matthew had to do was wait.

All of Annie's family and closest friends had previously arrived, as had Matthew's—everyone except Annie's sister, Ellee, her husband, Bret, and mother, Kiltie. The plan was that Ellee and her mom were to pick up Annie for dinner since they were *conveniently* in town. So they picked up Annie and took her to her favorite sandwich shop, but after that, Ellee mentioned wanting to go to Blue Blood to try the beer and possibly see the cave. As they headed that way, Matthew hid in the cave with the family and friends.

When Annie arrived at Blue Blood, Matthew's other brother, Micah, also a Blue Blood employee, was there to host. The group asked Micah if they could see the cave, and he conveniently pointed out one of the tour guides sitting at the bar. The guide graciously offered to give the tour, so they walked through the brewery and stopped at the cave entrance. When they opened the door and began to descend the stairs, there stood Matthew awaiting Annie. Matthew and Annie's song "The Heart Never Lies" by McFly played as she came down, and the look on her face was priceless! Matthew handed Annie a bouquet of flowers, held her tight, and they kissed. After telling her how much he loved her and wanted to spend the rest of his life with her, he knelt to one knee and proposed. Annie said yes!

After Matthew placed the sapphire ring on Annie's finger and gave her another kiss and hug, he told her he had one more surprise. The two then entered the first cavern of Robber's Cave only to find family and friends applauding and crying for them.

I'd like to thank Mathew and Annie for sharing their remarkable story. Congratulations, well done, and best wishes!

Trespassers and Sneak-ins

Those who have toured Robber's Cave recently notice that many carvings have been made after 2000. Through the late 1980s and 1990s, a padlocked door did little to deter trespassers and vandals. Nor did walling off the door frame with wood or obstructing it with concrete cinderblocks. Eventually, the city of Lincoln decided to bulldoze the entrance and cap the spot with concrete in 2000. Even then, determined youth still found ways into the tunnels by burrowing into the bluff from the west through an exposed two-by-two hole beneath the concrete slab!

At one time, online videos existed of daring teens who recorded their entire intrusion including the lengthy and strenuous, often comical, process of shimmying through the narrow opening in order to drop down to the stairwell. Actually, a few trespassers have returned in order to boast of their feats during tours. In retrospect, they admit youthful ignorance; others admit they had no idea what they were getting into and mistook the cave to be anything from someone's basement to a mine shaft!

Specific aspects of the cave's condition are revealed through such videos: in the room at the base of the steps, before entering through the north arch (what is now Blue Blood's barrel room) there are plastic bags, chains, wrenches, shoes, a mattress, rebar, and a tree stump. (Scarborough Jr. explained that he and his friends would drop heavy tree stumps into the cave through the "lunchroom chimney" to squat on during New Year's Eve parties).

In the far east tunnel (where the "blowhole" is located on the cave map) spray-painted walls, wire hanging from the ceiling, boards, aluminum cans, metal poles or pipes protruding from the wall, batteries, and latex gloves can be seen littering the cave floor. In the second tunnel, one can see bottles, lighters, candles, cinderblock, and even wood from the old stage.

While watching these online videos, humorous comments are not hard to come by. For example, "Dude, I seriously believe that someone had like some Satan witchcraft going on down here, because there's like, candles, everywhere!"

Standing at the top of the steps, one of the teens asks, "Was this a house? This had to be a house .

. . you go first!"

Imagine being along for one of these illegal, urban spelunking expeditions, and enjoy another one of the teen's humorous conversations I've transcribed. It conveys the juvenile explorers' astonishment, and quite possibly, their chemically enhanced imaginations. While entering tunnel number one, the dialogue begins, "This is huge! This goes on for miles!"

"These flashlights were, like, $4.50. We shoulda bought more. If these go out, we're f!@#$ed!"

"Look at this beam! This must've been, like, an industrial place."

"*Journey to the Center of the Earth*!"

"I feel like this would be, like, some historic place."

"Like a museum, yeah!"

"I can feel myself, like, being restricted."

"Yeah, you just have to calm down."

When one mentions the possibility of the cave being a mineshaft, one teen asks, "What do you mine in Nebraska? Limestone?"

Then someone answers, "No, dude, corn!"

They continue near the well, "I wanna, like, use this railing, but I don't want to get tetanus."

"Well, I got my tetanus, so I'm goodie!"

"What if this place is full of natural gas?"

"Dude, shut up, there's an arm showing up in my picture!

"That's your arm, bro."

"Oh."

During another break-in, as another group of kids peruse their way through the tunnels with a lantern, their recorded back-and-forth banter is as follows: "Dude, did miners work down here? I want to, like, find a million dollars! We need some dynamite . . . like, a lil' half-stick."

Other comical comments include, "If anything, there could be booby traps," followed by, "What would it be like if sandstone caved in . . . it'd be, like, sandy!" My personal favorite can be heard while one of the teens is carving something into the wall. A spider crawls out of a nearby hole, and he says, "Dude, I think it's a brown recluse!" and his friend nearby responds in a questioning tone, "So, let's leave?"

Many of the online videos have been removed recently, but they were entertaining to watch to say the least. On a more serious matter, these young intruders who thought they might find *buried treasure* as they explored *the mine* that they had *discovered* reminded me of a group of college girls from Bellevue, Nebraska, who are described in a 1904 *Omaha Daily Bee* article. When the girls explored the cave, because of previous rumors, they expected to find "trap doors, stacks of arms and treasure chests," but what they actually found supports the claim that Robber's Cave was likely used as a gambling den for some time after The Pioneer Brewery closed: "a card table of ordinary dimensions and a loose-joined, wobbly chair of a rather antique pattern, and small lamp" sat in one of the tunnels (6/10/1904).

Who Knew? Random Tidbits about Robber's Cave

Cold Storage

According to the 1938 *NSM* article, "For a while after the cave was abandoned by horse thieves it was used as a cold storage plant and ice house." This is logical given the cave's consistent cool temperature of 55-degrees Fahrenheit, but it might also explain why certain implements such as a large saw and cast iron ice block tongs were found in the cave (now on display in the barrel room). Before electric refrigeration, blocks of harvested ice were stored in warehouses or caves and insulated with sawdust.

The Pole Entrance

The Lincoln Evening Journal published a "Do You Remember?" section for the alumni of University of Nebraska—Lincoln. The list of memories includes classes in old U Hall, off-bounds Chicken Little Inn, picnics at Pen Woods, plays at the old Orpheum, and Frankie Sherman playing the piano at the Moon. But also included in the list: sliding down the pole at Robber's Cave. This article is the first reference I found of the pole entry, so I asked Scarborough Jr. about it during an interview. He explained that for a short while there had been a flagpole in the airshaft of the tunnel that connects tunnels one and two at the east end of the cave. This shaft is labeled the "blowhole" on the wooded map outside the cave's entrance. "We cut that out a long time ago—kids were landing on each other!" Scarborough Jr. laughed. The most recent reference I have of the pole entry is 1959.

This shaft is the same cylindrical chute that guests see when crawling through the tight passageway that leads from cross tunnel two back into tunnel number one. It always reminded me of something from one of my favorite movies, *The Goonies*. How was that shaft formed? Scarborough Jr.'s great-uncle had been a geology professor at Wynona College in Minnesota before becoming a photographer for *National Geographic* magazine. He explained that that particular shaft formed when saltwater rushed into the bluff, built up pressure, and eventually broke through a soft spot in the sandstone, creating a circular exposure. "The water flowing in from the west had to go somewhere," explained Scarborough Jr.

According to zoologist Michael Fritz, this same shaft that once featured the pole entry is now where many of the bats like to have their babies, or pups! Between the small nooks in the bricks is apparently ideal. The "blowhole" chute was also one of the passages of entry for some who snuck into the cave. Guests have explained lowering a soccer net into that shaft and descending into the cave. When they were ready to leave, they used the net to climb up and out, then simply pulled the net up with them, leaving no trace.

A Possible Fallout Shelter

In 1950, the city of Lincoln considered the use of certain locations throughout the city for bomb shelters. The Cold War increased interest in civil defense and the city considered Robber's Cave for one of the shelter locations. Other areas being considered for shelters were the Antelope conduit, the abandoned water storage reservoir in Van Dorn park and another reservoir near 32nd and X Street (12/29/1950).

Another fallout shelter search occurred in 1961. City–Council Civil Defense Director Richard Vestecka attended a three-day intelligence course at the Western Instructor Training Center at Alameda, California, and then a five-day conference of local CD directors at Los Angeles, California. Vestecka mentioned that a community shelter at 18th and Van Dorn Street would be completed by March. While engineering firms considered sites such as office buildings with adequate basements, the privately-owned [sic] Robber's Cave again surfaced as a possible shelter (10/30/1961). When I asked Scarborough Jr. about the cave's use as a shelter, he remembers telling the city that the cave would serve as a shelter for his friends and family only.

Beginning in 1922, Robber's Cave Featured a Dance Floor

Once, a guest inquired about the location of the cave's dance floor. The guest's grandmother had spoken of it, but I only had an idea of its location. So, to be sure, I asked Scarborough Jr. during one of our interviews. His response was, "It was right in front of the shit hook." When walking north from tunnel number two past what I call the "question mark" there is a prominent, raised ledge. Warning guests not to trip over this ridge is a must. That ledge actually is the edge of the old dancefloor—a large, flat slab of concrete installed in 1922. Envision a group of flappers dancing the Charleston as a band plays just around the corner on the little wooden stage. Even in June of 2017, a guest commented that that her grandparents square-danced in Robber's Cave from the 1960s up to the early 1970s!

Famous Visitors

Several notable Nebraskans are known to have visited Robber's Cave: Louise Pound, Leta Powell Drake, Sandy Dennis, Dick Cavett, Bob Devaney, and a slew of famous Nebraska Cornhuskers. When

I asked Scarborough Jr. if he knew of any celebrities that visited the cave his response was, "Hell yeah, Chuck Norris!" Scarborough Jr. reports that Norris, while laid over at Lincoln's Airport, must've noticed one of the many Robber's Cave ads that Vi Scarborough had posted at the airport because he came to tour the cave with a female friend and what appeared to be a bodyguard (did Chuck Norris need a bodyguard?) Scarborough Jr.'s son Scott Maybin led the tour while Scarborough Jr. waved from the window. I hope a photo surfaces someday in order to authenticate the story. When I sought verification from Maybin, he admitted that the guest did resemble the 1980s action star and then he complimented his stepdad's memory, which is remarkably sharp for an 88 year old.

Fred's Exotic and Tropical Fish Shop

Fred Scarborough sold exotic and tropical fish from a small room filled with homemade aquariums just north of the cave's entryway until the 1940s. Esther Scarborough kept an aviary off of the house to the west where she raised and sold canaries and parakeets. Some Lincolnites knew her as the "Bird Lady" and the "Canary Doctor." A 1942 *Lincoln Star* article that described the Scarborough's side business shed light on the location of a mysterious door. A few guests asked if I had known of a little door located at the landing between the two staircases. I had no answer until I came across the fish-shop article and confirmed its location with Scarborough Jr.:

> On the old foundations put in by a brewery in 1878 to keep the walls from caving in, Lincoln's most unusual store is located [. . .] Under a glass sky-lighted roof stand rows of tanks and aquariums in which swim the tiny, rare tropical fish which Fred Scarborough [. . .] sells and breeds.

At the time, Fred Scarborough ran the cave as a picnic place and sold tropical fish that he began collecting as a hobby while traveling. Also, an auxiliary greenhouse next to the aquariums held Fred's collection of plants. Customers came from Iowa, Oklahoma, and Colorado to purchase Fred's fish!

Injured in a 1930-railroad accident, doctors told Fred he would be paralyzed in six months, so he decided to stay on the farm where he and his father, John Wesley, had lived since they came to Nebraska. Fred began work on the fish room in 1936 by mixing the cement and constructing the tanks himself. "I didn't work with a square or drawings—I like to take the trowel and the cement and just start shaping it up," he said.

Since the tropical fish needed their water temperature to be between 65–85 degrees Fahrenheit, Fred designed and built heated tanks. Danios, gouramis, cichlids, swordtails, mollies, guppies, are just a few of the many varieties he kept in stock until he could no longer import them from Miami and Tampa, Florida. "There are a lot of varieties we haven't been able to get since the war started." I haven't met many guests who remember this business in the cave, but not only does it explain where that old door led, but it also provides insight into Fred Scarborough's personality.

"He can give the Latin name of each fish, tell its habitat and how specially bred varieties were obtained" (11/22/1942). Scarborough Jr. estimated the size of the fish room at 20 x 20 feet, while Esther's aviary just south of the house was about 25 feet long and about 10 or 12 feet wide. The fish room, as Scarborough Jr. refers to it, along with Esther's aviary, were destroyed in an explosion on the property in 1968 that also demolished the original home, along with several of Scarborough Jr.'s and his father's antique cars. The blast shattered windows on the south and west side of the second Scarborough home.

A Private Shooting Range

Scarborough Jr., an avid gun collector who held a class 3 firearms license, still used tunnel two as a private shooting range after the cave closed in 1973. He often invited his friends from the police department and sheriff's office to Robber's Cave for target practice. He liked to set up targets at the west end and fire toward the east (which explains all of the small holes that guests often ask about). Retired Lancaster County Sheriff's Captain Gary Juilfs corroborated the existence of this underground range as a guest on one of my tours.

Other "Robber's Caves"

In Austria and Germany, the Robber's Caves are known as *Räuberhöhles*. One is in Saxony–Anhalt, Germany, also called Daniel's Cave, and another is the Idstedt Robber's Cave (*Idstedter Räuberhöhle*), a passage grave in Schleswig–Holstein, Germany. In Austria there are *Räuberhöhles* in the Mollram Forest of Lower Austria, and in Spital am Semmering. There is a Robber's Cave in the Blaise Castle estate of Bristol, England, and there's even a river cave formation in Northern India called Robber's Cave.

Initiations, Rituals, and Ceremonies at Robber's Cave

Entire books have been written on the global practice of ritual cave use. From cavemen, Greeks, and Romans to Native Americans and college students, caves have been common places for initiation purposes for countless years for the simple fact that they partly offer seclusion and privacy in dark, quiet, and often hidden spaces. Reflect on what Walter Wright Arthen wrote about caves being a place between worlds in his essay "The Magic of Caves":

> Caves were very likely places for initiations [. . .] Young members of [a] community entering adulthood might have been blindfolded and led in darkness through [a] dangerous passage. They traveled into blackness and fear, facing the unknown, until the moment of revelation when they met the animal spirits. [. . .] Perhaps a vision quest or shamanic journey was played out in these lonely depths.

Although it is quite unlikely that anything to that extent occurred in Robber's Cave, the cave has seen it fair share of initiations over the years. At one point, the Scarboroughs were awakened by screams from a young man who had been tied to a sandstone pillar in the cave and then abandoned. The description of another such prank published in *The Nebraska State Journal* in April of 1898 is interesting, to say the least. The following story would have happened after the Pioneer Brewery closed, yet before J. W. Scarborough purchased and cleaned the cave. Keep in mind that, in this case, context to this story would definitely benefit the reader:

> The Tau Delta Omicrons were out seeing what they could do to a man without killing him outright, last night. Among other [things] they loaded him, bound and blindfolded, onto a motor bound for the penitentiary at an hour approaching that of midnight. They were bound for the old Robber's Cave out in the desolate suburbs. What the feelings and experiences of Raymond Pollard of Nehawka were [maybe] better imagined than described. Suffice to say that after surviving the ordeal of the cave and others too numerous to mention, he was taken back to town where it was attempted to finish him off by stuffing him so full of good things as seriously to endanger his life (4/16/1898).

*Raymond Clark Pollard, the brother of US Congressman Ernest Pollard, was born December 19, 1878, and passed February 11, 1968. Raymond is buried in Nehawka, Nebraska, at Mount Pleasant Cemetery.

In April of 1940, during a spring program held in the cave, eight geology students and two "teachers of science" were initiated in the University of Nebraska chapter of Sigma Gamma Epsilon (a national professional geology fraternity). John L. Champe, instructor in anthropology, and Emery L. Blue, science instructor at Irving Junior High School, were made associate members. The following students were taken in as full members: Elliot Bratt, Lyle Harvey, Joseph Kenny, and Wilbur Rogers, all of Lincoln; Guy Johnson, Hemingford; Harold Patterson of York; Carl Wahl of Eustis, and Jerome Wright of Chappell. Lester Ringenberg of Garland, president of the society, and Ray Harrison of Grand Island, pledge master, were in charge of the initiation (4/21/1920).

In May of 1929, the Nebraska State Junior Chamber of Commerce brought delegates to Robber's Cave where supper followed an initiation of nearly 50 out-of-towners. Six Lincoln men were also initiated. Carl Junge served as master of ceremonies (5/8/1929).

The Lutheran Club held informal initiation ceremonies at Robber's Cave for three hours in November of 1929. About thirty members were initiated in the presence of twenty old members. Reverend and Mrs. G. K. Rubrecht along with Mr. and Mrs. M. Hestenes chaperoned this affair (11/15/1929). A couple of years later, new members of the Lutheran Students' Club were initiated at Robber's Cave after meeting at the Temple Building. Reinhold Kildebeck provided the entertainment, Arthur Jenny headed transportation, and Magdalene Lebsack handled refreshments. Students were told to wear old clothes (11/6/1931).

In February of 1946, the members of Unit III, Beta chapter, of Nu Phi Mu business girls' sorority held a party at Robber's Cave at which four new pledges were initiated. Miss Patricia Thomas, social chairman, supervised (2/28/1946).

The Sigma Gamma Epsilon Earth Sciences Honor Society elected David M. Gradwohl in 1954. While a student the University of Nebraska, pledges were given wooden paddles to decorate and have signed by the geology department faculty members, active Sigma Gamma Epsilon members, and fellow pledges. According to Gradwohl:

> Our initiation rites started out in the basement of Morrill Hall. We were blindfolded and had to crawl around and under the display cases and through the hallways. Then we were driven to Robber's Cave out near the old Penitentiary. I think the pledges more or less played hide and seek with the actives, in and out of the sandstone tunnels and niches. I do not remember what all we did, except that the actives made the pledges chew tobacco.

In addition to David Gradwohl, here are the names engraved and inked onto the wooden paddle. Maybe you'll find someone you know: Ron Ohnoutka, Swanson, Don, Aram Sarkissian, R. Stacy, H. M. Heck, Alan L. Lamb, Ed Wedge, Rod Warren, Roger H. Barnard, J. R. Gifford, Robert Lantz, R. L. Cramer, H. S. Beardsley, E. F. Schram, William H. Gilliland, L. S. Tanner, John Leland Champe, C. B. Schultz, C. M. Riley, B. H. Burma, Henry Reider, A. L. Lugn, Roy Frankforter, John Howe, R. L. Marrs, W. J. Hunter, Wes, Barton, Carl Vondra, Paul Nygreen, Jerold Jesperse, Cyril Harvey, Paul O'Donnell, Willard E. Cox, Jim Lowel, Clark A. Mueller, Walt Sudbeck, A. McCrone, Hal DeGraw, Alan E. Peckham, James P. Garber, Stuart Watson, Rock H. Castellano, George J. Hugenberg, R. Lugn, Jay Ziegler, Al Osborne, Don Lorenz, John Harper, and Richard Renard.

The following story does not fall under the category of initiation, but it is a good old-fashion tale of revenge. The story happened while college kids used the cave after the Pioneer Brewery closed, yet before J. W. Scarborough bought the property. Historian Dale Nobbman extracted this tale from the 1907 *Cornhusker Yearbook*, and it recaps the "Class of 1907 History" beginning with freshman experiences in 1903.

One freshman in particular, Clarence Gardiner Johnson, "gave the sophomores in the fall of 1903 a little too much guff," according to Nobbman. The sophomores vindictively forced Johnson to spend the night in Robber's Cave (quite possibly alone) as a way to exact their vengeance. Remember that this happened a few years prior to J. W. Scarborough purchasing, cleaning, and lighting the cave—no doubt Johnson endured a cold and dark slumber.

Literary Society Gatherings

I'm often asked, "Just what exactly do literary societies do?" Well as of 1974, their meeting agendas hadn't changed much. They perform readings, skits, and music, give book reviews and impromptu speeches, and hold banquets, picnics and house parties. According to a UNL Alumni Association:

> Many of the earliest society members were future lawyers anxious to develop their talents in debates, plays and public speaking. Most prominent of those early members were Willa and Elsie Cather, Louise, Olivia and Roscoe Pound, and Rufus Lyman.

Cather is widely known as the Pulitzer Prize-winning American author of the Great Plains. Louise Pound gained notoriety as an American folklorist, professor, and incredible athlete. Her brother Roscoe Pound earned distinction as an American legal scholar and educator, not to mention Dean of Harvard Law School from 1916 to 1936. Rufus Lyman became the founding Dean of the University of Nebraska Medical Center College of Pharmacy and one of the most prominent leaders in US pharmacy education.

I know of just two photos that depict literary societies using Robber's Cave. One is of the Palladian Literary Society, which I purchased from Mr. Wendt at Bluestem Books in Lincoln, Nebraska. On the back of the photo it reads in cursive "UNL Palladian Party"). In 1974 the University of Nebraska—Lincoln's alumni magazine published another photo which shows the Union Literary Society (originally the Adelphian) on November 1, 1912, at the cave for a social meeting.

Of the many literary societies at the University of Nebraska—Lincoln over the years, the Palladian was the first. As of May 2017, *Nebraska U*, UNL's historical archives website, explains that UNL students founded the Palladian in 1871, and that the group would meet each week to practice declamations, read their own works, and debate. The first constitution of the Palladian Society states the group's purpose: "to help build up and perfect the moral and intellectual capacities . . . " Many graduates of this group went on to become statesmen, local officials, lawyers, and ministers. A dispute arose in 1873 that would divide the society. The poorer members known as Hay Seeds wanted to prevent those related to wealthy townspeople, known as the Aristocrats, from gaining total control of the group. The Aristocrats branched out on their own and formed the Adelphian Literary Society. After another dispute in 1876 about which students should be allowed to join, the Adelphians became the Union Society.

A third literary society emerged in 1889 called the Delian Literary Society, which included members of both the Union and Palladian alumni. The Delian formed the third group in order to control the society's increasing numbers. Eventually, the struggling Delian joined the thriving Union and formed the Delian–Union Literary Society in 1931, which existed until 1974. The Palladian Society lasted until 1969.

The Palladian Society photo is one of my favorites because upon looking closely, one can notice several details. A few individuals holding candles, a girl in the center of the photo with terrifying white eyes (most likely an optical illusion), and a young man can be found peeking up from "fat man's misery." The ribbon of color in the ceiling and certain large carvings can be seen in the photo which look identical today.

Initially, many thought Willa Cather was present in this photo standing along the wall in a large hat, so Jullia Grossman and I decided to investigate. We scanned the original photo I purchased from Mr. Wendt and sent it to Dr. Andrew Jewell, who is the Editor of the Willa Cather Archive at Love Library. If anyone would know, it would be Dr. Jewell. Here is his determination:

Thank you so much for sending this photograph to me. It is very kind of you, and I love seeing it. What a great picture!

I've looked over the picture pretty carefully, and I hate to confess it, because I really wanted it to be true, but I don't believe Willa Cather is in the photograph. The woman you mentioned does bear some resemblance, but after looking at hundreds of pictures of Cather from many angles, I feel with some confidence that it is not the same person . . . If the photo is of the Palladian Literary Society, you may be interested to know that Cather (when she was a student here in the early 1890s) was not in that group, but in a rival group, the Union Literary Society.

In 1912, Cather did travel to Nebraska from her home in New York City, and she was here in the spring briefly (April) and in the summer, but we only have a record of her being in Red Cloud, not in Lincoln. The folks in the photo also look like they are dressed for cold weather to me. I suppose it could just be the cool temperature of the cave—or a cool spring day outside—but it doesn't seem to be the season Cather was in Nebraska that year. I checked other years near 1912 when she was in Nebraska—1909, 1914—and the same is true.

Thanks again for sending me the photo. I have enjoyed this little investigation, and I look forward to being back at Blue Blood sometime soon.

Best,
Andy

Note: The group Cather belonged to, The Union, was photographed in the cave in November 1, 1912, for a social outing, but the months don't match up to place her in that particular photo. With that being said, I think that it is likely but not certain that at some point in her life the famed author would have visited Robber's Cave.

Other literary societies used the cave through the years as well. In October of 1910, the Everett and Willard Literary Societies journeyed to Robber's Cave for their annual Hallowe'en Celebration, and the Delian Literary Society gave a picnic at Robber's Cave in November of 1929. Twenty-five members and guests attended. Games were played and fortunes were told by one of the members dressed as a witch. Mr. and Mrs. L. K. Crown, Miss Mildred Larson and Miss Mary Gutherie chaperoned the party (11/17/1929).

The Ku Klux Klan's Presence

It could be said that the caverns of Robber's Cave have seen it all over the years. With such a varied and colorful history, it should come as no surprise that one of the many organizations to use the cave for initiation purposes was none other than the Ku Klux Klan.

In 1965, a congressional investigation of the Ku Klux Klan interested the public in Nebraska. At this time, a Nebraskan named Horace Mansell Davis, past president of the Nebraska Press Association and fellow Freemason, wrote a piece for *The Lincoln Star* regarding the KKK in Nebraska. Born in a sod house near Scotia, Nebraska, Davis became a teacher at Fish Creek as an eighteen-year-old. He would go on to become the deputy and state fire marshal for Nebraska. In his article, Davis explains that in the mid-1920s, the Klan put on a membership campaign in Nebraska, and there were about 25,000 voting Klansmen in the state. "One was elected to the railway commission, and there were at least two who held important appointive offices" (11/4/1965).

Davis's article further explains that three Klan leaders from Indiana set up mysterious headquarters in the Fraternity Building in Lincoln, now the Sharp Building, and leased Robber's Cave, near the Penitentiary, for initiation purposes:

> Membership in the Klan cost five dollars, which included a mask, shroud and cap for those who took the oath of affiliation, which seemed to be optional after the fee had been paid. The KKK was not militant in its Nebraska operations. There were a few burnings of crosses out of state and some rumors of financial blackmail that never reached the courts. After five or six years of active effort to get control of the state, the leaders quietly faded away and local members seemed to drop back into their normal status of citizenship.

Jim McKee outlined a brief history of the Ku Klux Klan and their presence in Nebraska in his April 22, 2010 *Lincoln Journal Star* article. Beginning in 1866, after the Civil War, a "social club" known as the Ku Klux Klan formed to prevent African Americans from voting. Originally formed in Pulaski, Tennessee, they were also known as "the Invisible Empire or Invisible Circle. The Klan's supreme leader was known as the Grand Wizard," and they often resorted to vigilantism.

"The central organization disbanded in 1869 and the Ku Klux Act or Force Laws of 1871 signaled the end of the original era," but in 1915 a second era of the KKK formed in Atlanta, Georgia. When African Americans moved north to seek employment opportunities, a new anti-black movement formed, "with the KKK moving out of the confines of the old Confederacy and claiming membership of 500,000 to one million." Membership in Nebraska grew at this time as well:

> In 1921, the first Nebraska Klavern opened in Omaha [at 41st and Farnam Street] with an agenda of expanding the anti-black plank to include Roman Catholics and all immigrants. That year, the KKK claimed over 1,000 members in Nebraska, 45,000 the following year and four million nationally by 1925.

Lincoln Klavern #11 formed in 1921, and Klan activity in the Capital City peaked during the period from 1924 to about 1929. Around 1924, the Klan purchased the "old Governor Butler house" at 1549 South Seventh Street to use for local headquarters. This location featured meeting rooms, a basement "Klanteen" that served coffee and sandwiches, and even had a full-time resident caretaker. "By 1924, the group had erected an 18-foot cross illuminated with electric lights, which was said to be visible for several miles."

Then in 1926, the Klan moved downtown and leased an office in the Brownell block at 139 South 11th Street. Although their brochures stated that the KKK was "Here Today–Here Yesterday–Here Forever," the Great Depression brought a sudden end to their "social club." The Seventh Street property became a private residence and the downtown office was listed as vacant. "The 1950s Civil Rights Movement saw a third-era organization, but by the 1970s total national membership had dwindled to less than 2,000."

Scarborough Jr. didn't have much to say about the matter but he did confirm the Klan's use of Robber's Cave for initiation purposes.

Injuries, Lawsuits, Parties, and Raids

Not only did I find references to injuries sustained by Robber's Cave visitors, but I discovered a few lawsuits as well. One example of the many injuries described in the *Lincoln Evening Journal* is as follows: "Poor Etta Mae Ruh was running in the cave with a glass in hand while attending the Methodist Sunday school picnic back in June of 1927. She fell and received a severe cut in her left hand requiring several stitches (6/1/1927). Some things never change as guests still trip, slip, and drop their glasses in the cave, albeit rarely.

Now for a few examples of the lawsuits. Fred R. Shroyer brought suit in district court against Mrs. Mary Scarborough and her son Fred who operated the cave in 1923. The suit was for $5,000.00 on account of injuries to Mr. Shoyer's six-year-old son, Delbert. Allegedly, Mr. Shroyer took his family to the cave for a picnic when his son fell twelve to fourteen feet down a stairway into a pit in the cave on September 20, 1922. Delbert rolled under the railing, breaking his right arm and fracturing his elbow resulting in $200.00 in medical bills. Mr. Shroyer alleged that due to the poor lighting and lack of proper railings guarding the stairways, his son fell. The only protection to prevent persons from falling off the stairs at this time was a single railing three to four feet above the stairway. Delbert's injuries compelled him to remain out of school that year!

The defendants stated that the child was in the care and custody of his parents and any mishap that occurred was due to their negligence. The trial began two years later on May 13, 1924, and Delbert was given a $690.00 verdict against the cave owners by Judge Stewart. $500.00 was awarded for the injuries and $190.00 allotted to cover medical expenses (5/1/1923).

Furthermore, in September of 1929, Lyell C. Hunt of West Point, Nebraska, was picnicking in Robber's Cave when he fell twenty feet into the old well fracturing his vertebra. He was in serious condition at Lincoln General Hospital under the care of Dr. Harry Everett. Hunt was placed in a cast, no signs of paralysis developed, and the *Lincoln Evening Journal* reported that he was "doing nicely" (9/3/1929). It doesn't appear that this particular accidental fall led to a lawsuit, but the same cannot be said for the following cave party in 1959.

Six sheriff's deputies raided a party of approximately 200 youth at Robber's Cave in January of 1959, which led to Esther Scarborough being charged with contributing to the delinquency of a seventeen-year-old girl who pleaded guilty to a charge of possession of alcohol. Altogether, nine teenagers (seven boys and two girls), were arrested according to Chief Deputy County Attorney Dale Fahrnbruch.

The incident became known because "someone squealed" to State Liquor Commission Agent Al Sipes. Pleading guilty before County Judge Herbert Ronin to possession of alcohol were eighteen-yearolds Daniel Young of North 24th Street, Jim Jacobson of North 25th Street, Ira Grierson of Hillside Street, and James Pardee of Calvert Street, and seventeen-year-old Janet Hergenrader of South 17th Street. Get this: the boys were fined $25.00 each, but Judge Ronin deferred sentencing Miss Hergendrader as she told the court she had only taken "one sip of beer." The other four pleaded innocent: nineteen-year-old William Carver of Woodsdale Street, nineteen-year-old John Stromer of South 11th Street, twenty-yearold Frank Teleen of South 15th Street, and eighteen-year-old Judy Swindle of Orchard Street. Hergenrader testified that the party was held to celebrate the end of first semester of high school classes, but none of the loyal and steadfast youth would disclose who bought the beer for them. One claimed that "an airman" had bought it for them (1/30/1959).

The January 1959 raid led to a crackdown by Sheriff Merle Karnopp, who was very concerned with the growing number of such "drinking led sprees." He planned to join forces with Police Chief Joe Carroll to halt such parties. (If the name Merle Karnopp sounds familiar to you, he is the Lancaster County sheriff who made the 900-mile round trip to Wyoming to bring mass murderer Charles Starkweather and his girlfriend Caril Ann Fugate back to Lincoln to stand trial in 1958. Karnopp is a member of the Nebraska Law Enforcement Hall-of-Fame.)

Judge Herbert Ronin dismissed the charge filed against Esther Scarborough on grounds of insufficient evidence after she pled innocent and passed a lie detector test! After four months, Judge Ronin dismissed the charges against the three boys who pled innocent as well.

The summaries of the lawsuits are not in any way meant to be an indictment on Esther Scarborough. She is largely remembered fondly:

The lady was like a den mother to all of us. She would gather up our quarters and all our sack lunches, and then turn us loose in the cave. When it was time for lunch she would switch the lights on and off. It's still not clear to me if the money we gave her was for entrance to the cave or the soda she always provided with our lunch.

The End of an Era

The Yeany family, who many know as the owners of Mary's Pet Shop and Fritz's Live Bait, the once popular pet shop just north of the cave, rented the Scarboroughs' home during the 1960s. Unfortunately, during this time, the cave fell into a state of disrepair (not that it was pristine to begin with). The cave's advertisements in the newspaper during the mid-1960s were as such: "Visit Historical Robber's Cave. Open Seven days a week. Under New Management." According to Scarborough Jr., the Yeany family simply hung a coffee can at the cave's entrance with a sign requesting a donation and just left it open. Visitors often stole the money, and activity in the cave became more and more chaotic.

Scarborough Jr. recalls, "Around 1972, Vi and I brought her visiting sister to the cave—it was trashed! It smelled horrible and there was paint all over the walls. I told my dad about the state of it, and he said that I'd have to take over. We warned the Yeanys to clean it up or they'd be evicted—it took us a year to get them out."

After Scarborough Jr. and his son Scott Maybin spent nearly a month cleaning what had become a health hazard, Edwin Scarborough Sr. ultimately decided to close the cave in 1973 due to concerns over the health and safety of visitors, not to mention the family's disgust with the repeated vandalism. By 1973, the Scarborough family had kept Robber's Cave open to the public for 67 years! "The cave's been open to the public for many years . . . but we just can't keep up with the vandalism" (8/16/1973). When Edwin Scarborough Sr. decided to close the Lincoln landmark in 1973 he stated, "I want people to understand that we're sorry it has to be closed, but my family's privacy is more important."

There were rumors that the entrance would be bulldozed, but Scarborough Sr. quickly quelled the gossip, "That's just a rumor that started and where it did I don't know. We're just closing the cave to the public. We couldn't bulldoze the cave, even if we wanted to, because of the physical nature of the structure," he said. Scarborough Sr. explained that his son, Ed Scarborough Jr., would soon move onto the property adjoining the cave, which had been rented out to the Yeany family for eight years. Mrs. Yeany said she liked living there because it was close to her pet shop, and she enjoyed the open air and being away from everybody. She did concede that the partygoers made life less than idyllic as her husband would often replace fourteen or fifteen light bulbs a day when the cave was in heavy use because of "free-swinging youth."

Shortly after Robber's Cave closed, the *Lincoln Evening Journal* printed an article about the letters and calls that Scarborough Sr. had received from fans attempting to change his mind about closing the cave. Scarborough Sr. explained that he was irritated by the publicity concerning the cave's closing and countered with a terse response, "It's been open to the public for so long that people think it belongs to them. But it doesn't. It's owned by my family, and we'd just like to have a little privacy now." He pledged that it would be preserved: "We wouldn't want to destroy a part of Lincoln history."

Having lived near Capitol Beach for so many years, I found it sadly coincidental Robber's Cave closed the same year that King's Ballroom burned to the ground. I often heard about the widely known dance hall by the lake growing up in that area. Suddenly gone in 1973 were two of Lincoln's sources for many good times and memories.

Reopening Robber's Cave in 1986

In 1986, Scarborough Jr. and his wife Vi decided to once again allow visitors into Robber's Cave. The cave officially reopened on Tuesday, April 1, 1986. "The cave was cleaned, paths leveled, and new lighting installed," Gary Soule explains in his *NSS News* article. One of the noteworthy documents that Scarborough Jr. gave me was his inspection map of the cave drafted June 12, 1984, by architect and structural engineer Jack Beers of Lincoln. Scarborough Jr. had begun making upgrades to the cave, and along with mapping a precise layout and measurement of the tunnels, Beers made an onsite inspection of the cave and certified that the tunnels were structurally sound. This needed to be done so that Scarborough Jr. could reopen, which he didn't necessarily want to do, but felt he needed to do in order to offset his expensive property taxes. The document clearly shows the location of the original Pioneer Brewery's foundation, which Scarborough Jr. and his grandpa Fred began to fill with destroyed antique auto parts around 1948 and then again in the mid-1960s. "In 1984, the state inspector took a tour and said before the cave could be reopened, I needed to put in handrails. I had Jack Beers draw the cave layout and dimensions—I was granted a permit to collect a fee for every person's visit."

Scarborough Jr. and his stepson Scott Maybin spent many hours cleaning the caverns. Unlike her husband, Vi Scarborough was very enthused and excited about reopening the cave. She had made print advertisements and dutifully posted them at rest stops along the interstate as well as at the Lincoln Airport. "Do you want to know how many showed up for the reopening?" Scarborough Jr. asked me, "Not a soul! Vi was absolutely floored." Similarly, Scarborough Jr. recalled that the *Journal Star* failed to send one photographer or reporter to the cave's reopening. Conversely, Jim Burnett of *The Omaha World Herald* came and photographed the cave. However, I do have documentation that the *Journal Star* took photos in the cave in February of 1986, before the cave reopened, as well as in April of 1986.

The reopening did not turn out to be a profitable venture for the family. Although cave bookings picked up in May, June, and July of 1986, they did not maintain through the year. In addition to charging $150.00 for a night's rental, plus a $100.00 damage deposit, the Scarboroughs decreased the price from $5.00 per adult and $3.00 per child to $3.00 per adult and $2.00 per child. When accounting for taxes and insurance, the cave simply didn't generate enough profit.

I have met several guests who remember having birthday parties at the cave in the 1980s. Others paid the small fee to explore the cave only to be scared off by older boys who hid out of sight to toss fireworks at passersby! Some simply remember how hot, wet, and smelly the cave would become during the keggers and college parties as bands often performed at the east end of tunnel number two.

As of 1987, Vi Scarborough had not regretted reopening the cave as Patty Beutler explains:

Some days, youngsters arrive in busloads from the western part of the state to clamber about . . . a couple from Iowa, in their 60s came back to the cave to relive their first kiss when both were students at the University of Nebraska . . . Individuals can explore the cave on their own after buying a ticket and stay as long as they like . . . We've had no bad experiences (4/13/1987).

During the first year that Robber's Cave reopened, the guests seemed to behave themselves. College fraternities and sororities held trouble free weekend celebrations. The partygoers would haul in kegs and live bands would perform. No one cared how loud the party became. "It's soundproof and we don't hear anything up here," Vi Scarborough indicated. "They come here expecting to have a good time and they do."

Unfortunately, it didn't take long for the youth to disregard the family's expectations and the chaos returned. One event had as many as 500 guests! Groups began losing their damage deposits when they left the cave a disaster. In that event, Scott Maybin would have to awake early, walk through the entire cave with trash bags, and dutifully clean up after everyone before 11 A.M.

A few years after reopening, Vi Scarborough's enthusiasm had diminished, and the family posted a "For Sale" sign on the property in 1988. "I want out," she stated in David Swartzlander's *Journal Star* article, "I'm tired of it. My husband's tired of being in business. We want to travel a little." Initially, the Scarboroughs thought Lincoln's Parks and Recreation Department might find a use for the longtime attraction, but "the department, unsure what it would do with the cave, showed little interest" (8/16/89). The Scarboroughs' original asking price for the cave, their house, and the highway frontage was $322,000.00. By 1989, Mimi Cotton of Woods Bros. Realty confirmed that two contracts had been signed for a smaller amount. One of the signers was president of Continental Financial Services Corp. Tom White, who had intentions to use the frontage along 10th Street and keep the cave open. "Maybe it would be promoted differently. I anticipate it staying open," White stated.

By this time, Scarborough Jr. had sold his gun shop, Capitol Shooting Supply, to Harvey Dahlberg, who changed the name to the Powder Keg Gun Shop. Dahlberg planned to move his shop elsewhere by January of 1990. Referring to Dahlberg's gun shop, which faced 10th Street, White said, "The idea is to clear out the ground and do something else with the front." Vi Scarborough and Cotton thought White had intentions of building a restaurant in addition to subdividing the land. Scarborough Jr. recalled that in 1989, he sold the cave and 2.5 acres to Tom White, a partner with Ridge Development Co. for around $285,000.00. Records indicate that Robber's Cave, along with the Scarborough family's prairie-style home was sold in 1990 to J. C. Braeger. Scarborough Jr. explained that someone had interest in relocating the house to an acreage "way out east of the penitentiary," but as soon as the house became vacant, trespassers vandalized the house beyond repair, and eventually the new property owners razed it.

After 30 Years, Scott Maybin Visits Former Childhood Property

One familiar face in many of the cave photos I've obtained is Scott Maybin, Vi Scarborough's son. Scott, who spent many years of his childhood living on the cave property, accepted my invitation to return to his old stomping grounds in January 2018 for conversation and a walkthrough. I was curious to hear his thoughts and comparisons of what's become of the area. He very generously accepted and brought photos and articles of his own. Scott moved to Lincoln from Florida after his mom met Scarborough Jr., and for sixteen years Scott called the cave property home. Picking berries, climbing trees, playing in the cave with friends and family after birthday parties, he holds plenty of fond memories of the place.

I am thankful to have had the chance to walk the tunnels with Scott, as plenty of memories flooded back to him once we headed downstairs and through the stone arch. He hadn't been to the cave in nearly 30 years, and after entering tunnel one, the first change he noticed was a difference in the color of the walls; they seemed much darker now. He also noticed that portions of "fat man's misery" had widened considerably since 1989. The tunnel, still quite tight, used to be significantly narrower all the way through. The walls could have widened from 30 years of trespassers rubbing their way through to reach the bottom of the well. He also explained that the small tunnel at the bottom of the well's stairs, now filled with dirt, actually extends farther. The tunnel continues down, curves to the right and leads back into the well space forming a complete circle around a wide sandstone pillar.

When Scott provided short twenty-minute tours of Robber's Cave, he would let the guests roam after he had finished. While walking people through the cave, he'd warn visitors not to use their keys to etch their names. He knew of instances when people couldn't start their automobiles after tours because they had worn down and altered their key! He'd also point out the bullet holes from his grandpa and stepdad shooting targets at the end of tunnels two and three:

Well, back in the mid-80s, my mom was charging $5.00 and $3.00 for guided tours, quite a bit back then! I gave the tours for a few months, but they were short-lived. I didn't make much, so I got another job. After that, she let people go in by themselves for $3.00 and $2.00.

Unlike his mom who claimed that there weren't any problems as of 1987, Scott remembers that the very first event booked at the cave after reopening was a party organized by the University of Nebraska's Kappa Sigma fraternity. Let's just say they didn't get their deposit back. Scott recollects:

> She [Vi] also rented out the cave for keggers at the rate of $200.00/night with a $150.00 cleanup deposit, which they got back if the cave was left in satisfactory condition. I'd say about one third of the parties ended early because the cops would shut them down. The college kids would charge admission at the door, let minors in, and someone would narc on them.

Scott also had the unpleasant task of walking the tunnels with a trash bag the following mornings after college parties. He'd work to clean the mess while Ed Jr. would repair the electrical components. Scott chuckled when we neared the "question mark" tunnel during our walkthrough as he recalled Ed Jr. entering the tight space with a flower pot filled with vinegar and water to pour into the slick and stinking stream that ran from the tunnel after large parties.

Before Robber's Cave reopened in 1986, Scott and Ed Jr. worked together to make a few improvements: installing railings and lights, fixing steps, and moving sand. They removed the stage, which by that time had been painted blue, and relocated much of the sand that had accumulated beneath the stage over to cross tunnel number two. Their intent was to create a soft ramp in order to decrease the height of the step. This high step is just north of the "question mark" and leads past the "blowhole" airshaft back into tunnel one. Once they did reopen, "someone showed up and gave us a little souvenir sand bottle. They had acquired it from the cave's gift shop long ago and wanted us to have it."

Having Scott back at the cave helped answer a few questions. The Model A frame guests often remember seeing was used as a support near the landing of the entrance staircase. The cylindrical, metal chute chimney above tunnel three's fire pit was gone by 1973, and I was surprised to learn that the ladder, currently where the fire pit is, had to have been installed sometime after 1989, the year the Scarboroughs sold the property and moved. Scott does remember the presence of a pole near tunnel one, and he also recalled there seemed to be more bats in the 70s and 80s. So many, in fact, it wasn't uncommon while walking through the cave to have one fly directly into his chest and fall stunned to the sandy floor.

Of course one of Scott's reminiscences had to include an attempted break in. He recalled noticing a boy around fourteen years of age near the family smoke house, which used to sit atop the third tunnel's airshaft (currently a bat box located at the entrance to the restaurant's overflow parking lot). The kid had a green ski rope and was looking to sneak in. Scott retrieved Ed Jr. and they confronted the boy who fumbled up the lie that he was trying to help a friend who had been stuck in the cave. Scott and Ed Jr. knew that no one was in the cave, but Scott checked anyway. The boy realized he was caught, and Ed Jr. scared him off after yelling a few choice words. The kid even left his green nylon rope, "I think we still have it!" Scott laughed.

Developers Attempt to Seal the Cave

Until 2000, the shack which served as the public entrance to the cave could still be found in the overgrown lot just east of the grain elevators. The hut-like, frame structure angled into the ground and led into a stairwell with two flights of steps that descended to the stone arch entry. The shack was not a pretty sight—spooky actually. It should come as no surprise that this mysterious entryway became a magnet for vandals. Eventually, the owners needed to take action. "We are taking extra-strong measures to secure the entrance to the cave," said Lincoln attorney Kent Seacrest, who represented Ridge Development Company and visited the cave as a youngster. Ridge Development, who had previously spent nearly $25,000.00 attempting to secure the doorway, planned to bulldoze the entrance, cover it with truckloads of dirt, and cap it with a concrete slab. Seacrest explained that the operation would be done in such a way to allow future access to the cave if an opportunity arose.

The developers had good intentions in their attempt to prevent sneak-ins but to no avail. While the frame entrance still stood, trespassers simply broke the lock on the door to enter. When cinderblocks were stacked in front of the door, trespassers smashed them to enter the cave. Once the developers knocked down the frame entrance, filled the area with dirt, and placed a slab on top, trespassers burrowed and shimmied beneath the large hunk of concrete to drop into the stairwell. When describing the methods of those who just couldn't resist sneaking into the cave, I'm reminded of the proverb: "Where there's a will, there's a way."

A Walkthrough of the Cave

Entering from the Barrel Room

As soon as I open the door to the barrel room and guests begin to descend the steps, they immediately comment about the cellar-like smell and the abrupt cool temperature change. I happen to like the smell of the barrel room. The fragrant oak barrels used to age some of the Outlaw Series brews overpower the slightly musty cave aroma, in my opinion. From the barrel room, the Scarborough house stood above and a bit to the north. Scarborough Jr. does not recall the "Fluoridation Kills" sign mentioned in *The Guide to the Ghosts of Lincoln,* but many visitors on the cave tours claim to. Guests describe that particular sign being displayed when Esther lived on the property, and because that sign displayed a skull and crossbones along with a warning, it added a sense of ominousness to the atmosphere, as if the coyotes didn't add enough already.

The slanted wood-frame structure that angled into the ground to the west would lead to what is now the barrel room space via two staircases (the remnants of which can be seen today). At one time, Fred Scarborough's fish room, which later became a garage and store room, was located directly north of the white, hut-like entrance. Once at the bottom of the staircase, one could enter the cave through the archway to the right. To the left was a square room with a picnic table and fireplace where birthday gatherings were often held. Today, that space is the barrel room where one will find many of the items found in the cave sand displayed on a ledge: a horseshoe vice, ice tongs, a pickaxe head, a drive shaft, a saw, a steering wheel, etc. Facing the entrance into the first tunnel, one notices a stone wall and archway that comprise the south wall of the room. This stone wall and entrance were an addition built off of the first tunnel after 1908; however, I find it conceivable but not likely that this wall might be what's left of the north side of the Pioneer Brewery structure. The stonework matches the wall pictured in the one-and-only photo of the old brewery.

Tunnel One—Original Entrance and Natural Ceiling

Gary Soule reports in his *NSS News* article that quarrying partly destroyed Robber's Cave's natural entrance. When standing in the first tunnel, there are remnants of the natural entrance being stoned up at the west just beyond what appears to be a door frame and wooden entryway at the base. Running water did not form this tunnel entirely, as Andra lowered the floor; however, this tunnel has the only peaked ceiling without pickaxe markings. The majority of geologist agree—and I've asked several, that the first tunnel's formation began by floodwater, probably from Salt Creek, flowing in from the west through a pock in the bluff.

Tunnel number one is often guests' first impression of the cave, as it is where we begin the tours after entering through the barrel room's archway. This first tunnel is also the space that would have housed any pioneers seeking refuge in 1862, and it would have been the site for the late 1867 duel.

Cross Tunnel One

An opening to the south at tunnel one's midway point descends into the first cross tunnel. In this particular connecting tunnel, the sedimentary layers in the sandstone become very evident, and one can see variations in the stone's color. The dark ribbons reveal iron ore, and the lighter yellow shades indicate limonite. There is an uneven set of steps that lead south from tunnel one to tunnel two farther down into the cave, and remnants of the original lighting system can be seen in the ceiling. Scarborough Jr.'s map on the wooden board labels this spot "sink hole." I found this particular tunnel creepy to pass through during the Halloween lantern tours, as the many faces carved into the wall illuminated as I walked past them with a lantern. A former Nebraska football player explained that oftentimes kegs lined the wall of this particular tunnel during Cornhusker football parties in the 1960s, as it served as the cave's central location. In this tunnel, one can find ELS 48' (former owner Ed Sr.'s mark), and of course ABBA among countless others.

Tunnel Two—Bands, Movies, and Who Knows What Else

Passing through cross tunnel number one leads us into tunnel number two. One can notice the ceiling's drastic change in shape—from a teardrop peak to the curved arch. Andra's pickaxe marks are very evident at the east end of this tunnel. As previously mentioned, two of my favorite photos in the cave are of literary societies both in tunnel two: the first is of the Union Literary Society in 1912 standing on the staircase looking east, and the second is of a larger group of the Palladian Literary Society circa 1910 facing west, standing snug, and holding candles.

Mixed with clearly fresh carvings from 2014 and 2015 are plenty of older markings. Many of the deep, Greek letter carvings that can be seen in the early 1900s photographs are still easily found in this tunnel, along with Heike Gang and the Lorenz Gang, as well as where Gardner Moore (the original owner of Ideal Grocery) left his mark over 100 years ago. Tunnel two is where the Scarborough family's mushroom pits were located in the early 1900s and also where Scarborough Jr. had his private gun range in the 1970s.

If one were looking to the west in this tunnel in the 1930s, a wooden door that at one time led into the cellar of the Pioneer Brewery, could be seen at the terminus of the tunnel. A wall of stones that can be seen in photos from the 1980s replaced the wooden door. It is likely that Fred Scarborough or Ed Scarborough Sr. would have been who stoned up that opening since it was done sometime after 1932 but before 1973. At the east end of tunnel two sat the wooden stage for musical acts. A sphinx head used in a Union College sorority's initiation rituals long ago remains visible high on the north wall. Last, at this spot, a group of young men were photographed around

1910 crouched and rolling dice, engrossed in a game of craps. This scene is often recreated by guests who pose in the exact location of the photo during holiday parties, company parties, and class reunions.

Fat Man's Misery and the Well

At the west end of tunnel two next to the staircase, one will find the infamous "fat man's misery." This narrow tunnel, now off limits to the public, used to lead visitors approximately 30 feet deeper into the well area. Jacob Andra dug this well for the Pioneer Brewery as it served as the brewers' water source for lagering. As previously mentioned, Andra described finding petrified pecans and embedded antlers while digging the well deep into the sandstone.

In 1937, the *Lincoln City Guide* reported the lowest point of the cave was 62 feet, whereas a 1987 Robber's Cave brochure would later mark the well's depth at about 60 feet. This area of the cave is not part of the regular public tours as it is tight, cramped, slippery, wet, and muddy. Scarborough Jr. reported kids either crawling to the bottom of the well to relieve themselves, or kids falling into the low area and becoming stuck. He complained about having to go into the cave on several occasions to pull kids out. The Scarboroughs eventually filled the well as best they could with sand and dirt to deter such incidents. Scarborough Jr. then covered the open portion of the well with the metal bars that once covered the back windows of his gun shop, Capitol Shooting Supply, to prevent further accidents and lawsuits.

Tunnel Three—Lunch Room, Fireplace, Bat Cave, and Robber's Roost

For many years, guests referred to tunnel number three as the "lunch room" because it featured a 30-foot picnic table and fireplace chimney. This tunnel, the second largest, served various social functions, steak roasts, fish fries, BBQs, and birthday parties. The airshaft ascending from the third tunnel used to be covered by a smoke house, where the family also used to store firewood. Scarborough Jr. would drop tree stumps down the shaft on occasion for friends and family on which to sit during New Year's Eve parties.

A 1966 ad in the *Lincoln Star* stated, "30 ft. picnic table—grill your steaks or hot dogs right here!" At one time after 1973 when the cave closed, transients utilized this tunnel to camp. At one time a heavy manhole cover enclosed the top of the shaft. A wooden ladder now leads up and out of this tunnel. Robbers Cave LLC constructed a wooden hut above the shaft's exit for the bats that now covers the shaft's opening at ground level.

Like tunnel two, tunnel three was stoned up at the west end. If one knew where to place their feet, they could climb into a small square room with a sandy floor known as "robber's roost." Children playing hide-and-seek could never be found once they crawled onto that ledge and into the little room. This area is filled in with dirt today, but carvings can be seen all the way back and around the corner. Of course legend has it that this secluded mini-room hid not only kids playing hide-and-seek, but infamous thieves and robbers. Remember that tunnel two and three were stoned up at the west, which is a main reason why so many guests with active imaginations claim the tunnels continued farther to the penitentiary and regional center. In reality, the two tunnels led to the Pioneer Brewery's cellar.

The Second Cross Tunnel—Oldest Carving, Question Mark, Dance Floor, and Blowhole

Standing at the east end of tunnel two where the stage for bands sat, one can pass into a shorter tunnel to the north. When walking into this space, guests will notice two interesting finds at their feet: a long, flat slab beneath the sand that creates a ledge a few inches high, and the other is the oldest carving found in the cave: *Sam Dalton May 1875*. I learned from Scarborough Jr. that the flat slab is the old dance floor installed in 1922. (See the dance floor ad in photo section.)

Just past the Dalton carving on the opposite side is a bas relief high on the wall that is the only carving of its type found in the cave. It reads DAKOTA SANDSTONE in perfect block lettering. The possibility of it being a geological surveyor's carving has been mentioned.

Halfway into this tunnel, a short, narrow passage curls into the east wall. This is known by many as the "question mark." Scarborough Jr., on the other hand, candidly refers to this tight space as the "shithook." The Pioneer Brewery might have used this space as a small storage area—I'll leave it up to the imagination to determine the fraternities' and sororities' purpose for this space. On private tours, I'll let visitors peek and take a look, but generally it's off limits due to the fact that only one or two people at a time can fit.

Believe it or not in the 1960s, some parents used Robber's Cave as a type of daycare system. Children would be dropped off with a sack lunch and "Old Lady Scarborough" would let them run around the cave, sometimes all day. Logically, she knew that all of the tunnels connected so she couldn't lose anyone, and she flicked the lights on and off when the time came for the kids to leave. Many guests that were a part of this system remember Mrs. Scarborough fondly as she often provided sodas. However, some describe how dark, smelly, and wet certain nooks of the cave were. A few returning visitors even remember that older kids would throw fireworks from these hidden, tight spaces. Visitors also used the "question mark's" small space as a bathroom—hence Scarborough Jr.'s label for the closet-sized nook.

Continuing north, one passes directly beneath a large KKK carving. The tunnel then tightens as guests must step up, duck, and proceed back to tunnel one. In doing so, they'll pass the "blowhole" airshaft on their left, which is described in the section entitled "The Pole Entrance."

"Scarborough Jr.'s great uncle, a geology professor at Wynona College, asserted that saltwater flowing into tunnel one from the west built pressure and ultimately created an opening in a weak spot in the sandstone.

The Scarborough Family— Four Generations of Cave Ownership

The Scarborough name will be forever linked to Robber's Cave. After all, the property had been in their family for four generations beginning in 1906. The family reached Nebraska from Ohio, and John Wesley and Mary Scarborough purchased the then 4.2-acre property that has since been divided into three lots. The lot today is approximately 1.5 acres. By the time the Scarboroughs came to own the cave property, the Pioneer Brewery had come and gone. The empty brewery structure turned into a sporting house or dance hall and in turn, gained a reputation for being, at least by one account, the "toughest place in the country." Such a status led to the building being burned (thanks to the Anti Horse Thief League).

John Wesley Scarborough

John Wesley Scarborough purchased the land that included Robber's Cave on June 15, 1906, and that property went on to be in his family for generations to come. J. W. owned the cave for sixteen years before dying at his home on the property in 1922. An illness paralyzed him during the last year of his life. I learned that J. W. was also a Freemason as he first joined Rawalt Lodge No. 138 on February 8, 1890, and later joined Lancaster Lodge No. 54 A.F. & A.M. on July 4, 1913. He was even a Past Patron of Lincoln Chapter No. 148 Order of the Eastern Star (which coincidentally held initiations at East Lincoln Lodge No. 210, the lodge I served as Worshipful Master in 2018) and Rawalt No. 138 of Oxford, Nebraska. (On February 22, 2018, after requesting and being granted dispensation by the Grand Master of Nebraska, I moved my lodge's charter to the cave and East Lincoln No. 210 became the first lodge of
Freemason's in the world to hold a meeting in Robber's Cave in over 100 years.)

J. W. passed away on July 11, 1922, and was survived by his wife and two sons, Fred C. of Lincoln and R. J. of Winona, Minnesota. He was given a Masonic funeral service by Lancaster

Lodge No. 54., Reverend Charles Shepherd officiated, and he was interned at Wyuka Cemetery in Lincoln (7/11/1922). More information about J. W. Scarborough is revealed in Harold J. Moss's 1938 interview with Fred Scarborough in the next section.

Fred Carl Scarborough

Born in Salem, Iowa, on October 10, 1877, Fred had English Quaker ancestry. His wife, Esther Belle, was alive at the time of the interview; however, his father, John Wesley, had passed. Fred graduated from a grade school in Mount Pleasant, Iowa, in 1882, attended country school in Frontier County, Nebraska (whose county seat is Stockville, north of McCook). After he graduated high school in 1894 in Oxford, Nebraska, he became a sergeant with Company L in the US Army during the Spanish–American War, which ended in 1898. Fred served with the 3rd Regiment of Nebraska with whom he traveled to Cuba and also the Philippine Islands. On his Spanish War information card, he is listed as a painter, but he became a conductor for the CB and Q Railroad and conducted a train either from McCook, Nebraska, to Denver, Colorado, (according to newspaper accounts) and/or Oxford, Nebraska, to Brush, Colorado, (according to his grandson Ed Scarborough Jr.'s accounts) into the early 1920s.

Scarborough Jr. confirmed that Fred was also a farmer, teacher, and rancher. In 1923, Fred moved to Lincoln and began operating the cave property, raising birds, chickens, and fish as a hobby and commercially. He didn't belong to a particular church, but mentioned activities with the Freemasons.

In 1932 when Fred filed as a petition candidate for state representative in the 36th District, the *Lincoln Journal Star* included the following information:

> Mr. Scarborough stated that he approved of the taxpayers' league and its principles. He finished high school and taught country schools, then served in the 3rd Nebraska Volunteer Infantry during the War with Spain. He worked twenty years for Burlington and resigned to go into business. At the time, he was an active member of the VFW and commander of the William Lewis Camp US Spanish War Veterans. The other district candidates were Miss Sarah Muir and Charles C. Spangler.

I also learned from Scarborough Jr. that Fred was wounded in the Spanish War by what he called a "fallback bullet" that entered Fred's shoulder and went down into his hip. This injury gave Fred a distinguishing physical attribute as it caused him to walk with a noticeable limp. Once Fred finished his service, he raised horses for cavalry on his ranch in Brush, Colorado, until his father requested help with the cave property, so he sold his ranch and moved to Lincoln.

Harold J. Moss Interviews Fred Scarborough—1938

Local author and historian Dale Nobbman shared with me an interview transcript on file at the Library of Congress that was included in *American Life Histories: Manuscripts from the Federal Writers' Project, 1936–1940*. Lincoln native Harold J. Moss conducted an eight-hour interview with Fred Carl Scarborough, John Wesley's son, in the cave and at the Scarborough residence on September 26 and

30, as well as on October 13 of 1938. Reading the transcript of this incredible interview provided insight into the Scarborough family's history, what the cave was like when they first bought it, and what they discovered while cleaning it. First, Fred remembers his father John Wesley Scarborough:

> My father was a Quaker and attended Quaker College in Salem, Iowa. He married at Salem in 1876, Mary Wilmeth. He came to Nebraska in 1884 and settled near Cambridge. He was interested in decoration work for expositions throughout the country. Finally, he took over this old historic cave [. . .] and was active in research work to gather data about it.

Fred goes on to explain what his father learned about the cave during his research, along with his reasons why he believes so many visitors are drawn to the cave:

> It had served as a refuge in time of storm, winter blizzards, Indian hostilities, and white man depredations. As people came to know of it, it became a point of great interest as it presents still the atmosphere and surroundings of the romantic early days. And one can in its cavernous depths be carried back and relive the dramatic moments of those earlier days. Such life was lived at this spot, which can only be imagined. The people as a group living near here had numerous ideas about this opening in the earth and were possessed of varying emotions concerning it. Today it is still a place for entertainment, education, and traditional inspiration.

Next, Fred defines the original intent for the cave and how gossip of buried treasure led to crowds arriving to watch his dad clean the cave:

> He acquired title to the cave about 1906 and started to clean [it] out for the purpose of raising mushrooms. (Scarborough Jr. later showed me the location of the mushroom pits in tunnel two on the Beers Architects map.) But the people began to gossip and thought he was digging for buried treasure. They came in crowds to watch him and his operations. They believed anyway that there was treasure buried about the cave.

Fred then defines what he and his dad found while cleaning Robber's Cave's caverns:

> In the larger cavern they carved out the figurehead of the Sphinx. [This can still be seen today at the east end of tunnel two]. This was a sort of shrine in some of the rituals of the University Students of those days. We have found many old bones embedded in the sandstone wall of the caverns and also in excavating the floors. Many old lead slugs were dug up in one part of the lower cavern, which were crude—counterfeits of $1.00 and 50-cent coins. The cave was, we believe, the hideout of counterfeiters in the early days. The first cow brand used in Nebraska is cut out into the walls. The JETJE. Thompson "Jet" Brand. [This particular etching has yet to be found, and there is a good chance it has been carved over.] In 1908, an old cowhand visited the cave and claimed this was one of the most important brands ever used in Nebraska and he said, the first.

J. W. did in fact grow mushrooms in the cool, damp, and dark cave for a short time. The two three-by-eight pits were in tunnel two along the north wall. Fred then recounts to Moss an unsubstantiated story about local youth from a nearby orphanage stealing items from the cave and being caught later by the home's overseer:

There is a story about some boys from the boys' home just north of here. [Jim McKee helped to clarify that the boys' home north of the cave was most likely the Nebraska Orphanage on the southeast corner of 11th and South Street.] About 1904 they got into the cave one day and dug around. They returned to the home that night [with] some gold watches, breast pins and gold pieces. These were supposed to have been taken from them by the attendant or overseer at the home.

Fred then comments on the Pawnee use of the cave (which I later learned was unlikely). Accurate or not, here Fred contends during the Moss interview, "It is likely that only Pawnee Medicine Men and chiefs came to this cave. The Indians in the tribal or colony ranks would hardly dare to venture near the spirit world." In actuality, the small Pawnee presence in Lancaster County was for the purposes of hunting or gathering salt near what is now Capitol Beach Lake. As previously mentioned, the Otoe-Missouria were the main group in the area closest to the cave.

Moss even provides a unique (and comical) description of Fred Scarborough the individual:

Medium height (he actually stood just 5'5"), trifle stout, regular features, smiling expression, ruddy complexion, with a very pleasing personality. He was congenial yet firm and had many characteristics of a railroad trainman: somewhat detached, and very direct, with executive ability. Very intelligent, with an analytical mind and imagination. Enthusiastic as to the cave and takes great pride in it as well as the birds and fish. Is not boresome.

Fred explains to Moss how his English ancestors lived in the United States before the Revolutionary War. He mentions a Masonic letter dated 1763 with the original hand seal of wax still attached (a letter such as this might have been carried when one traveled place to place, much the same as ID cards are used today.) Then he elucidates how his great-great-great-grandfather, who lived in Orleans County, New York, west of Rochester, was killed in 1860 "in his own yard, upon his return from delivering a group of runaway slaves to the next depot near Keokuk, Iowa, (perhaps this information served as the genesis of the unlikely Underground Railroad tie to Robber's Cave). He had a blind cellar dug to one side of the house that was entered by pulling out a "dummy table" from the wall. Apparently, being a small boy, Fred's great-grandfather also "carried messages through the timber to friendly forces."

Last, Fred provides an especially interesting comment that affords some detail as to the cave property's description in the late 1800s. The brewery business had closed, but the abandoned wood and stone structure still stood atop the cave at this time. Fred Scarborough states:

Along about 1879 the entrance to [the] cave was through the basement of an old dance hall and sporting house, which stood here. This place was a thieves' hangout [. . .] and in 1885 the Anti Horse Thief Association burned it down. The fire was set by White caps [sic].

The dancehall and sporting house that Fred Scarborough refers to would likely have been the abandoned Pioneer Brewery structure because both buildings sat atop the cave at corresponding dates, and both offered entrance to the cave through a basement or cellar.

The Ricochet Incident

Given what I learned about J. W. and Fred Scarborough, and later about Ed Sr. and Ed Jr., it is safe to say that there was never a dull moment on the Scarborough property. Consider the following close call that occurred at their home in the spring of 1945. Esther sustained injuries about her legs, forehead, and one of her arms when Fred's shotgun accidentally discharged. She was treated for shock and nineteen buck shot wounds! Dr. F. W. Blumer reported her condition as "fine" three days later. How did this happen? According to the police report, Esther and Fred were chasing a rat at the back of the farmhouse near Esther's lily ponds. When Fred fired his weapon, the buckshot glanced off a rock striking Esther.

Fred passed away in the Scarborough home on July 24, 1949, but Esther would go onto to live until June 5, 1965.

Edwin L. Scarborough Senior

Steve Newnom, the Newnom family's genealogist, informed me in 2018 that Edwin's father, Ora Albert Newnom, was born March 29, 1882, in Westland, Ohio, and married Esther Belle Stevens on November 28, 1906. After Edwin Lee Newnom was born on August 17, 1909, Ora died in Cambridge, Guernsey County, Ohio, on September 7, 1909, from typhoid fever when Edwin was just three weeks old. Esther Belle Stevens Newnom remarried Fred C. Scarborough on March 18, 1914, in Sidney, Nebraska, and the two adopted and raised Edwin as a Scarborough.

By the way that Scarborough Jr. describes his dad, one can assume that Edwin Sr. was quite the character, just like his son. A pilot and flight instructor, Edwin Sr. survived being shot down twice in WWII: once by a German dive bomber while flying a C47 from Casablanca to Egypt, and a second time while he flew a Douglas A20 for the 15th Air Force. The second time, the US Navy accidentally shot down Edwin Sr. during a mission over Sicily to bomb a particular bridge!

Scarborough Jr. shared a memory of his dad in the *Journal Star's* section "Lessons Learned from Dad" in 2013:

> When my father came home after the war, he began to teach me to fly at Arrow Airport. He told me: "Fly the airplane, don't let it fly you." Many years later, I bought a Cessna 170B in Pulaski, Wisconsin. On the way home the snow began. I trimmed it out on a compass heading, then let it fly itself—hands off. It flew us out, right to the airport. We landed for gas, then on to Lincoln. So it seems, Dad, that the airplane can fly all by itself, too. I told him. "Yes, but you still have to be there," he said.

It is evident that toward the end of his life, Edwin Sr., retired warden of the Men's Reformatory, had had enough of the cave. He did not believe the Jesse James and Underground Railroad stories that surrounded his cave, and he actually preferred that people quit bringing them up. He stated in 1976, "It was a haven for people who needed shelter from time to time. Anything beyond that is speculation." Edwin Sr. closed the cave due to vandalism and safety concerns in 1973. Visitors often damaged the electrical system and the grounds around the entrance. "It wasn't worth it. I got tired of repairing it."

Edwin Sr. passed away on October 31, 1983, in Lincoln, Nebraska. At the time of his death, he was married to Jessie Rosena "Scottie" Craig Wilkinson Scarborough, a retired Goodyear employee and member of the Gladiolus Society. Census records indicate that Ed. Sr. lived in the Beverly Hills, California, area for some time managing a laundry mat in the 1940s, but he and "Scottie" were married in Lincoln in 1948. Ed Sr. had been previously married to Agnes Elizabeth Carter in 1928. Agnes was an employee at Miller and Paine's in Lincoln and is Ed Jr.'s mother.

Edwin L. Scarborough Junior

I am very fortunate to have had success contacting John Wesley Scarborough's great-grandson Ed Scarborough Jr., and I'm thankful that he has agreed to meet with me time and time again. Visiting Scarborough Jr. at his home and conversing with him has been unforgettable, to say the least. He has answered my questions, recounted many stories, and shared several of his scrapbooks and photo albums. Each time I'd call him to schedule a visit, he'd say, "I have to show you something; you're going to love it!" He even gave me two old bottles filled with the red, brown, and white sand from Robber's Cave that his grandma, Esther, made with a straw. These decorative pieces used to be sold at the cave's gift shop.

Scarborough Jr. has also given me numerous photos of the cave property, along with a photo of the 1873 Winchester Model rifle he discovered as a boy while digging in the ruins of the burnt horse barn just south of the cave. "It had a low serial number on it, and I eventually sold it to Dick Headly and made a pretty penny!" remembers Scarborough Jr.

Edwin Lee Scarborough Jr. was born in 1930 in Lincoln, Nebraska, but he lived in Glendale and Burbank, California, as a young boy while his mom managed a manor or apartment building that he claims was owned by Basil Rathbone of Sherlock Holmes fame. He describes being put on a plane when he was nine or ten to return to Nebraska to help his Grandpa Fred on the farm and with the cave. These were some of the best years of his life as he describes the beautiful view of the valley descending west from the cave, the sunsets, and learning to drive and plant corn with his Grandpa Fred. When Earl May was still located on O Street, Scarborough Jr. recalls going there to purchase mulberry tree saplings, which he and his grandpa planted in a row at the north side of the property (this row of mulberry trees still exists). Scarborough Jr. shared one particular memory about how he used to climb into one of his mulberry trees to watch birds until once he noticed a big bull snake in the tree with him!

Ed Jr. was in the Lincoln Model Airplane Club with Vince Goeres, author of *Wings Over Nebraska*, in the mid-1940s. Ed Jr. flew for Lincoln Aviation and for the Lockheed Corporation in Burbank, California, the American aerospace company founded in 1912. In 1943, Lockheed began, in secrecy, development of a new jet fighter at its Burbank facility, the Lockheed P–80 Shooting Star. Scarborough Jr. worked in Lockheed's Advanced Development Division, more commonly known as "Skunk Works." Specifically, he installed outboard engines on Lockheed's Constellation aircraft (he calls them "Connies"), which were propeller-driven, four-engine airliners. He also worked many years in Lincoln at Lancaster Research and Development Corp., which became Concept Engineering.

Capitol Shooting Supply—June 1954

In addition to owning Robber's Cave, Scarborough Jr. operated the Capitol Shooting Supply business that sat east of his home on the west side of what is now 10th street turning into Highway 2. Ed Jr. recalls the many issues visitors to the cave caused if they decided to crawl down into the well area, which measured 62 feet deep. "They'd get stuck and we'd have to go in and help them climb out. Finally, I took the bars from the back of my gun shop and blocked the area."

Ed Jr. as I've come to know him, enjoyed riding motorcycles, building and driving old cars, flying planes, jumping out of planes (he belonged to the Black Hawk Skydiving Club), hunting, and collecting. He maintained his love of firearms long after he closed his gun shop. His stepson explained to me that at one time Ed Jr. owned close to 60 guns and referred to them as his children! To say Ed Jr.'s a colorful character would be an understatement. A former sheriff stated that when Ed Jr. was in his younger days, he'd cruise Lincoln and end up at King's Drive-In in a black, 1938 Cadillac LaSalle hearse! I also learned from this former sheriff that at one time Ed Jr. may or may not have dropped a watermelon from his plane while flying over O Street as a prank long ago. Did I mention Ed Jr. is interesting to talk to?

The Explosion in Old Fish Room A.K.A. "The Mishap"

During one of our visits, I asked Scarborough Jr. what had happened to the original house that his great-grandpa built. He explained that the original house became a garage in which he used to build his 1932 Ford Roadster. Scarborough Jr. also stored his 1941 Ford Deluxe, his 1924 Buick Touring, and his 1929 Model AA truck in this garage at one point or another. After a deep breath, he recounted how the family's original house-turned-garage met its demise:

> During the time when the Yeanys were renting the property from us [this would have been around 1968], they were using a cement block incinerator to burn some weeds. The fire spread from the weeds into the straw from my coyote pen. Now, I had two twelve-pound black powder kegs and a bunch of ammunition stored in my grandpa's old fish room. When that caught fire it blew everything to hell. [Be sure to read the section about Fred's exotic and tropical fish shop.] I heard it [the explosion] from South 14th Street at the time, and I thought the two big bangs were sonic booms from jets flying over or something. That [explosion] ruined a few of our antique cars and the original house burned in that fire. You're bringing back some bad memories, boy.

Scarborough Jr.'s memory served him well. His recounting of what happened closely corroborates with the *Lincoln Evening Journal's* July 1, 1968 report:

> Inspectors are probing the cause of an explosion and fire that resulted in damages to a storehouse and its contents located over Robber's Cave. The building housed several thousand rounds of ammunition, gunpowder, and three antique motor vehicles. The cave was not damaged in the mishap.

To make this story even crazier, consider the conditions that the firemen faced that morning. Fire chief Dallas Johnson described, "exploding ammunition which sent projectiles flying around the area" in addition to the normal firefighting hazards. Bullet casings were recovered hundreds of feet away from the storehouse.

Little's Pioneer Market

Many visitors to Robber's Cave will remember a fruit and vegetable stand that stood at the front of the Scarborough's property just off of 10th Street. In 1927, an ad in *The Lincoln Star* simply read, "TOMATOES—help yourself, Robber's Cave, 3200 So. 11th." Eventually, that fruit stand would either become or be replaced by Bob Little's Pioneer Market. In 1953, their *Lincoln Evening Journal* ad read, "We have our own irrigated truck garden. Two loads weekly from Denver." In 1955, their advertisement had "CHAS BOYD, truck gardener since 1940. Open every day from 11 AM–9 PM and 9 AM–9 PM on weekends." They sold Bing cherries, apples, potatoes, watermelons, beans, sweet corn, tomatoes and many other items. "All kinds of flowering and vegetable plants, grown in our greenhouse. Also fresh vegetables and fruits" (5/27/1960).

Lincoln writer Cindy Lange-Kubick reminisced about Bob and Elaine's market in her May 2017 *Journal Star* article: "She was a part of my childhood, wiry and browned by the sun, like a Dorothea Lange photograph come to life on 10th street." Bob Little, who also ran a greenhouse and nursery with Elaine at 1st and Pioneers Boulevard, constructed the wood-frame market that featured slanted bins, a striped awning, and eventually a second structure for the sweet corn that "their customers clamored after, emptying gunny sacks for customers to paw through." What a business this must have been! The Littles were open seven days a week, 8 A.M. until dark, and on Mother's Day, they gave free petunias to all mothers. Scarborough Jr. remembers how difficult it was to break the news to the Little family that the property had been sold and that they'd need to relocate.

The Scarborough House

There were actually two houses on the property until the 1968 explosion and fire destroyed J. W. Scarborough's original homestead; however, most people remember the larger, two-story home complete with sun porch, coyote pens, windmill, lily ponds, and aviary. Scott Maybin remembers a stone marker on the property that stood at the top of an airshaft. At three to four feet tall, it was made up of smaller stones that individually weighed approximately ten pounds each. These stones were cemented together around a center pipe.

I also learned from Maybin that there were three chicken houses as the family had about 200 chickens. Scott mentioned that he kept a few bantams as pets. Robber's Cave, along with the Scarborough's home was sold in 1990 to Tom White of ZSA Realty Group but as soon the family moved, the house was vandalized beyond repair. Scarborough Jr. understandably was disgusted by what happened. He laments, "It was a prairie-style house, see, and someone had interest in moving it to an acreage way out east of the penitentiary."

The Display Case

Scarborough Jr.'s wife, Viola, was from Miami, Florida. She met Ed Jr. via correspondence and moved her family to Lincoln, and after living in a few different homes, they moved onto the cave property. When Vi and Scarborough Jr. reopened the cave in 1986, they exhibited a display case of cave objects just outside of their front sunporch on a fence. Objects included an old kerosene lamp, a pickaxe, and some of the coins found in the cave sand. Vandals broke the antique block and tackle and most of the objects were stolen, so when college kids rented the cave, the display case was the first thing Scarborough Jr. brought inside.

The Wooden Sign with Map Returns

Other items dotted the cave property to aid visitors. Scarborough Jr. erected a snow fence near the entrance shack from which his hand-painted layout of the cave once hanged. The wooden relic details safety hazards and provides specific cave locations with names: the old Pioneer Brewery's foundation, the fireplace chimney, "fat man's misery," two sink holes, and an airshaft just to name a few.

Forrest "Frosty" Chapman, former executive director of the Nebraska Liquor Control Commission, decided to drive his two children past the cave property in the early 1990s in order to show them his old hangout. By that time, the lot had become run down and overgrown with weeds. However, the old frame entrance still stood, and a sign indicated that the property had recently sold. While Frosty walked the area with his kids, he noticed the wooden sign upon a trash heap and immediately thought, "That does not belong in the garbage." He called the number posted on the sold sign with intent to return it, but he received no answer. Frosty kept the sign in his garage for over twenty years before kindly returning the wooden map to Robber's Cave shortly before the brew house and cave opened! Thanks to Frosty, this unique object, remembered by many, once again hangs next to the entrance to Robber's Cave.

Frosty also happens to be a talented painter known to many for his imaginative witticisms and infinite optimism. (He retired in 2003, but then became the state liaison for the Alcohol and Tobacco Tax and Trade Bureau and founded the TTB Newsletter.) The sign he returned fits right in with the old cans, bottles, tools, and a rusted, mangled wheel displayed—all found in the sand and mud while cleaning the cave's tunnels (I've included more specific descriptions of many items found in the cave in the later chapter "Identified Buried Objects"). Down in the barrel room near the cave's stone arch entrance, there is a ledge with even more rusted items discovered in the cave on display: a drive shaft, a pickaxe head, a steering wheel, ice clamps, and even a blacksmith's post vise or leg vise.

The sign that Frosty Chapman returned isn't the only sign that Scarborough Jr. created. He also built a larger four-by-eight sign that provided a brief history of the cave. Scarborough Jr. displayed this particular sign from two four-by-four metal pipes that he set in concrete just east of the boulder-covered base of the family's windmill cistern. Perhaps one day, someone will return another missing piece of the cave's history to the property.

"Treasures" Found in Robber's Cave

Listed in Gary Soule's *NSS News* article are the contents of what the Scarborough family found as they cleared the caverns of debris in preparation for their mushroom garden: "human bones, counterfeit coins and actual silver dollars from 1878 to 1882, a rifle, copper tubing, gambling devices, pocketbooks, a tanning stone, and Indian artifacts. Most were exhibited at the cave." Scarborough Jr. describes how the process of cleaning the cave brought many visitors, "My grandpa [Fred] explained it as [pause] people became suspicious when they saw him [J. W.] digging all this [expletive] out of the cave. Rumors spread about what was going on."

Scarborough Jr.'s description corresponds closely with Soule's statement that, "Stories of hidden treasure brought so many visitors to the place that the plans were changed, and the cave was kept open for sightseers and picnics."

Folklorist Louis Pound explains in *Selected Writings*, "In the American West, giants and ogres and dwarfs are replaced by Indians, train robbers, and horse-thieves in need of hideouts, and by men concealing or looking for buried treasure." Indeed, the cave has no shortage of tales, but descriptions of documented finds do exist. It is a shame so much has been stolen, especially the objects found and displayed near the Scarborough's sun porch. Excluding the many cave relics that Scarborough Jr. sold or gave away, the whereabouts of many others are still unknown. He did happen to show me a document titled "Coins found by original entrance site in 1948" which included photos of the coins dating from 1850 to 1911.

Shortly after J. W. Scarborough purchased the cave in 1906, L. C. Oberlies published an article in *The State Journal* under the headline "UNEARTHING OF TREASURE—mysterious visitor to penitentiary caves disinters an iron box from an underground vault":

There has been recently discovered an interesting little excavation about 12 by 16 inches across and 18 inches deep near the deep end of the long tunnel. This square hole cut out of the solid rock had been covered over with sand and debris for apparently many years, and it was but recently that the owner in taking a party of friends through the caves, came to know of this encouchment [*sic*] for jewels, gold, and bond.

In 1911, in a section of *The Valentine Democrat* called "Lincoln, State Capital Chat," a "Treasure Trove" in South Lincoln is described:

> During a series of explorations made while clearing out the debris in Robber's Cave, near the penitentiary, south of Lincoln, a number of articles are being brought to light that seem to bear out the theory that the cave at some time was the rendezvous of a gang of desperadoes as well as a well-known spot to the Indians of years ago. Among the finds are jewelry of every description, money, some of it counterfeit, firearms of antebellum make—among them a rifle barrel 46 inches long, rusted and decayed—a peck or so of keys in singles, pairs and bunches, arrowheads and stone weapons of a remote time, and the rusted and rotted remains of purses, grips and old-time carpet bags. The present owner of the cave has equipped it with electric lights, and it is becoming quite a popular resort for Lincolnites as well as visitors to the Capital City.

The items listed in *The Valentine Democrat* are similar to what Scarborough Jr. described finding while sifting the sand through a screen in the later process of cleaning the tunnels with his grandfather Fred, sans the stone weapons of a remote time. However, it could be possible that J. W. found that elongated pinkish stone with handle while clearing the cave (referenced earlier in the chapter "Legends of Native American Use"). Scarborough Jr. said it belonged to Fred, his grandpa, and that he donated the object along with several other items to the Nebraska Commission of Indian Affairs.

On the subject of found treasures, there is a reasonable chance, albeit by happenstance, that a guest in Robber's Cave actually found a gold watch beneath the sand in one of the tunnels because in 1923, C. C. Burston reported to police that his wife "lost a gold watch" while visiting the cave. I'm sure if Mr. Burston's wife's watch had been recovered, an entertaining tale of found treasure surfaced with it. The 1938 *NSM* article tells of an old carpetbag that was found in the mid-1930s that contained 43 silver dollars, three counterfeit. The most recent date on any of the coins was 1875. Also stated, "later remnants of an old gunny sack was [*sic*] unearthed and with it 183 pairs of shears and some two dozen glass cutters."

In addition to the 1873 Winchester Model rifle Scarborough Jr. found, repaired and sold, the next object described is another significant find. With the aid of a metal detector, Professor E. E. Blackman of the Nebraska State Historical Society, who led an informal archeological reconnaissance of the area around Roca, Nebraska, found a Civil War bayonet and half of a horseshoe buried four feet down in an old posthole at the cave (*NSM* 1938).

Researching Blackman, I learned that "in 1901, with the help of J. Sterling Morton, Blackman became the first archeologist at the Nebraska State Historical Society." Under his leadership, interest in archeology grew in Nebraska as, correspondingly, did the number of artifacts that the society received. So I decided to ask Nolan Johnson with the Nebraska State Historical Society if he knew what happen to the bayonet Blackman found in Robber's Cave. Laura Mooney, Senior Museum Curator at the NSHS, looked into the matter but found nothing in E. E. Blackman's file about an object from Robber's Cave. However, Mooney did find one of the souvenir bottles of cave sand from about 1913, the *Souvenir Booklet*, a Robber's Cave handbill (printed advertisement), and the fraternity paddle mentioned in David M. Gradwohl's description of the initiation rites for the Sigma Gamma Epsilon earth sciences honor society.

The last description of "treasure" described can also be found in the 1938 *NSM* article, and it might seem a bit outlandish to most: "Protruding from one of its walls of sand some forty feet beneath the top can be seen the bones of some prehistoric animal." Dinosaur fossils are very rare in the Dakota Formations and most of them come from Kansas; however, a large ornithopod femur is known from Burt County, Nebraska, as well as fossil dinosaur tracks from Jefferson County. In my research, I did find a description of petrified pecans and antlers found embedded in the sandstone near the bottom of the well, but nothing to the extent of a prehistoric creature. I'm sure that such a find at the cave would have been well documented.

Identified Buried Objects

While cleaning the cave, as well as during construction, owners Sam Manzitto and others excavated several tubs of objects from Robber's Cave.

Chemical, pharmaceutical, and apothecary bottles:
-Early 1900s medicine bottle manufactured by Obear–Nestor Glass Co., East St. Louis, Illinois
-Early 1900s 4 oz. cough syrup bottle
-1933 apothecary bottle manufactured by Owens–Illinois Glass Co. in Clarion, Pennsylvania -
1934 chemical or pharmacy bottle manufactured by Fairmount Co.

Beer bottles:
-Circa 1906–1915 bottle from Davenport Brewing Co. made by American Bottle Co. -
1938 bottle manufactured in Alton, Illinois, by Owens–Illinois Glass Co.
-1960s Michelob bottle
-Anheuser Busch Budweiser bottles from 1965 through 1971

Whiskey bottles:
-National Distillers whiskey bottle made in Cincinnati, Ohio, from 1918 through
1944 -1947 whiskey bottle manufactured by Owens–Illinois Glass Co. -1949
whiskey bottle manufactured by Fairmount Glass Co.

Soda bottles:
-1938 Nesbitt's Soda bottle
-1941 RC Cola bottle manufactured by Owens–Illinois Class Co. in Streator, Illinois
-1942 Hire's Root Beer bottle
-1947 Canada Dry Ginger Ale bottle manufactured in Fairmont, West Virginia, by Owens–Illinois Glass Co. -Lincoln, Nebraska, embossed Coca Cola bottle

Water bottles:
-Early 1900s spring and mineral water bottles
-Early 1900s Shogo Lithia Springs Co. water bottle from Lincoln, Nebraska

Food jars:
-1939 food bottle manufactured by Owens–Illinois Glass Co. Huntington, West Virginia
-1970 32 oz. food jar
-1971 food jar manufactured in Alton, Illinois, by Anchor–Hocking Glass Corp.

Other bottles:

-1925 Nehi Beverages bottle

-1931 bottle manufactured Owens–Illinois Glass Co. in Fairmount, West Virginia

Legendary Late-Night Host Dick Cavett Returns to Robber's Cave

Mentoring highly gifted students at Irving Middle School has many rewarding benefits. Not only does it allow me to read great books repeatedly, I have an opportunity to meet and challenge bright and motivated sixth, seventh, and eighth grade students all seven periods of the day. Many have joked with me that working with middle school students is the reason I have a second job at a brewery, but it's not. I've thoroughly enjoyed my twelve years with Lincoln Public Schools and look forward to many more.

One of my former students, Christopher Peñas-Hull, is currently in the International Baccalaureate program at Lincoln High School. I mentored Christopher from sixth to eighth grade in English, and he was not only smart and full of energy, but humorous and kindhearted. I assigned Christopher to enter a writing contest in sixth grade called Letters About Literature. The task: compose a letter to any author, living or not, about how their book changed your life or your view of the world. Christopher wrote his letter to Jules Verne about *20,000 Leagues Under the Sea* (Christopher's letter is archived at the Jane Pope Geske Heritage Room of Nebraska Authors at the Bennett Martin Library).

I have Christopher to thank for meeting his grandfather, Nebraska Educational Telecommunications pioneer, Ron Hull. During National Library Week, since Christopher's letter won the LAL contest for his division, he and I were invited to the proclamation-signing ceremony at the State Capitol to meet Dave Heineman, Nebraska's governor at the time, then enjoy lunch high above Lincoln at the Nebraska Club. Christopher and his grandfather have always been very close, and Mr. Hull joined us for lunch along with his parents. Mr. Hull thanked me many, many times for my work with Christopher and, having friends the likes of Ken Burns, Sandy Dennis, and Mari Sandoz, he supplemented our lunch with many entertaining stories.

That same year, Christopher gave me the gift of a signed copy of his grandpa's autobiography *Backstage*. Lunching with Mr. Hull that day, as well as reading *Backstage*, I learned that he and Dick Cavett had been friends for many years. I had heard of Cavett, but I wasn't very familiar with him. It didn't take long for me to understand why this famous Nebraskan is such a late-night TV legend. The list of guests he interviewed on his program, *The Dick Cavett Show*, from 1968–1974 is remarkable: musicians Ray Charles, Jimi Hendrix, and John Lennon; comedians Groucho Marx, Lucille Ball, and Jerry Lewis; actors Marlon Brando, Henry Fonda, and Katharine Hepburn; and athletes Muhammad Ali, Joe Namath, and Jackie Robinson. Cavett even had a cameo in Tim Burton's movie *Beetlejuice*! Well, I had come across a *Journal Star* article by L. Kent Wolgamott in which Cavett lamented Robber's Cave being closed. I thought to myself, *well, it isn't anymore, I'm going to make this happen!* Here is how it all came together.

In January of 2016, the Capitol Beach Association rented Blue Blood's brewery floor for their annual holiday party. (I would later learn of an interesting coincidence between Scarborough Jr. and Capitol Beach: not only did he and his buddies ride their motorcycles on the dry portions of the salt lake, his aunt Harriet is the grandmother of my childhood friend who lived on Capitol Beach lake, Mike Burden, owner of Burden's Surplus Center on West O Street.) Back to the Cavett story: I had an absolute blast giving the Capitol Beach crew their cave tours. Barb Hoppe, a neighbor who involved me in teaching for Bright Lights Summer Learning Adventures, and also Leta Powell Drake, known to many as Kalamity Kate, encouraged me to pursue my idea of contacting Cavett. (I remember Drake having really unique items for sale at her Capitol Beach garage sales on Lakeshore Drive when I was little.)

Mr. Hull passed along my invitation to Cavett and a short time later I received a call from Cavett's assistant in New York to discuss our possibilities. Cavett was scheduled to be in Lincoln, Nebraska, for a show at the Lied Center with comic, author, and actress Paula Poundstone that February (2017), and Cavett had events scheduled in Wayne and Hastings, Nebraska, as well. Cavett's assistant explained that Dick really wanted to visit the cave if we could make it work. I liked our chances. Coincidentally, I met Mr. Hull, Christopher, and their family a few nights later while having dinner at Wilderness Ridge in Lincoln. Hull, too, reiterated that Cavett really wanted to see what had come of Robber's Cave. I told Mr. Hull that anytime Cavett was available I'd be glad to provide a private tour.

The weekend Dick Cavett came to Lincoln I made sure to keep my phone nearby because I knew I could be receiving the call at any time. That call came Sunday, February 19, 2017, the morning after Cavett's Lied Center show. His wife Martha asked if I'd be available to give them a tour around noon that day (before leaving Nebraska, Cavett wanted to visit long-time friend Roger Welsch in Dannebrog, too). I accepted and then remember immediately going outside to remove my daughter's car seat so I could vacuum and clean my car. My daughter, Brooklyn, sent me off with good luck wishes and a colorful painting that she created for the Cavetts.

I picked up Dick and Martha Cavett from their hotel—Martha politely complimented me on the cleanliness of my Camry—and we met one of Cavett's childhood friends, Freddy, at the cave. Coworker Colby Coash came to welcome the Cavetts and after a few photos, Jamie Schack, and I accompanied Dick, Martha, and Freddy into the cave for what would be an unforgettable experience to say the least. Jamie, who's also my younger sister, photographed the reunion between Cavett and cave.

Cavett's parents, Dorcas and Alva, were highly respected educators in Lincoln, Nebraska. Dorcas taught at Prescott Elementary in 1948 and Bancroft Elementary in 1953, while Alva taught English at Lincoln High School for 28 years. (Cavett Elementary in Lincoln is named in their honor.) It should come as no surprise that Dick Cavett graduated from Yale. The spry comic quoted

Mark Twain and shared a witticism about every 30 seconds that day in Robber's Cave. Being back in the cave reminded him of when Sir Laurence Olivier's once described a nightmare about doors leading to other doors. Even at 80, Cavett maneuvered and meandered through the nooks, crannies, and crevices as if he had barely aged. He later claimed to be more proud of his gymnastic feats than his three Emmy wins. (Cavett is a two-time Nebraska state high school pommel horse champion.) After our time in the cave, Jamie and I sent the Cavetts off with a t-shirt, souvenir booklet, Brooklyn's painting, and a great memory. Cavett even signed an item to be displayed at the restaurant. He made my day when he sent Jamie the following email a few days later:

Jamie,

Thanks to you and Joel and one special little girl for making our visit to my favorite cave so memorable, nostalgic and just plain fun. I can't stand to take the T-shirt off, even in the shower. Joel's knowledge, presentation skills and scholarship merit a big raise. My wife Martha has already commandeered Brooklyn's painting for our family scrapbook. Good luck and great success to all of you.

Yours spelunkingly,

Dick Cavett

Dick Cavett and Ron Hull were on stage together the following night at Wayne State College in Wayne, Nebraska, so I took the opportunity to visit my grandparents, aunt, and uncle in nearby Wisner, Nebraska, and made the short drive to Wayne to attend Cavett's second event. The stories he told about Bob Hope, Groucho Marx, Audrey Hepburn, Fred Astaire, Henry Fonda, and Bette Davis were unforgettable. My favorite however involved Marlon Brando, a paparazzo, and a wicked punch. Read Cavett's *Brief Encounters: Conversations, Magic Moments, and Assorted Hijinks* if you're interested in the details.

When Cavett saw me after the show at Wayne State, he commented, "We meet again. Where was it, Paris?" I could only chuckle as I had him sign a program for a fellow Irving Middle School mentor and Cavett fan, Nancy Svoboda.

Dick Cavett—from childhood pranks near his South 23rd Street neighborhood in 1950s Lincoln, Nebraska, to late-night mischief with Marlon Brando in 1970s New York City—how thankful I am that he accepted my invitation and let me be a part of his nostalgically gratifying return to Robber's Cave. We enjoyed an unforgettable Sunday afternoon, and my personal goal of bringing Dick Cavett back to Robber's Cave had been accomplished.

Underground Birthday Parties, Why Not?

Sandra 'Sandy' Dennis was an American theater and film actress. At the height of her career in the 1960s she won two Tony Awards, as well as an Oscar for her performance in *Who's Afraid of Virginia Woolf?* Although she was born in Hastings, Nebraska, she lived in Lincoln and attended Lincoln High School with Dick Cavett (they both graduated from LHS in 1955). The Tony Award-winning actress even celebrated her birthday in 1952 with a party in Robber's Cave!

Janice Sherman reminisced about Robber's Cave in Mary Jane Nielsen's *Lincoln Looks Back*: "I was there [just once] when I was invited to a birthday party given by Sandy Dennis in 1952. We both attended Everett Junior High, and I had just moved here from Beatrice. I remember the bats and the smell, and having a good time."

In October of 1957, guests enjoyed an Indian-themed birthday party for Derry Vandewege's eighth birthday at Robber's Cave. The youngsters spent the entire time exploring the cave but took a break to eat a cake decorated as an Indian drum. The eight guests were all from the Eastridge neighborhood: Kenny and Neil McCabe, Jake Shapiro, Terry Mazurak, John Rogers, Stuart Smith, Rodney Taylor, and Alan Spencer. Derry's siblings Vikki and Brad were present as well (10/26/1957).

Tommy Lemm, son of Mr. and Mrs. Theodore Lemm also from Lincoln's Eastridge neighborhood, celebrated his ninth birthday in May of 1958 with a cookout, scavenger hunt, and trip to Robber's Cave (5/13/1958).

Also in 1958, Harry Meginnis Jr. met twelve friends at Robber's Cave to celebrate his seventh birthday party. Harry Meginnis Jr.'s father, Harry Sr., owned a Lincoln Ford dealership in the 1970s. He also owned the local Hertz franchise and qualified for the US Open Golf Championship as a teenager.

Bob Reece, his brother Tom, and their friends motored to Robber's Cave in July of 1968 for a birthday party (7/2/1968).

Carol Jacob toured the cave in June 2017, and after the tour she told me about a frightening occurrence during her Robber's Cave birthday held in the cave in the late 1960s. In tunnel number three, known to many as simply "the lunch room," Carol's mother lit a fire and began to roast hotdogs. It didn't take long for the smoke to ascend into the airshaft sending many bats flying down and out of the chute! Carol's birthday party quickly turned into a frenzied scene as the lunchroom tunnel filled with the shrieks of screaming children that scattered, ducked, and dodged the bothered bats.

What to Make of the Cave's Folklore?

I'm often asked how much of the cave's folklore I believe. Considering that we've likely all seen how a simple story with a bit of truth can develop into a grand tale over time, I have come to believe that the stories specifically involving the Pawnee, escaped slaves, and Jesse James, although possible, are highly unlikely to be factually accurate. I appreciate this folklore and share it with others to keep it alive. It is entertaining; however, I never forget that folklore by definition is the beliefs and stories of a community passed through the generations by word of mouth and should not be simply accepted as truth.

Historians, with good reason, doubt the authenticity of the cave's legends, yet Robber's Cave maintains a unique and intriguing history. After searching for, finding, and reading nearly all that has ever been written or reported on Robber's Cave and considering what has been found in and around the cave over the years, I do find the cave's usage by early settlers, Coxey's Army, and later, horse thieves and gamblers to be quite convincing. A horse barn did stand just a few hundred feet south of the cave, which burned sometime before 1931, and in the charred ruins of that horse barn a young Scarborough Jr. dug through and discovered a blackened 1873 Winchester Model rifle. It might not have belonged to Jesse James, but that's still quite the find!

Furthermore, when considering the presence of the brewery, then later the sporting house/dance hall (quite possibly a brothel), usage by the Ku Klux Klan, along with the sheer number of parties and accidents at this space, there is plenty to indicate that the cave and surrounding area possess quite a colorful past. Even after J. W. Scarborough opened the cave to the public, there were issues with trespassing, vandalism, underage drinking, sexual assaults, and injuries. One can only imagine what has happened in the dark, unsupervised, underground tunnels through the years.

How about the cave's ghosts? I still contend that for people who view spirits simply as memories floating alongside the present, you'll find them everywhere. As for the other type of ghosts—ask one of the twelve Lincoln priests who have blessed the cave.

The Renaissance of Robber's Cave Tours

I'll admit, I had always remained hopeful that Robber's Cave would reopen to the public. Although, I had never imagined I'd have the opportunity to be such an integral part of the renaissance of Robber's Cave. I have met really wonderful people giving tours, and I especially enjoy presenting to guests who are thankful that the cave has reopened. Often times, even after a tour has ended, I'll remain in the cave and converse with the guests that get it—the ones who truly appreciate what a unique place the cave is to Lincoln, Nebraska. Not because it's incredibly historical, although it has its share of history, but because of the memories Robber's Cave evokes for them. Some guests have returned for tours five or six times!

Dale Nobbman is one of the many guests for whom one tour was not enough. He wrote on his history blog about how I made his birthday a very special day when I gave him and his wife a private tour in March of 2017:

> There was no place I would have preferred to be than in a part of Lincoln that was already here before Lincoln was Lincoln in 1867. My guide was Joel Green—nobody knows more about Robber's Cave than Joel!

When Matt Hansen, the LEED architect at the Capitol Preservation office came for a second tour, he conveyed how interested he had been in the cave as a youngster. We shared frustrations regarding the lack of information that publicly existed about the cave, and he expressed how much he appreciated someone documenting the stories and putting forth the time and effort to record it for future generations.

Robbers Cave LLC's cave tours have played a huge part in making the cave accessible once again to the public. In an interview with Taylor Barth on *10/11 Now*, Ed Zimmer stated, "The city's interest in participating in this project has really been all focused on the cave and wanting to help make that available again to the public in a safe, productive way." The Lincoln Chamber of Commerce President Wendy Birdsall agrees: "You've married it with a historic spot and made it a destination, so folks will come […] to participate in a piece of history" (8/27/2015).

Each Carving Marks a Story

From floor to ceiling, nearly every inch of Robber's Cave's soft, sandstone walls are covered with carvings. Most of the etchings fall into the following categories: names and initials, Greek letters, faces, hearts, and peace signs, but there are even feathers, bas-reliefs, and a Sphynx head. Nearly every decade going back to the 1870s is represented (Sam Dalton 1875 being the oldest found). From the large Sigma Alpha Mu (one of Lincoln's few Jewish fraternities) right at the entrance to Metallica, ABBA, and the Kool-Aid man, it's amusing to think of the circumstance behind each impression. Unfortunately, along with the etchings that express teenage crushes and mischievous memories, several indecent and contemptible engravings are peppered throughout: human anatomy, marijuana leafs, middle fingers, swastikas, pentagrams, and profanity.

I once noticed a guest in his mid-60s meticulously combing the walls during a tour. Once the tour ended, the gentleman approached me holding a digital camera and asked if I'd be willing to take him back into the cave so that he could have his photograph taken next to a Zorro carving he made many years ago. He explained that he grew up an absolute Zorro fanatic (Zorro is a masked, heroic outlaw created in 1919 by Johnston McCulley), and the guest had many memories of running through the cave pretending to be the skilled sword fighter.

I escorted his return into the cave so we could capture a photo of him standing next to his giant Z cut into the sandstone long ago. I'll never forget the elation displayed on the gentleman's face as we walked up the stairs to leave. Like most of the carvings, I had passed that Z so many times without thinking twice. Now, I'll never look at it the same way after knowing its origins. When I walk through the cave's tunnels, it's amusing to guess the circumstances behind certain etchings.

As more and more people tour the cave, I gain additional insight behind so many of the mysterious markings. Scarborough Jr. once told me of a very old carving he knew of located near "fat man's misery." Founded by Garner Moore in 1920, Ideal Grocery had been a mainstay at 905 South 27th Street, and it was Lincoln's oldest grocery store when it burned in May of 2016. Scarborough Jr. reported that in 1906, Moore hopped up on a picnic table and put a deep carving of his name in cursive high on the north wall. The century-old carving is in excellent condition and can plainly be seen today.

Sharing My Story

I consider myself immensely lucky to have been able share the story of Robber's Cave along with my connection to it with thousands of people. In addition to writing this book, I have been asked to submit articles to newspapers, interview for local TV shows, and provide private and public cave tours for magazines, schools, Girl Scouts, high school reunions, fraternal organizations, anniversaries, birthdays, bachelor and bachelorette parties, rehearsal dinners, holiday parties, company parties, association gatherings, bands, and season ticket holder events. Recently I've been accepting invitations to speak about the cave for various organizations and businesses. Sometimes, after an event, an audience member will graciously offer to show me an old photo or two of Robber's Cave. I've attained so many wonderful images and memories simply by meeting others who share a common interest in the cave.

A Timeline of Social Use— Recording the Cave's Popularity

Before Robbers Cave LLC reopened the cave for tours and events, most people seemed to remember Robber's Cave because of Boy Scouts, birthday parties, college keggers, and bands; however, the cave had been used for so much more. In order to give an idea of the cave's numerous uses through the years, I created a timeline to detail what the cave was used for and when. So many organizations, social clubs, churches, and youth groups have used the cave. Maybe you'll recognize a name or two! Even if you don't, what a snapshot this timeline is of just how different social life in Lincoln was in the early to mid-1900s. I selected a variety of uses from several decades in an attempt to document the cave's popularity. Currently, 30 guests can be in the cave at once, so to learn of gatherings that featured hundreds in attendance bewilders me.

1909   The JUK Club gave a party at Robber's Cave in November of 1909. Games were played and refreshments were served. This info was posted directly above a bolded announcement that I found amusing: Over-Eating: It is a crime against nature and most inexcusable!
(*The Nebraska State Journal.* November 7, 1909, p. 7.)

1910   Epworth Leaguers and friends were instructed to board Penitentiary Car at 10th and O St. at 6 P.M. to explore caves and "lunch with the young people in this historical place."
(*The Nebraska State Journal.* September 18, 1910, p. 21.)

Mrs. Roach of St. Paul Methodist Church chaperoned 41 young people on a trip to Robber's Cave in September of 1910. They enjoyed exploring the cavities and hearing the interesting stories as to the jewelry, knives, and various other articles found in the cave.
(*The Nebraska State Journal.* Sept 25, 1910, p. 20.)

Vine Camp held an outing and luncheon at Robber's Cave in October of 1910.
(*Lincoln Daily News*. October 19, 1910, p. 12.)

1911 The following is a sweet little story called "Visit to Lincoln" written by nine-year-old Viola S. Hansen of West Point, Nebraska. Remember, the cave did not feature electric lights until after *The Omaha Daily Bee* published this story on Sunday, January 29, 1911:

One day Harry and John, who live in Fremont, came home from school all out of breath.

"What is it children?" asked Mrs. Gray

"Miss Green said, 'school is to leave next Tuesday afternoon,'" said they.

Tuesday afternoon soon came; they were very glad, as were all the children in the school.

Their mother said that she had a grand surprise for them; they were anxious to find out what it was. A few days later they were told that they were to spend half of their vacation in Lincoln with friends. Soon their mother began to pack their trunks.

In an hour they were at Lincoln; their friends were at the depot to meet them.

Harry's father worked for the railroad company. So they had a free ride to Lincoln. It was about evening when they got there. The next day they went out to look about the city. Peter, one of their friends, said, I will show you Robber's Cave."

They walk on and on until they came to 3000 South Eleventh Street, where they saw a hill with green grass and flowers upon it. On the side of this hill there was a low entrance, not high enough for a tall person to go through without bending. They saw many sights, but this one interested them the most. The guide carried a lantern. At first they were frightened but soon found out that it was very dark inside; it was just as dark as night. The walls were of many colors and the ground was as smooth as a floor. Then they went into other tunnels of Robber's Cave and saw men with lanterns sitting on benches talking.

People when going into this cave took lanterns with them, because it is very dark. They saw many beautiful things, but the time was altogether too short. Before leaving they thanked their friends for entertaining them while they were there.

They soon were on their way home again. Their father and mother were waiting for them. The rest of the vacation was spent in telling their friends about their visit to Lincoln. Vacation was soon over and everyone was back to school again.

1912 On November 1, 1912, members of the University of Nebraska Union Literary Society held a social meeting at Robber's Cave.

(*The Lincoln Star*. August 15, 1976, p. 13.)

1913 About 50 Boy Scouts took a trip to the "penitentiary woods," Robber's Cave, and the old paper mill in August of 1913 under the leadership of Scout Master Beck of University Place. While on the trip the scouts studies woodcraft and played scout games.
(*Lincoln Daily News*. August 4, 1913, p. 3.)

In November of 1913, the Epworth League of the Havelock Methodist Episcopal Church served supper in Robber's Cave.
(*The Lincoln Star.* November 30, 1913, p. 23.)

1914

Miss Gladys Ashworth entertained informally for Mrs. Williams of Grant, Nebraska, in July of 1914. Games and music were furnished; Mr. Joe Granger won the royal prize for being the best at the guessing game; refreshments were served on the porch which had been "prettily decorated with Japanese lanterns." A picnic was given at Capitol Beach in their honor and a party was given at Robber's Cave before they left for home.
(*The Lincoln Star.* July 5, 1914, p. 22.)

In August of 1914, Mrs. Calvert, who was in charge of the junior work for the WCTU (Woman's Christian Temperance Union) led 187 children to Robber's Cave to sign a pledge to refrain from the use of intoxicating liquors or narcotics in any form.
(*The Lincoln Star.* August 12, 1914, p. 10.)

State Superintendent James E. Delzell took his office force to Robber's Cave as it is known for a picnic dinner in October of 1914. Something interesting about Mr. Delzell is that his father became totally blind from exposure serving for the 142nd Infantry of Indiana, so James secured his own education and assumed the burdens of the family. Delzell became the superintendent of public instruction for Nebraska in 1911.
(*Omaha Daily Bee.* October 7, 1914, p. 3.)

1915

The Lincoln Star advertised picnics at Robber's Cave—fires every night in December.
(*The Lincoln Star.* December 5, 1915, p. 10.)

In December of 1915, The Sansgelt Club, a woman's bridge and social club, had a party at Robber's Cave requesting "all old members" to attend.
(*The Lincoln Star.* December 12, 1915, p. 2.)

1916

The Lincoln Traction Company advertised a route that would carry passengers to Havelock, "The largest railroad shops west of Chicago, College View, Antelope Park, City Park, Penitentiary, Asylum, and Robber's Cave.
(*The Lincoln Star.* August 13, 1916, p. 43.)

1919

Mrs. S. R. McKelvie, wife of Nebraska Governor Samuel McKelvie, entertained houseguest Miss Bessie Love in November of 1919, and members of Alpha Tau Omega and 70 other friends were guests. Alpha Tau Omega entertained Miss Love with a wiener roast at Robber's Cave.
(*The Nebraska State Journal.* November 3, 1919, p. 10.)

1921

During the Epworth Assembly in August of 1921, under the direction of Mrs. C. O. Bruce, the children hiked to Robber's Cave. The hike occurred while the adults listened to Dr. Burns lecture about how there needed to be the following laws for the home's protection: a uniform prevention of marriage for the unfit, and a national board of movie censorship.
(*The Nebraska State Journal.* August 9, 1921, p. 5.)

About twenty former Wayne Normal and Wayne High School students attended the wiener roast given by the Wayne Club at Robber's Cave. The following members were elected: Hugo Serb, president, Ira McDonald, vice president, and Dorothy Huse, secretary.
(*The Nebraska State Journal.* October 16, 1921, p. 22.)

Alpha Kappa Psi members enjoyed a wienie roast at Robber's Cave in October of 1921 after meeting at the Social Science building.
(*The Nebraska State Journal.* October 22, 1921, p. 9.)

The Cudenaang Camp Fire Girls with Gladys Sidles as guardian held their "council of spooks" at Robber's Cave in October of 1921.
(*The Nebraska State Journal.* October 30, 1921, p. 22.)

1922

Pukwana Camp Fire Girls planned a hike to Robber's Cave in March of 1922 with Miss Ruth Wood who was president of the club at the time.
(*The Nebraska State Journal.* March 12, 1922, p. 19.)

After a meeting at the home of Marie Dahlberg, the Mojag Camp Fire Girls took their breakfasts and hiked to Robber's Cave.
(*The Nebraska State Journal.* July 23, 1922, p. 17.)

As part of the recreation program for the Nebraska Epworth Assembly, Mrs. C. O. Bruce planned hikes to Robber's Cave for games, stunts, and races.
(*The Lincoln Star.* July 31, 1922, p. 14.)

Fifty VFW members with their families and friends "drove out in automobiles" to a wienie roast at Robber's Cave in September of 1922.
(*The Nebraska State Journal.* September 28, 1922, p. 7.)

The Veterans' Club of the Lincoln Business College gave a wienie roast at Robber's Cave in October of 1922. An enjoyable evening was reported.
(*The Nebraska State Journal.* October 16, 1922, p. 5.)

The Westminster Presbyterian Church, located at 23rd and Garfield Street at the time, held a Hallowe'en party at Robber's Cave. I enjoyed reading the sermon topics for that

week: "The Divine Remedy for Human Feverishness" and "A Saloonless World and How to Get It."
(*The Nebraska State Journal.* October 29, 1922, p. 10.)

1923 "All young people" of St. Paul Church and congregation were invited to the "Hard Times Hallowe'en Party" at Robber's Cave in October of 1923.
(*Lincoln Evening Journal.* October 27, 1923, p. 3.)

1924 The YMCA organized a busy program for the boys' department during the spring vacation of March 1924. In addition to Bible examination, ping pong, and checkers, the organization planned a hike to Robber's Cave as well.
(*Lincoln Evening Journal.* March 27, 1924, p. 17.)

In April of 1924, Siwihono Camp held a meeting at the home of Sylvia Mosher, and plans were made for a hike to Robber's Cave.
(*The Lincoln Star.* April 13, 1924, p. 26.)

On December 27, 1924, a headline in the *Lincoln Evening Journal* read A CAVE FESTIVAL FOR BOY SCOUTS: Famous Tuocs Gang to Exhibit Wild Ways Before a Large Gathering at Monday Night Feast. "Boy Scouts to Frolic at Cave: Robbers' Rendezvous to be Scene of Evac Screbbor . . . " headlined *The Lincoln Star.* The local paper built up the event by printing the following:

> Every feature will be snappy, [. . .] bring your CSS & D-cup, saucer, spoon and dime—or at least bring something to drink out of, eat from and eat with, whether it is tin, wood or whatnot. You will be astounded to see what the real characteristics of this terrible band of Tuocs are. They have promised to come clean, in all their methods, intrigues, secrets, even to the pass word of their organization [. . .] The Tuocs band has so many traditions and unusual customs that it will require the cooperation of all to make the Evac Screbbor a success.
> (*The Lincoln Star.* December, 1924. Pg. 2).

The account of the event is quite amusing. Humorously, one of the "Grand Tuocs" submitted a description of the gang (spell Tuocs backwards and you'll start to catch on) along with their plans for the feast and entertainment at Robber's Cave, which featured 300 scouts:

> The famous Tuocs gang of pioneer western days, once more in captivity through the efforts of no less dignitary than our own chief of police, Peter Johnston. The very wildest of this gang will be on exhibition at the cave, perhaps in chains, so ferocious are they. It is reported that they eat dogs alive and carry knives in their teeth! No fear—as Chief Johnston has them well trained and daily workouts are given to the entire band in preparation for the revival of an ancient robber

festival held always just before the beginning of the New Year at one of their places of refuge and safety. More details of the program will appear in the Sunday papers. As only three hundred scouts can be entertained it is very essential that you get in touch with your scoutmaster before sunrise Monday that he may make sure of your reservation. You may be too late. The Tuocs gang promises hot and heavy, rough and ready, regular robber food, and a rip-snorting spooky program, and a visit through one of Lincoln's most notorious and interesting institutions [. . .] Special car service is being arranged for [. . .] Rain or shine, snow or sleet, the Evac-Screbbor will not be held up by any rival elements. The cave will be warm, dry, and have adequate police protection.

Executive Tuocs Willard Yates and J. E. M. Thomson were named guards of the exits, and the Lincoln Traction Company furnished free transportation for the evening. This had to have been quite the ordeal! The follow-up story in the *Lincoln Evening Journal* three days later disclosed a bit more of what went on at the "Impressive Evec Screbber" bandit banquet:

> Three hundred boy scouts representing each of the 35 Lincoln troops with over 50 other guests. Dr. E. H. Barbour, Willard Yates, Lloyd McMasters, and Chief Johnston were among those who played the parts of robbers in the festival, which was a portrayal of the lives of legendary bandits who once lived in the cave. Guides were furnished to direct groups through the cave and tell wild tales of bandit deeds. On entering the cave the boys signed their names on the roster in blood as the robbers were accustomed to do, and then were sworn to absolute secrecy about what they saw and heard in the cave. After being taken [through] the cave's various tunnels, the scouts gathered in a large chamber where they served as a court to try the robbers. Ralph McDermott, chief scout executive, served as judge and sentenced the robbers after they were convicted.
> (*Lincoln Evening Journal*. December 30, 1924, p. 6.)

1925

In honor of Miss Lucille Wachter who was leaving for Denver, Colorado, about 21 girls from the University Publishing Company hosted a wiener roast at Robber's Cave. "The affair was in the nature of a Hallowe'en party."
(*The Lincoln Star*. October 29, 1925, p. 16.)

In December 1925, *The Lincoln Star's* Havelock Notes included Miss Grace Walker and Paul Van Valkenburgh taking their Sunday school classes to Robber's Cave for an evening picnic.
(*The Lincoln Star*. December 13, 1925, p. 36.)

1926

In January of 1926, Miss Marie Wilson and Ernest Harris hosted members of the Hoot Owl Club at Robber's Cave. Miss Bertha Craig and Clyde Davis were taken in as new members.

(*The Lincoln Star*. January 3, 1926, p. 25.)

First Baptist Church held a BYPU (Baptist Young People's Union) party at the cave in February of 1926.
(*The Lincoln Star*. February 28, 1926, p. 24.)

In April of 1926, under the "WHAT'S DOING TONIGHT" section of the *Lincoln Evening Journal*, the congregation of Mt. Zion Baptist Church advertised a picnic in the cave.
(*Lincoln Evening Journal*. April 26, 1926, p. 14.)

In May of 1926, Juniors of Union College entertained the seniors at a picnic at Robber's Cave and later Crete Park. More than 100 students made the trip.
(*Lincoln Evening Journal*. May 11, 1926, p. 4.)

Included in the "YWCA Notes" of *The Lincoln Star* in June of 1926, The Federation Girls had a picnic at Robber's Cave.
(*The Lincoln Star*. June 6, 1926, p. 21.)

The Nebraska State House's Department of Agriculture spent the evening exploring Robber's Cave after a picnic for 45 members in September of 1926.
(*The Lincoln Star*. September 30, 1926, p. 6.)

1927

The Optimist Club fried hamburgers and toasted marshmallows at a social event in Robber's Cave. Bread, coffee, pickles, onions and mustard were furnished. Each family was to bring potatoes to roast . . . and a pie. Games for the children followed.
(*Lincoln Evening Journal*. October 3, 1927, p. 11.)

Chaperoned by P. L. Gaddis and Reverend F. I. Finch, 40 high school-aged members of the First Methodist Church made their annual excursion to Robber's Cave for a picnic the afternoon of October 29, 1927.
(*The Lincoln Evening Journal*. October 25, 1927, p. 5.)

1928

On April 6, 1928, Sigma Gamma Epsilon, an honorary geological fraternity, hosted a national convention at the Hotel Lincoln. President Decker was in charge of the morning meeting at which time Professor Schramm presented the address of welcome. That evening, after touring the campus and the city, they held a barbecue at Robber's Cave.
(*Lincoln Evening Journal*. April 6, 1928, p. 28.)

As described in the "University Notes" section of *The Lincoln Star* in 1928, the department of geography featured a number of field trips to points of interest in and near Lincoln. The out-of-town trips included the lower Platte Valley with its fish hatcheries, stone

mines, sand dredging plants, cement works, and pottery factory. Another excursion visited the Blue Valley near Milford, rich in Indian legends and scenic beauty. Lincoln locations included the capitol, Robber's Cave, and the state museum. Doctor N. T. Bengtson and Shipman were in charge of the excursions.
(*The Lincoln Star*. July 8, 1928, p. 26.)

On Wednesday, November 7, 1928, Spanish War veterans held their belated Hallowe'en party in Robber's Cave. The time was spent telling ghost stories at a wiener roast, then the ladies served donuts and coffee in the cave.
(*Lincoln Evening Journal*. November 7, 1928, p. 5.)

The Owasaka Camp planned a hike to the cave in December 1928 during their meeting at Marion Brown's.
(*The Lincoln Star*. December 16, 1928, p. 27.)

1929

Merrie Gold Camp Fire, their guardian and guests, Mrs. Erwin Hopt, Mr. Morgan, Mr. and Mrs. Young and Miss Woods, enjoyed a supper cooked over fires in Robber's Cave after they visited the Yankee Hill Brick Yard and clay pits.
(*The Lincoln Star*. April 7, 1929, p. 23.)

The alumnae members of Theta Sigma Phi had a picnic in the cave on April 23, 1929. Miss Jacqueline Stice and Miss Dorothy Colburn were in charge of arrangements. They must've had fun because a few days later, the same sorority returned where members prepared supper on the fireplace and played games. Miss Norma Carpenter was in charge.
(*Lincoln Evening Journal*. April 27, 1929, p. 7.)

Star Study was the newest activity for members of the NH Club of the YWCA in April of 1929. The club held evening meetings to study legends of the stars and picnicked at Robber's Cave.
(*The Lincoln Star*. April 28, 1929, p. 28.)

The Junior Chamber of Commerce members entertained fifty visitors from around the state in May of 1929 by taking them to Robber's Cave where the Lincoln Pep Group played, and initiatory ceremonies preceded a Dutch lunch.
(*Lincoln Evening Journal*. May 6, 1929, p. 6.)

In July of 1922, 300 delegates came to Lincoln for the 12th annual Epworth League Institute's program. The institute brought young people of the Methodist church from Lincoln, northern Kansas, Beatrice, and Hastings together, and in addition to education classes, tours to Robber's Cave, Capitol Beach, the capitol, and Nebraska Wesleyan University were organized. "The Measure of a Man" was the subject of Clark A. Fulmer's address before a crowd of 250 in the open air auditorium.
(*The Lincoln Star*. July 22, 1929, p. 4.)

In August of 1929, *Lincoln Evening Journal* reported that the Elm Park Methodist's High School League had a picnic supper at Robber's Cave.
(*Lincoln Evening Journal.* August 23, 1929, p. 12.)

1930   Following a visit to the Burnham Brick Yards, about 100 summer school students took the department of geography's educational excursion to Robber's Cave in June of 1930.
(*The Lincoln Star.* June 29, 1930, p. 32.)

In July of 1930, the Epworth Board planned their entertainment features including a tennis tournament and a trip for the juniors to Robber's Cave.
(*Lincoln Evening Journal.* July 29, 1930, p. 10.)

Kappa Sigma Pi and Delta Omega Phi both held luncheons, afternoon sports, and a watermelon feed at Robber's Cave in September of 1930.
(*Lincoln Evening Journal.* September 17, 1930, p. 8.)

The Cotner seniors entertained the sophomores at a wiener roast at Robber's Cave in November of 1930.
(*The Lincoln Star.* November 2, 1930, p. 12.)

1931   A Hallowe'en party for boys at the YMCA was held in October of 1931 that culminated with game tournaments, over-night hikes and trips to the penitentiary and Robber's Cave. The boys were to come masked to the party.
(*The Lincoln Star.* October 28, 1931, p. 13.)

1932   Nebraska and Des Moines chapters of the Military Order of the Cootie surprised Arthur D. Dodds on his birthday and "After the Des Moines members had partaken of a chicken dinner at the home of Mr. Dodds, 3411 Cable, they joined the Lincoln group at Robber's Cave."
(*The Lincoln Evening Journal.* May 21, 1932, p. 4.)

In a *Lincoln Star* article by Fred L. Fassett in June of 1932, he describes the danger of moral lapses when children are allowed to run loose after supper. President Roosevelt is credited with saying, "If a fellow goes to the devil, he goes after supper." Fassett explains the need for good, clean, wholesome activities for youth so that they can become honest, upright people—a credit to themselves, their family and community—one of that great mass known as the typical American, the foundation of a nation. The city challenged leaders to organize and fulfill an intensified summer program of stimulating activities. The Boy Scouts of America were mentioned as the organization that knew better than any other the full significance of keeping the idle time of boys filled with activities that were pleasurable and educational. Scoutmasters were challenged and in order to aid their holding the interest of the boys, the vacation program committee arranged a number of attractive features that were to appeal to every scout.

Included in such activities were free admissions to several of Lincoln's most appealing recreation places: Robber's Cave, Landis Field, Capital Beach, the Apple Blossom miniature golf course, and the State Theater, the "new" municipal building, the university, Modern Cleaners, and the auto club park. I sure hope these outings helped to "properly bend the little twigs into sturdy oaks, straight, upright, and kingly." Don't you just love the vernacular of the time?
(*The Lincoln Star*. June 26, 1932, p. 26.)

In July of 1932, under the supervision of Leonard Hartnett, scoutmaster of Troop 57, a large group of Boy Scouts enjoyed visits to not only Robber's Cave, but to Curtis, Towle, and Paine, Grainger Brothers, Nehi Bottling Works, the Beatrice Creamery, the Lincoln Hatchery, Lincoln Telephone Company, and, get this, the city sewage disposal plant!
(*The Lincoln Star*. July 17, 1932, p. 14.)

1933

The local VFW auxiliaries entertained the visiting ladies at a Robber's Cave party during a Cootie "scratch" in July of 1933. The Military Order of the Cootie is a non-profit Veterans' Service Organization.
(*The Lincoln Star*. July 2, 1933, p. 4.)

The Epworth League Institute had 392 members in 1933. In August of that year, members visited Robber's Cave, Nebraska Wesleyan's and UNL's campuses, Bryan Memorial Hospital, and the Men's Reformatory.
(*The Lincoln Star*. August 6, 1933, p. 4.)

1934

Mrs. Gerald Vallery entertained her Sunday school class at a wiener roast at Robber's Cave in
April of 1934.
(*The Lincoln Star*. April 29, 1934, p. 21.)

Under the direction of Betty Lois Wheeler, the Zhonta Camp Fire Girls had a breakfast and meeting at Robber's Cave before playing nature games in June of 1934.
(*The Lincoln Star*. June 17, 1934, p. 17.)

The Aktatci Camp Fire group cooked their supper over an open fire and had a Hallowe'en party and treasure hunt at Robber's Cave in November of 1934. This after Miss Helen Emig gave a presentation on trees complete with slides of the Mariposa big trees. She also gave a talk on gown decoration.
(*The Lincoln Star*. November 4, 1934, p. 18.)

1936   The Epworth League high school class went to Robber's Cave for an outing in March of 1936.
(*The Lincoln Star.* March 15, 1936, p. 11.)

The Entre Nous club enjoyed its annual spring party in May of 1936 when members drove to Lincoln for a wiener roast at the cave. After exploring the cave, they spent the remainder of the evening playing Monopoly at the home of Mr. and Mrs. W. A. Keitges.
(*The Lincoln Star.* May 22, 1936, p. 11.)

1937   Fifty employees of the land utilization division of the resettlement office honored Neill Robb at a farewell picnic party at Robber's Cave in April of 1937. Mr. Robb had been transferred to the resettlement office in Washington D.C. Irene Nelson, Maxine Fillman, and Joy Deuser were in charge.
(*Lincoln Evening Journal.* April 27, 1937, p. 7.)

1938   About 40 attended the Optimists Club's post Hallowe'en masquerade party at Robber's Cave. Mr. and Mrs. Stuart Lesse won prizes for the best costume, while Mrs. Heath Griffith and Marian Bohling tied for first place in the treasure hunt.
(*The Nebraska State Journal.* November 4, 1938, p. 6.)

1939   The Harmony Club enjoyed a picnic at Robber's Cave in April of 1939.
(*The Nebraska State Journal.* April 9, 1939, p. 28.)

Job's Daughters held a picnic at Robber's Cave in June of 1939.
(*The Lincoln Star.* June 21, 1939, p. 6.)

Twenty members of Boy Scout Troop No. 14 attended a Hallowe'en party at Robber's Cave in 1939. George Mann, George J. Franklin, and Harvey Davis organized the lunch and activities which included bobbing for apples, a treasure hunt, and a "sham battle."
(*The Lincoln Star.* November 2, 1939, p. 6.)

In December of 1939, members of the Lincoln Outdoor Club met at the Municipal Swimming Pool building to take part in a program planned by Mr. and Mrs. Chet Swearingen, Mr. and Mrs. Gil Steele, and Mr. and Mrs. Myron Wylie. The party went to Robber's Cave for supper.
(*The Nebraska State Journal.* December 10, 1939, p. 24.)

1940   Members of the Business Girls' League had a picnic in the cave where league representatives made their reports on a recent business girls' conference held at Lake Okoboji. Irene Yates and Greta Hagemann provided cars.
(*The Nebraska State Journal.* July 21, 1940, p. 22.)

Te Ha Tu Camp Fire held a Hallowe'en party at Robber's Cave in the fall of 1940. The committee in charge of the party was Geraldine Garrett, Shirley Mercer, Betty Egger and Jean Schwartz.
(*The Nebraska State Journal.* November 3, 1940, p. 23.)

1941   A picnic was given at Robber's Cave by Miss Doris Neidhamer and her brother, Byron, and David McShane, honoring Miss Phyllis Wilson. Miss Wilson was leaving for Kansas City and Poplar Bluff, Missouri, to spend a few weeks visiting relatives before joining Mr. Wilson in Washington, D.C. where they would make their new home.
(*Lincoln Evening Journal.* May 30, 1941, p. 5.)

Twelve seniors from Roseland and their sponsor, Mrs. Louis Douglas, wife of the Roseland superintendent, couldn't get into the state penitentiary Tuesday while they were visiting places of interest in Lincoln on senior sneak-day. They did roam about Robber's Cave, however, and visited the zoo, the state house, and a bottling plant among other places. Luncheon was provided at the chamber of commerce, where they met another sneak-day group of 32 seniors from Osmond, chaperoned by Principal M. G. Roach. This group toured the university campus, the Journal, Roberts Dairy, the Lincoln Flying School and the Telephone Company. Footballer Warren Alfson was a guest at the luncheon, with Chet Avery, Art Bailey and Ken Boshart of the Chamber as hosts. Bailey was master of ceremonies. Piano music was provided by Betty Jean Horner from the University.
(*The Nebraska State Journal.* April 9, 1941, p. 4.)

In April of 1941, the YMCA's boys' department hiked to Robber's Cave after tumbling and gymnastics, and just before a father and son swim.
(*The Lincoln Star.* April 13, 1941, p. 4.)

Trinity Methodist Church held an intermediate picnic at Robber's Cave following their Fellowship Kensington luncheon in October of 1941.
(*The Lincoln Star.* October 21, 1941, p. 6.)

1942   Belknap Juniors No. 3 auxiliary to Belknap Women's Relief Corps held an April Fools' party at Robber's Cave in April of 1942. Audrey McClure as Queen Fool, and her attendant, Jeryce Gunn, conducted a program of tricks and jokes. Bonnie Bintz, won the spelling contest and was made lady-in-waiting to the queen. Other guests were Mrs. Charles McClure, Darleen Weaver, Beverly Paine, Lois Gillespie, Jane Kidney, and Janice Wroth.
(*The Lincoln Star.* April 5, 1942, p. 16.)

The Epsilon Chapter of Beta Sigma Phi enjoyed a wiener roast at Robber's Cave in October of 1942. Nine members attended with Mrs. Lillian Hahn and Mrs. Evelyn Pothast. Miss Virginia Ann Poor was the rushee of the evening.

(The Lincoln Star. October 9. 1942, p. 8.)

Wo An Ka group held a bicycle hike to Robber's Cave in October of 1942.
(The Lincoln Star. October 18, 1942, p. 20.)

In November of 1942, in addition to her story about the cave (see below), Joanna Jorgensen submitted to *The Lincoln Star* the following puzzle called the "ROBBERS' CAVE SCRAMBLES": 1- OKSYOP 2- TYEMSRY 3- POSC-NDA-BRESORB 4- NULTNE 5- CETESR-SAASPEGS.
(The Lincoln Star. November 12, 1942, p. 12.)

*If you must know the answers to the above scramble: 1- SPOOKY 2- MYSTERY 3- COPS AND ROBBERS 4- TUNNEL 5- SECRET PASSAGES Six seniors from Beatrice spent quite the sneak day in Lincoln in November of 1942. They visited Robber's Cave, the Lincoln Chamber of Commerce, and the Lincoln Airport where four of the seniors took flight in an airplane! (Could you imagine this happening today?) Mrs. Ivan Hedge and John Ferdig furnished cars, Superintendent Brown and Mrs. Brown accompanied the group as sponsors. After lunch, the group visited numerous stores, the capitol building, and the zoo. Evidently the day wasn't very "sneaky" but what a day!
(Beatrice Daily Sun. November 30, 1942, p. 8.)

1943 Numerous parties were held in July of 1943 for soldiers. Charles A. Fraley Post and auxiliary invited 50 soldiers to a wienie roast at Robber's Cave. They toured the cave, had a treasure hunt, and closed the evening with a ball game at Van Dorn Park.
(The Nebraska State Journal. July 2, 1943, p. 5.)

"Robber's Cave"
By Joanna Jorgensen,
November 19, 1942

Robber's Cave is a good place to go when you want a spooky place to play games. It is a cave dug out of sandstone by underground rivers. To reach it you go down a long stairway something like going into an out-door cellar. There are many long halls. Some of them are lighted, but more of them are dark and spooky, so when you go there you would need a flashlight. Most of the walls are covered with carved initials, so we put ours there, too.

"Fat man's misery" is a long and narrow tunnel that turns many corners and has steep and difficult steps. An old well runs through "fat man's misery" and you come out on it three times as you go through the tunnel.

Cops and Robbers is about the best game to play. Half of us were [cops] and half of us were Robbers. We all had sticks for guns. The Robbers would make [scary] noises and then run and hide and the [cops] would chase them. We would all chase and shoot at each other, and once when we were trying to find the cops in "fat man's misery," we stumbled over another robber that was supposed to be a corpse and was trying to scare us. The light that came down from the top of the well shone on her face in such a way that it did look [scary].

When we got hungry we went to the dining-room cave. The owner dropped wood down through the long chimney to the fireplace for us to burn and roast our [wieners] with. We ate at the long benches. Then we lighted the candles on the birthday cake and everyone sang "Happy Birthday" to me. We had ice cream with cake. Finally, the owner came down and we went home. Our legs were stiff from climbing so much, but we all had lots of fun.

*The previous story appeared in the "Kiddies Korner" section of the November 19, 1942 copy of *The Lincoln Star* on Pg. 6. Joanna sent the story for Halloween, along with the scramble puzzles.

The Le Wa Ta Na group of the Camp Fire Girls organization were entertained at a Robber's Cave party in May of 1943. Mrs. James DeRyke and daughter, DeLores, were in charge of arrangements.
(*The Nebraska State Journal.* May 23, 1943, p. 19.)

All teenage girls in Lincoln were invited to take part in a supper hike to Robber's Cave as planned by the YWCA's teenage outdoor committee in July of 1943. Girls wishing to attend were to meet at City Hall at 5:00 P.M. and that afternoon they were to hike to the cave for supper and exploration. Janice Cochran, chairman of the trip, suggested wearing old clothes.
(*The Nebraska State Journal.* July 20, 1943, p. 3.)

At a time when the Lincoln Boy Scouts assisted in war service projects such as the collection and salvage of scrap rubber, metal, and tin cans, they were rewarded with supper-hikes to Robber's Cave in September 1943. Lincoln had 735 former Scouts in the armed services, including 204 commissioned officers at that time!
(*The Nebraska State Journal.* September 19, 1943, p. 27.)

Twenty-five soldiers were entertained at Robber's Cave by Charles A. Fraley post No. 1450 VFW and its auxiliary. Fred Scarborough, the cave's owner at that time, told the cave's history which at that time covered 50 years.
(*The Nebraska State Journal.* November 14, 1943, p. 5.)

1944   (I love the names of these gals in the following "Girl Scout News" section. They all seem as if they could be characters from AMC's award-winning series *Madmen*.) Elizabeth Garner, Betty Lou Northway, Ruth Richmond, Evelyn Waddell, Jean Ward of Troop 14, and June Greer of Troop 7 worked on their cyclist badge requirements as Mrs. William Moore accompanied them on a bike ride to Robber's Cave for a cookout in October of 1944.
(*The Lincoln Star.* October 1, 1944, p. 18.)

Churches of all denominations entertained university students in September of 1944 at the annual all-university church night, which emphasized a closer relationship between students and church. Presbyterian students met at the student house on campus before

attending a picnic at Robber's Cave planned by Westminster Church, but the party was moved to the church annex after the cave became too crowded—the overflow crowd had reached 75! Pvt. Arthur Frackenpohl, ASTRP student, played piano numbers.
(*The Lincoln Star.* September 29, 1944, p. 5.)

While working on requirements for their cyclist badge, Girl Scout Troop 7 and Troop 14 cycled to Robber's Cave accompanied by Mrs. William Moore.
(*The Nebraska State Journal.* October 1, 1944, p. 18.)

Girls working on the torch bearer rank fulfilled the geological requirements and nature honors when guardian Mrs. G. A. Ackerman escorted the Wa Lu Ta Camp Fire group to Robber's Cave in December of 1944.
(*The Nebraska State Journal.* December 24, 1944, p. 15.)

A number of Girl Scouts from troops 2, 6, 8, 9, 18, and 20 were guests of Boy Scout troop 43 at their annual Robber's Cave picnic in December of 1944.
(*The Nebraska State Journal.* December 31, 1944, p. 17.)

1945

The girls of Wa Lu Ta Camp Fire group met at Mrs. Louise Ackerman's to discuss and demonstrate habits for beauty, but not before Anita Ackerman shared a report of the group's recent visit to Robber's Cave.
(*The Nebraska State Journal.* January 14, 1945, p. 20.)

Troop 6, under the leadership of Miss Betty Vlasnick, hiked to Robber's Cave for a wiener roast in January of 1945.
(*The Nebraska State Journal.* January 21, 1945, p. 16.)

In May of 1935, the senior class of Odell High School with their sponsor Mrs. Royal Elf (what a name!) Ward Finch, and E. E. Vance "sneaked" to Lincoln to visit Robber's Cave, the state penitentiary, Morrill Hall and *The Lincoln Journal*, where they watched the evening edition being printed. They also enjoyed a chicken dinner at the Cornhusker Hotel.
(*Beatrice Daily Sun.* May 3, 1945, p. 5.)

A group of Camp Fire girls from the Southwest Community Center day camp included a trip to Robber's Cave among their activities.
(*The Lincoln Star.* July 18, 1945, p. 8.)

1946

The O Ki Ci Ya Camp Fire girls had a cookout at Robber's Cave with Mrs. Vivian Bush as guardian in April of 1946.
(*The Lincoln Star.* April 21, 1946, p. 20.)

In May of 1946, Troop 7 of Vine Congregational Church planned a hike to Robber's Cave after the girls made corsages to be used at a church dinner under the instruction of Mrs. Ruth Fleming.
(*The Nebraska State Journal*. May 19, 1946, p. 20.)

Troop 1 of South Street Temple lunched at Van Dorn Park then hiked to Robber's Cave in June of 1946. Marilyn Maca and Louise Asmus assisted.
(*The Nebraska State Journal*. June 9, 1946, p. 18.)

The Odako Camp Fire group visited Robber's Cave before picnicking at Van Dorn Park. Clarice Priefert, Phyllis Weeden, and Marilyn Boisen were the new officers, and Barbara Jean Van Allen and Mrs. Martin Boisen were the guardians for the group.
(*The Nebraska State Journal*. June 23, 1946, p. 18.)

The YMCA's Thursday Evening Club had a picnic at Robber's Cave in July of 1947. Ida Pleines was in charge of the food.
(*The Lincoln Star*. July 20, 1947, p. 26.)

1947   Members of the Business and Professional Girls League of the YWCA hiked to Robber's
Cave for a picnic meeting. Venetha Jurgena made the arrangements.
(*The Lincoln Star*. July 6, 1947, p. 22.)

1948   The seniors of Barneston High School made Robber's Cave a part of their ambitious sneak day in May of 1948. They began in Blue Springs and headed out by 1 A.M! After a pre-dawn breakfast in Valparaiso, they reached Omaha to visit Boys Town and the WOW building. When they returned to Lincoln in the late afternoon, they visited Robber's Cave and saw a show. Lastly, they had a midnight snack at Beatrice.
(*Beatrice Daily Sun*. May 6, 1948, p. 7.)

In July of 1948, the "Fraternals" section of *The Nebraska State Journal* advertised a Robber's Cave picnic for Business and Professional Women of the YWCA.
(*The Nebraska State Journal*. July 28, 1948, p. 9.)

1949   In October 1949, a YM–YW coed club was organized at the YMCA which emphasized outdoor recreation. Al Larson was named chairman and Jack Shubert, Shirley Svarc, and Betty Wallace were chosen as members of the club's executive committee. The club's first event was a Halloween party at Robber's Cave.
(*The Nebraska State Journal*. October 13, 1949, p. 14.)

1950   The West Oak Sewing and Cooking Club met with their families at Robber's Cave in June of 1950. Officers of the club were: Joan Westfall, Sharon Larson, Carol Olson, and Marilyn Lawson. Also in attendance were Cleora Carnes, Shirley Lange, and Sonja Udeen.
(*The Lincoln Star.* July 3, 1950, p. 21.)

1953   The pupils of District 14 (Hamilton Country) with their parents and teachers motored to Lincoln in March of 1953 to visit The Nebraska State Penitentiary, Gooch's Mill, Roberts Dairy, The Burlington Hump, The Lincoln Telephone and Telegraph Co. and Robber's Cave. Those in the group were Miss Phyllis Brinkmeyer, Mr. and Mrs. John Wiebe, Robert and Jimmie; Mr. and Mrs. L. B. Penner and Marilyn; Mr. and Mrs. Orville Stevens and Lynn; Mr. and Mrs. Walter Gaman, Lou, Doris, Hazel, Russell and Della; Mrs. Calvin Wiebe and Susie; Mrs. Carl Schmidt, Mr. and Mrs. John Von Riesen, Danny and Judy; Mrs. Paul Penner, Leona and Gene.
(*Beatrice Daily Sun.* March 24, 1953, p. 10.)

Under "Clatonia News" in April of 1953, Miss Carol Uhlman took her District 3 pupils to Omaha to visit Boys Town, the School for the Deaf, and the zoo, but they stopped in Lincoln first to saunter through Robber's Cave. The group was accompanied by Mr. and Mrs. Willie Schlake, Mr. and Mrs. Rankin Duitsman, and Mr. and Mrs. Leonard Uhlman.
(*Beatrice Daily Sun.* April 15, 1953, p. 14.)

1954   "The Jones Boys" men's discussion group held their annual mystery scavenger party in May of 1954 "with wives invited." The event began with a clue announced over the radio or printed in a classified ad. Members gathered these clues as the week progressed and the event culminated at Robber's Cave for supper.
(*Lincoln Evening Journal.* May 25, 1954, p. 12.)

1955   Centenary Methodist at 6th and Elk St. in Beatrice, Nebraska, brought sack lunches and took an intermediate excursion to Lincoln to visit Robber's Cave after the 11 A.M. sermon "A Pair of Jesus' Glasses" in September of 1955.
(*Beatrice Daily Sun.* September 16, 1955, p. 8.)

1958   The Havelock YWCA Y–Ettes met at Robber's Cave in in April of 1958.
(*The Lincoln Star.* April 7, 1958, p. 5.)

The Wa-Ne's Camp Fire Girls, comprised of Meadow Lane fourth graders, had their first cookout of the year at Robber's Cave led by Mrs. Jessie Haith and assisted by Mrs. Robert Ore. Other members included Sandy Lehl, Marilyn Welch, Martha Martens, Kathy Stokes, Janet Regler, Peggy Koenigsman, Mary Ellen Ore, and Barbie Haith.

(*The Lincoln Star.* January 12, 1961, p. 12.)

1961   Many young men from Lincoln's Air Force Base, along with men from the area's two Nike–Hercules anti-missile bases at Agnew and Crete, were in town celebrating the USO's 20th anniversary in January of 1961. In addition to the dance at the Cornhusker Hotel, the military men toured the railyards and explored Robber's Cave.
(*Lincoln Evening Journal.* January 29, 1961, p. 42.)

1965   In April of 1965, the seventh and eighth grade of Burchard, Nebraska, accompanied by their teacher, Mr. Richard Pflanz, and bus driver, David Wilkinson, made a field trip to Lincoln where they visited the Air Base, Robber's Cave, and Morril Hall.
(*Beatrice Daily Sun.* April 14, 1965, p. 7.)

1966   The following "rollicking event" was described in the "TALK around the Town" section of *The Lincoln Star* in March of 1966. The affair was a "Flintstone Party" at Robber's Cave hosted by Mr. and Mrs. Richard Endacott and Mr. and Mrs. James Haberlan. Two hundred guests enjoyed a buffet and entertainment by a strolling musician!
(*The Lincoln Star.* March 11, 1966, p. 17.)

In October of 1966, five girls from Boulder, Colorado, visited Lincoln. Lincoln's Kitowando Horizon Club entertained the group with a dinner at the Patio Drive-Inn. The next day, they toured the state capitol, camp fire office, Sheldon Art Gallery, and lunched at Robber's Cave. They also visited various Lincoln high schools, attended a Northeast vs. Lincoln High football game, and had a slumber party at the home of John Lux. Finally, they visited Camp Kiwanis near Milford before returning to Colorado.
(*Lincoln Evening Journal.* October 27, 1966, p. 8.)

Epilogue—The Last Legend

While perusing the vacant Robber's Cave property in the early 1990s, the aforementioned Frosty Chapman found a .45 caliber bullet from the 1920s or 30s. When he sent me a photo of the bullet, he included in his message, "Few people outside of law enforcement would have had use for that caliber. Mostly carried by thugs and cracks at that time. Sure makes you wonder."

Chapman had the bullet made into a necklace and gave it to his daughter for Christmas that year. On Christmas Eve, however, Chapman penned his own legend to correspond with his find. One could say that Frosty's story he wrote December 24, 1991, is "The Last Legend" of Robber's Cave.

"Jesse James's Last Christmas (1891)"

By Frosty Chapman

As Jesse hobbled out of the cave, the glare of the harsh, winter sun momentarily blinded him. Did he see something or was it just two old eyes playing tricks? Age gripped him tightly, and the effort of climbing out of his sandy tunnel of a home had tired him. The cold air burned his throat, and the snow crunched underneath his worn leather boots. After just a few steps, he stopped to gather his breath.

It was Christmas day, and like so many others, he was alone. As he gazed at the faded jean-blue sky, he thought of all the evil he had done. Tears streamed down his old, leather face as dark memories flooded his heart. No family, no friends, just a long nightmare of grief and pain brought to others. The burden seemed heavier than ever to his aching, old soul.

Suddenly, Jesse realized he was not alone. Standing in front of him was Gabriel, a small boy from a dirt-poor family who lived in the shack of a cabin not far from his cave.

"Mr. James, we want you to spend Christmas with us. We don't have much, just some rabbit stew, but please come and share what we have." Then the little boy handed him a small carved wooden horse. It was all he had received for Christmas, and Jesse knew he had to receive it. Before the day was through, however, he would receive an even more precious gift, but taking this small offering opened his heart to receive the greater gift.

"Son, thanks for the horse. It's been a while since I had one, and this one I could even ride." They laughed together, and the tension was gone.

Trembling, arthritic hands then removed his beloved .45 Smith and Wesson Schofield revolver from the old holster. Jesse removed the bullets carefully. He gazed at the small messengers of death for only a moment, then threw them as far as he could. Then he handed the gun to the now wide-eyed boy.

"Son, I done a lot of bad with this, and you're too young to have it now, but you tell your Pa to hold on to it till next Christmas. I reckon some darn fool will want Jesse James's gun, and you folks won't have to eat rabbit stew for the big day."

"Thank you, Mr. James," Gabriel said, taking the gun with both hands.

The old man placed his hand gently on the boy's shoulder, and together, they headed home.

"The only way to fight nostalgia is to listen to somebody else's nostalgia."

–Pete Hamill, *Tabloid City*

References

Abourezk, Kevin. "Robber's Cave Plans Moving Forward." *Lincoln Journal Star*. March 5, 2015, p. 1.

Altenbach, Scott J., Freeman, Patricia W., Geluso, Kenneth N. University of Nebraska State Mammalogy Papers: "Nebraska's Flying Mammals." University of Nebraska State Museum. University of Nebraska—Lincoln, 1997.

Arthen, Walter Wright. "The Magic of Caves." Fire Heart, 1996.

Aucoin, Jim. "Settlers, Revelers Used Robber's Cave." *The Lincoln Sunday Journal and   Star*. August 15, 1976, p. 3.

Barbour, E. H. 1931. "Evidence of dinosaurs in Nebraska." *Bulletin of University of Nebraska State Museum*. 1:187–190.

Bartels, Alan J., "Nebraska's Coolest Caves." *Nebraska Life Magazine*, 21, no. 3 (May/June 2017), 20.

Barth, Taylor. Interview with Ed Zimmer. *10/11 Now*. August 27, 2015.

Baugher, Joe. "Lockheed P–80/F–80 Shooting Star." USAF Fighter, July 16, 1999.

Becker, Jim. Personal Interview on November 3, 2017.

Beck, Bill and Don Schaufelberger. *The Only State: A History of Public Power in Nebraska*.

"Belmont Students Explore Robber's Cave," *EdLines*, April 28, 1986, 1-3.

Beutler, Patty. *Lincoln Journal Star*. April 13, 1987, p. 8.

Boardman, Mark. "The Anti Horse Thief Association." January 13, 2017. *True West Magazine*. https://truewestmagazine.com/anti-horse-thief-association/

Boggs, Johnny D. "The Great Escape." *True West Magazine*. September 4, 2015.

Boye, Alan. *A Guide to the Ghosts of Lincoln*. Saltillo Press. Eugene, OR: 1983.

Bristow, David. "Lane's Army." *The Iowan*. Summer, 1997.

Campbell, Joseph. *The Way of the Animal Powers, Historical Alias of World Mythology*. Vol. 1. Alfred Van Der Marck Ed. USA, 1983.

Clock Tower. Union College Heritage Collections, 45, no. 9, (November 13, 1970).

Clock Tower. Union College Heritage Collections. 25, no. 10, (March 3, 1950).

"Dakota Environments." jpg. Image by Ank-man 20:30, (UTC), self-made by Ank-man. April 22, 2007.

Daly, Judi. "The Anti-Horse Thief Association: Protect the Innocent; Bring the Guilty to Justice." The Long Riders Guild Academic Foundation. 2014.

Davis, Horace M. *The Lincoln Star*. November 4, 1965, p. 4. Donning Company
      Publishers, 2010.

Duggan, Joe. "Jesse James wanted slice of the Good Life." *Lincoln Journal Star*.
      October 18, 2007.

Federal Writers' Project, Nebraska: A Guide to the Cornhusker State. New York, NY:
      1939, p. 197.

Gates Jr., Henry Louis. "Who Really Ran the Underground Railroad?" *The Root*.
      http://www.pbs.org/wnet/african-americans-many-rivers-to-cross/history/who-really-ran-
      the-underground-railroad/

Green, Joel. Personal correspondences with current cave owners, archive files, brochures, and cave
      site research visits from 2015-2017; Lincoln, NE.

Green, Joel. Interview with Edwin Scarborough Jr. Lincoln. March 15, 2017.

Green, Joel. Interview with Edwin Scarborough Jr. Lincoln. March 26, 2017.

Green, Joel. Interview with Edwin Scarborough Jr. Lincoln. April 3, 2017.

Green, Joel. Interview with Edwin Scarborough Jr. Lincoln. April 9, 2017.

Green, Joel. Interview with Edwin Scarborough Jr. Lincoln. May 10, 2017.

Green, Joel. Interview with Edwin Scarborough Jr. Lincoln. May 30, 2017.

Green, Joel. Interview with Edwin Scarborough Jr. Lincoln. May 4, 2017.

Green, Joel. Interview with Edwin Scarborough Jr. Lincoln. October 22, 2017.

Green, Joel. Interview with Matt Hansen. May 3, 2017.

Grinspan, Jon. "How a Ragtag Band of Reformers Organized the First Protest March on
      Washington D.C." May 1, 2014. https://www.smithsonianmag.com/smithsonian-
      institution/ how-ragtag-band-reformers-organized-first-protest-march-washington-dc-
      180951270/

Gurnee, Russell H. and Howard N. Slone. Visiting American Caves. Crown Publishers Inc. New
      York, NY: 1966, p. 123.

Hansen, Matt, email message to author, July 7, 2017.

Harrington, Judy. *Lincoln Journal Star*. October 7, 1960, p. 8.

Historical Perspective. "History of Public Power in Nebraska." Nebraska Interactive.
      2017. http://www.powerreviewboard.nebraska.gov/prbmanual/2.html

Hoverson, Doug. "Land of Amber Waters: The History of Brewing in Minnesota." University of
      Minnesota Press: Minneapolis, MN: 2007.

Joeckel, R. M., Cunningham, J. M., Corner, R. G., Brown, G. W., Phillips, P. L. and   Ludvigson, G.
      A. 2004. "Late Albian Dinosaur Tracks from the Cratonic (eastern) Margin of the Western
      Interior Seaway, Nebraska, USA." *Ichnos*, 11:275–284.

Johnson, Nolan, email message to author, April 9, 2017.

Jorgensen, Joanna, *The Lincoln Star*. November 19, 1942, p. 6.

The Kansas City Public Library. *Civil War on the Western Border: Bushwhackers Demand Surrender of
      Lexington*. Accessed November 13, 2017.

Lancaster Country Register of Deeds. Personal correspondence and access to subdivided cave
      property plat map. (December 2017).

Lange-Kubick, Cindy. *Lincoln Journal Star*. April 29, 2017.

Levy, Rachel G. *Religious Conception of the Stone Age and Their Influence on European Thought*. Harper and
      Row. New York, NY: 1963.

LeBlanc, Maurine. Photo: Merle Charles Karnopp. 1971.
    https://www.findagrave.com/memorial/137464849

The Lincoln Daily Star. November 1, 1914, p. 1.

Lincoln Evening Journal. Monday, July 6, 1925, p. 1.

Lincoln Evening Journal. June 1, 1927, p. 4.

Lincoln Evening Journal. August 20, 1927, p. 4.

Lincoln Evening Journal. September 3, 1929, p. 2.

Lincoln Evening Journal. "Cooties Stage a Surprise." May 21, 1932.

Lincoln Evening Journal. September 24, 1932, p. 2.

Lincoln Evening Journal. February 11, 1937. p. 4.

Lincoln Evening Journal. December 15, 1937, p. 13.

Lincoln Evening Journal. December 29, 1950, p. 1.

Lincoln Evening Journal. October 26, 1957, p. 3.

Lincoln Evening Journal. May 13, 1958, p. 8.

Lincoln Evening Journal. January 30, 1959, p. 14.

Lincoln Evening Journal. May 27, 1960, p. 19.

Lincoln Evening Journal. October 7, 1960, p. 8.

Lincoln Evening Journal. October 30, 1961, p. 8.

Lincoln Evening Journal. July 1, 1968, p. 8.

The Lincoln Journal Star. January 7, 1914, p. 4.

The Lincoln Journal Star. September 24, 1932, p. 2.

The Lincoln Journal Star. August 16, 1989, p. 1.

The Lincoln Star. December 30, 1913, p. 10.

The Lincoln Star. January 2, 1915, p. 7.

The Lincoln Star. Tuesday, July 11, 1922, p. 19.

The Lincoln Star. Oct 15, 1922, p. 12.

The Lincoln Star. May 1, 1923, p. 9.

The Lincoln Star. May 13, 1923, p. 30.

The Lincoln Star. June 10, 1923, p. 26.

The Lincoln Star. August 30, 1925, p. 66.

The Lincoln Star. May 8, 1929, p. 2.

The Lincoln Star. November 15, 1929, p. 20.

The Lincoln Star. November 17, 1929, p. 28.

The Lincoln Star. July 23, 1930, p. 4.

The Lincoln Star. November 6, 1931, p. 2.

The Lincoln Star. April 21, 1940, p. 28.

The Lincoln Star. November 22, 1942, p. 30.

The Lincoln Star. February 28, 1946, p. 9.

The Lincoln Star. March 13, 1946, p. 6

The Lincoln Star. August 29, 1949, p. 1.

The Lincoln Star. March 3, 1950, p. 1.

The Lincoln Star. July 2, 1968, p. 10.

The Lincoln Star. August 16, 1973, p. 1.

The Lincoln Star. "Union Literary Society Photo." August 15, 1976, p. 13.

Loope, David & Kettler, Richard & Weber, Karrie & L. Hinrichs, Nathan & Burgess, D. (2012) "Iron-Oxide Concretions: Hallmarks of Altered Siderite Masses of Both Early and Late Diagenetic Origin." *Sedimentology*, 59, (October 2012) 1769–1781. Accessed August 29, 2017.

Mayhew Cabin and Historic Village and John Brown Cave. "The Underground Railroad." Accessed May 11, 2018. http://www.mayhewcabin.org/education-history.htm

McCormick, Chris and Green, Len, eds. "Crime and Deviance in Canada: Historical Perspectives." 1st ed. Toronto: Canadian Scholars' Press Inc., 2005, p. 54. https://www.nwhc.usgs.gov/disease_information/white-nose_syndrome/

McKee, Jim, email message to author, February 28, 2017.

McKee, Jim, email message to author, May 15, 2017.

McKee, Jim, email message to author, December 4, 2017.

McKee, James L., Arthur E. Duerschner. *Lincoln: A Photographic History*. J & L Lee Co., 1980.

McKee, James L. "A New Chapter on Robber's Cave." *Lincoln Journal Star*. March 18, 2001, p. 2.

McKee, James L. *Visions of Lincoln: Nebraska's Capital City in the Present, Past and Future*. TankWorks, 2007.

McKee, James L. *Lincoln: The Prairie Capital*. Windsor Publishing, 1984.

McKee, James L. *Remember When . . . Memories of Lincoln*. J & L Lee Co. Lincoln, NE, 1998.

McKee, Jim. *The Lincoln Journal Star*. January 26, 2013.

Meek, F. B., and F. V. Hayden, 1861, Descriptions of new Lower Silurian (Primordial), Jurassic, Cretaceous, and Tertiary fossils, collected in Nebraska Territory, with some remarks on the rocks from which they were obtained: Proceedings Academy Natural Philadelphia, p. 415–447.

Mezzy, Dick. *Lincoln Evening Journal*. September 12, 1967, p. 6.

"Minnesotans nearly wipeout the James/Younger gang." *A+E Networks*. 2009. http://www.history.com/this-day-in-history/minnesotans-nearly-wipeout-the-james-younger-gang.

Moss, Harold J. Interview with Fred C. Scarborough. Series: "Folklore Project, Life Histories, 1936–39" Call # MSS55715: Box A717. Library of Congress Source Collection: US Works Projects Administration, Federal Writers' Project. Repository: Manuscript Division.

"Native Americans Meet Challenges." Nebraska Studies.org. Accessed July 16, 2017.

"Nebraska During the Cretaceous Period." http://eas2.unl.edu/ Accessed April 8, 2016.

The Nebraska Sheriff Magazine. February 1938, reprinted in Vol. 59, no. 2, (November 1989) 29.

Nebraska State Historical Society. "E. E. Blackman." July 13, 2009. Accessed April 15, 2016. http://nebraskahistory.org/libarch/research/manuscripts/family/blackman.htm.

The Nebraska State Journal. April 16, 1898, p. 6.

Nebraska Statesman—Lincoln, June 26, 1869, p. 3.

Nebraska U: A Collaborative History. "Literary Societies." Accessed June 22, 2017. http://unlhistory.unl.edu/exhibits/show/1900-1909/students/literary-societies

Nielsen, Mary Jane, Jonathan Roth, Gil Savery. *Lincoln Looks Back*. Nebraska Printing Press, 2009.

Nin, Anais. In Favor of the Sensitive Man, and Other Essays. Harcourt Brace Jovanovich. San Diego, CA: April 1976.

Oberlies, L. C. *The Nebraska State Journal*, 36. (July 29, 1906) 7.

Oberly, James W. "Military Bounty Land Warrants in the United States 1847–1900." University of Wisconsin—Eau Claire, Inter-university Consortium for Political and Social Research, Eau Claire, WI: 1991.

Olberding, Matt. "Bringing Back the Brews." *Lincoln Journal Star.* February 16, 2015, p.1. *Omaha Daily Bee.* June 10, 1904.

Parminter, Debra. "Andreas' History of the State of Nebraska-Lancaster County." NEGenWeb Project. Part 8, Musical Societies. http://www.usgennet.org/usa/ne/topic/resources/andreas/lancaster-p8.html. Accessed February 6, 2018.

Parsons, Dan. "Pints and Politics." Podcast Episode #6. Blue Blood Dank-A-Licious IPA craft beer, Libertarian Legislator, Stories from Robber's Cave, Player FM, April 2016. https://player.fm/series/pints-and-politics-with-dan-parsons. Accessed September 21, 2017.

Parsons, Dan. "Pints and Politics." Podcast Episode #12. Blue Blood Dank-A-Licious IPA craft beer, Live at Blue Blood with Mayor Beutler, Player FM, August 2016. https://player.fm/series/pints-and-politics-with-dan-parsons. Accessed September 21, 2017.

Polenberg, Richard. "Hear My Sad Story: The True Tales That Inspired Stagolee, John Henry and Other Traditional American Folk Songs." *Cornell University Press.* November 2015, p. 118.

Pound Louise. *Nebraska History*, 29. no. 4, (December 1948) 305.

Pound, Louise. *Selected Writings.* University of Nebraska Press, 1949.

"Rocks and Minerals of the American Indians." Accessed August 4, 2017. https://www.rockology.net/10-rocks-and-minerals-of-the-american-indians/

The Raab Collection. "Authenticity: secretarials, machines." February 23, 2011. www.raabcollection.com/blog/authenticity-secretarials-machines

Ray, Robert. "Following the James Younger Gang." *True West Magazine.* September 7, 2001.

Reilly, Michael R. "Waukesha County Detective Society." Sussex–Lisbon Area Historical Society, Inc. January 12, 2006.

Reist, Margaret. "Robber's Cave: Closing up a Lincoln Legend, Developers Planning to Seal up Cave." *Lincoln Journal Star.* July 20, 2000.

Ruggles, Rick. *Omaha World Herald.* September 4, 2016.

Schwaniger, Mark. *Lincoln Journal Star.* June 6, 2016.

Soule, Gary K., email message to author, February 4, 2017.

Soule, Gary K., email message to author, February 7, 2017.

Soule, Gary K., "Nebraska's Historic Robber's Cave." National Speleological Society News, 75, no. 2, (February 7, 2017) 14-19.

Souvenir Booklet of The Cave at Lincoln, Nebraska. Accessed at Bennet Martin Public Library, Jane Pope Geske Heritage Room of Nebraska Authors in September 2005 and at Ed Scarborough Jr.'s home in 2017.

SSO–GLO Plat and Note Search. Accessed December 6, 2016. Analyzed field notes with Dr. Joeckel. http://www.sso.nebraska.gov/maps/gloindex.html.

Steil, Mark. "Following the trail of Jesse James." *Minnesota Public Radio.* September 7, 2001.

Taylor, Troy. "Robber's Cave, Lincoln Nebraska." *The Cave Conservationist*, 22, no. 2, Hot Springs, SD: (2003) 3.

Union College – Golden Cords Yearbook. Lincoln, NE. Class of 1960, p.125

The Valentine Democrat, October 12, 1911, p. 7.

Wagner, Nancy. "Caves of Sandstone in Minnesota." *USA Today.*

Wahlmeier, Tess. *Diocesan News*. "Hidden Goods in Robber's Cave." August 5, 2016.

Waldinger, Joel. "Man Goes Deep to Explore, Preserve the Hidden Treasures of Door County's Caves." *Wisconsin Public Television*. October 14, 2014.

Wallace, Anthony F. C. "Jefferson and the Indians: The Tragic Fate of the First Americans." Belknap Press of Harvard University, Cambridge, MA: 1999.

Watkins, Albert (1913). History of Nebraska: From the Earliest Exploration of the Trans Mississippi Region. III (First ed.). Lincoln, NE: Western Publishing and Engraving Company.

Weyers, Jack. "Robber's Cave Status." *The Cave Conservationist*, 22, no. 3, Hot Springs, SD: (December 2003) 6.

Wolgamott, L. Kent. Interview with Dick Cavett. *Lincoln Journal Star*. October 25, 2014.

Wolter, Tim, email message to author, December 28, 2017.

Zimmer, Edward, email message to author, February 21, 2017.

Zimmer, Edward, email message to author, March 13, 2017.

Zimmer, Edward, email message to author, June 10, 2017.

Zimmer, Edward, email message to author, July 15, 2017.

Zimmer, Edward, email message to author, December 15, 2017.

Acknowledgments

To the thousands of guests that have followed me into Robber's Cave for tours, I am very grateful. Your support and encouragement to publish this book has been invaluable. I must thank Sam Manzitto Sr. and the members of Robbers Cave LLC for reopening and reviving Robber's Cave, and especially my sister Jamie Schack, who introduced me to the business; Jullia Grossman; Bruce Smith; and Ralph Allen for initially showing me the ropes, Colby Coash for sharing info about films and ghosts, and Riane Murphy who has always done and continues to do an incredible job scheduling so many tours for me.

To Phil Whitmarsh and everyone at Redbrush for helping me to navigate the publishing process.

To Frosty Chapman for returning the Robber's Cave map after so many years and for writing the foreword to this book. I appreciate your support and enthusiasm. Believe me, it has really helped! Although we just met, it seems as if we've known each other for years. I have enjoyed trading tales over coffee and our chess matches at The Mill. Thank you for being so willing to share your talents with me for this project.

To Dale Nobbman for writing the preface for this book. Thank so much for your advice, information, photos, and time.

To Tony Bertino, Jordan Lambrecht, Karley Johnson, and Ally Frame at Pixel Bakery Motion Studio for the one-of-a-kind book cover and colophon. I couldn't be happier with them!

To Jim McKee for reviewing my book and providing praise.

To Peter Salter and Gwyneth Roberts at the *Lincoln Journal Star* for the front-page article about my book and tours.

To Ron Hull for helping me to bring Dick Cavett back to Robber's Cave.

To Kristen Stohs and everyone associated with the *Live and Learn* show for helping bring the story of my book and tours to a television audience.

To the businesses, organizations, churches, and clubs that have invited me to speak and give presentations about the cave, thank you for your interest.

Although I enjoy reading, researching, interviewing, recording stories, and compiling information in an attempt to clarify much of the cave's lore, I am not a trained historian. Therefore, I must thank preservation architect Matt Hansen, historians Jim McKee, Ed Zimmer, Dr. Kieren Bailey the library director Union College, and cave specialists like Dr. Matt Joeckel and Gary Soule, all who have been kind enough to provide unique insight and expertise.

Much gratitude is owed to everyone who contributed photographs to my project: Ed Scarborough Jr., Scott Maybin, Martha Brown, Mary Toren, Matt Norsworthy, Dale Nobbman, and Jim McKee. I owe thanks to Nolan Johnson, Marty Miller, and Laura Mooney at the Nebraska State Historical Society for helping me search for articles, photos, and collections as well.

I'd like to acknowledge my wife, Tiffanie, for putting up with all of my folders, photos, and articles that were often strewn about our dining room table during the writing process, and for understanding that this book was something I simply needed to do.

A huge, heartfelt thank you goes to my daughter, Brooklyn, for cheerfully donning her Vala's Pumpkin Patch headlamp to assist me on so many tours. You have been the perfect sidekick, and your Daddy loves you more than you will ever know. I can't wait to read your books in the near future.

About the Author

Joel Green, the proud son of legendary auto mechanic Dwight Green and once aspiring astronaut Jacque Green, had been collecting information about Robber's Cave for years before he decided to finish this book for Nebraska's 150th anniversary. A Lincoln High School alum, Green visited seven countries as a high school student ambassador and became the first in his family to graduate college. He worked for NBA Hall-of-Famer Harvey Pollack of the Philadelphia 76ers, and then became an associate editor for the Cleveland Cavaliers. Green mentors highly gifted students in writing for Lincoln Public Schools, and he is very involved in Lincoln's community as a Freemason and Lakeview Elementary School volunteer. He is a two-time recipient of the VFW Citizenship Education Award. Although Green's interests include traveling, conversing with wise people, and exploring abandoned places, there's nothing he loves more than being a father. He is an avid Husker fan and lives in Lincoln, Nebraska, with his wife, Tiffanie, and daughters, Brooklyn and Savannah. He continues to give public and private tours of Robber's Cave when he's not teaching.